South Carolina:
Deed Books
16, 17, 18

Abstracted by
Carol Wells

HERITAGE BOOKS, INC.

Other Heritage Books by the author:

Robertson County, Tennessee, Court Minutes: 1796 - 1807
Rutherford County, Tennessee, County Court Minutes: 1811 - 1815
Sumner County, Tennessee, Court Minutes: 1787 - 1805 and 1808 - 1810
Williamson Co., Tenn., County Court Minutes: May 1806 - April 1812
Williamson Co., Tenn., County Court Minutes: July 1812 to the end of 1815
Rhea County, Tennessee, Circuit Court Minutes: Sept. 1815 - March 1836
Rhea County, Tennessee, Tax Lists and County Court Minutes, Vol. D
Edgefield County, South Carolina: Deed Books 13, 14, 15

Published 1997 by
HERITAGE BOOKS, INC.
1540E Pointer Ridge Place
Bowie, Maryland 20716
1-800-398-7709

ISBN 0-7884-0670-1

FOREWORD

Edgefield clerks who found such counties as Linkhorn and Ogle Thorp, GA; Granvill, VA; Lawrence, SC; and the state of Tenecy could also do interesting things to family names. All names written in the original books are given here. Readers doubtful of an interpretation of the handwriting, please check the old books.

Although these deeds were recorded from 1798 to 1800, the years in which they were written stretch from the 1760s. Many chains of title reach back to the 1750s and may tell of land sold, disputed, and inherited; they name heirs, kinfolk of other surnames, remarriages, residences in different states and counties, and may state exact or approximate dates of arrivals, departures, deaths, and marriages. Locations are identified by names of nearby watercourses and by names of adjoining landowners. Names of witnesses and surveyors give further details. Besides land conveyances, deed books include mortgages, releases of dower rights, powers of attorney, depositions, bills of sale for slaves and other possessions, and conditional sales that provide care of the aged until death.

Edgefield County then included parts of present Aiken, Greenwood, McCormick, and Saluda Counties. Much commerce across the Savannah River with businessmen and planters in several Georgia counties is documented.

ABBREVIATIONS

adj	adjoining
admr	administrator
cr	creek
DS	deputy surveyor
gdn	guardian
JP	justice of the peace
L&R	lease and release
P/A	power of attorney
R	river
rec	recorded
S	south
/s/	signed
wit	witness, witnesses

p.1-4 [much obliterated on this page] Ephraim Franklin to Henry Wise. Deed, 17 August 1798, £100 sterling, 171[?] acres on waters of Littlehouse creek, part of 200[?] acres granted to sd Ephraim Franklin 6 Feb 1786; another [unreadable] granted to sd Ephraim Franklin 2 Oct 1786; another granted [unreadable]. Wit -- Franklin, -- (x) Franklin Jr. /s/ Ephraim (I) Franklin. Judge Joseph Hightower certifies release of dower by Anne Franklin wife of Ephraim Franklin 17 August 1798. /s/ Anne (x) Franklin. Proven 17 August 1798 by Isham[?] Franklin; Joseph Hightower.

p.4-6 Jesse Pitts & wife to Joel Brown. Deed, $100, 100 acres on Little Saluda being part of [obliterated] granted to Jesse Pitts 4 June 1792 [next pages unreadable]

p.6-8 William Howle of Wilks County, Georgia, to William Shin--. Deed. 6 May 1798, $[unreadable] being land granted unto sd William Howle on Stephens Creek adj Moses Lucus land now held by John Hill, by Evan Morgan, William Stringer and vacant land, plat certified by David Burk D.S. 10 August 1785. Wit John Swillivan, Thomas Oden. /s/ William (x) Howle. Proven 10 Oct 1798 by John Swillivan; Chas Old JP. Rec 9 Oct 1798.

p.8-11 John Savage of Richmond County, Georgia, to Daniel Nail Senr. Deed, 17 July 1798, £[?], 125 acres bounded by land of William Evans originally granted to [obliterated] Richardson, Casper Nail Junr, Casper Nail Senr, being part of land originally granted to Benjamin Harris late of Georgia and conveyed by sd Benjamin Harris 21 Aug[?] 1787 to Casper Nail Junr, and by Casper Nail Junr to John Savage. Wit [obliterated] Nail, [obliterated] Zinn. /s/ John Savage. Judge Joseph Hightower certifies relinquishment of dower by Elizabeth Savage wife of John Savage 13 [obliterated] 1798. /s/ Elizabeth Savage. Proven 13 Sept 1798 by Casper Nail; Joseph Hightower JCE. Rec 9 Oct 1798.

p.11-14 Hugh Young atty for Hugh Ross of Charleston, SC, to John Rowe. Deed, 15 [obliterated] 1795, 105 acres, £20 SC money, little Stephens Creek adj lands of John Taylor, James Williams. Wit William Young, Silvs Walker. /s/ Hugh Young. Proven 16 Sept 1795 by Silvanus Walker; John Davis JP. Rec 9 Oct 1798.

p.14-16 Isaiah Blackwell to the Church. Deed of Gift, 21 April 1798, for goodwill, unto the Church of the Reverend Charles Blackwell decd, one acre on Plumb branch. Wit Enoch Breazeale, Jesse Hill, Joab Blackwell. /s/ Isaiah (x) Blackwell. Proven 9 Oct 1798 by Jesse Hill; Rd Tutt JP. Recorded 9 Oct 1798.

p.16-19   William Reynolds & wife Peggy to John Searls. Deed, 8 May 1797, £50 sterling, to John Surls 150 acres adj lands of James Picket, John Roberson, Thomas Roberson, Robert Jennings, Joseph Jennings, John Surls line, part of 300 acres granted to Morris Calleham by Gov Wm Moultree 3 April 1786. Wit Thomas Bazmore, Thomas Cason. /s/ William Reynolds, /s/ Peggy (x) Reynolds. Proven 23 May 1797 by Thomas Bazemore; Henry Key JP. Rec 9 Oct 1798.

p.19-23   Samuel Carter to David Rush. Deed, 25 May 1798, 50 pds, 198 acres, part of 962 acres originally granted to sd Samuel Carter 3 June 1793, on Little Creek of Cuffeetown creek of Stephens creek. Wit Davis Williams, John Gibson, Daniel Rush. /s/ Samuel Carter. Certification by Shadk Stokes D.S. that John Lyon D.S.laid off 962 acres on Little Creek of Cuffeetown Creek on 27 January 1792 signed by Gov Wm Moultrie, of which Stokes laid off 198 acres. Proven 25 May 1798 by Davis Williams; James Harrison JP. Recorded 9 October 1798.

p.23-24   Elizabeth King to Sarah Dinkle. Bill of Sale, 9 October 1798 for $20, one Negro girl Molly and one cow. Wit Burrel (x) Johnston, Thomas H Howle. /s/ Elizabeth (x) King. Proven 9 Oct 1798 by Thos H Howle; H Middleton JP. Rec 9 Oct 1798.

p.24-25   Elizabeth King to William King. Bill of Sale, 9 October 1798 for $20, Negro boy Dave. Wit Burrel (x) Johnson, Thos H Howle. /s/ Elizabeth (x) King. Proven 9 Oct 1798 by Burrel Johnson; Rd Tutt JP. Rec 9 Oct 1798.

p.26-28   John Gormon to Cullen Lark. Deed, 8 October 1798, £45 sterling, 150 acres originally granted to Nicholas ---ting (on the bounty) 6 ---ember 1768 when surveyed in Berkley County but now in Edgefield, on a branch of Saluda river now called Fosetys creek. Wit Paul Abney, Willis Borrum. /s/ John (I) Gorman. Proven 9 Oct 1798 by Willis Borum; Russell Wilson JP. Rec 9 Oct 1798.

p.28-30   Henry Wilson of Abbeville County to Richard M Dozer. Deed, 22 April 1797, £60 sterling, 250 acres on Big Creek of Little Saluda river bounded by lands of Rowlen Coatney, surveyed for Isaac

Crowther 6 September 1784 and granted to Thomas Dozer 4 January 1796 on 17 April 1797. Wit Jno Wilson, Thos Steele, Thos Dozer. /s/ H Wilson. Proven 29 Sept 1798 by Thomas Dozer; Russell Wilson JP. Recorded 9 October 1798.

p.31   Rebeckah Devour to Edmund Watson. Renounciation of Dower. Judge Joseph Hightower certifies that Rebekah Devour wife of Matthew Devour relinquished unto Edmund Watson her right of dower, 9 October 1798. /s/ Rebekah (x) Devour. Rec 9 Oct 1798.

p.32-34   Thomas Dozer to Henry Wilson of Abbeville County. Deed, 17 April 1797, £40, 250 acres on Big Creek of Little Saluda river adj Rowlen Coatney; surveyed for Isaac Crowder 6 Sept 1784 & granted to Thomas Dozer 4 Jan 1796. Wit Jas Wilson, Thomas Steele, Richd M Dozer. /s/ Thomas (#) Dozer. Proven 29 Sept 1798 by Richard M Dozer; Russell Wilson JP. Rec 9 Oct 1798.

p.34-36   Gibeon Burton to Samuel Crowe. Deed, 29 August 1798, £75 SC money, one stud horse, household goods. Wit Joshua Weeks, John (x) Weeks. /s/ Gibeon Burton. Proven 30 Aug 1798 by Joshua Weeks; Russell Wilson JP. Rec 10 Oct 1798.

p.36-44   Peter Morgan, planter, and Annemeriah his wife to Jesse Scruggs, planter. L&R, 9 March 1791/10 March 1791, £50 sterling, 200 acres in Edgefield County formerly Granville County, SC, on a branch of Turkey Creek called Beaverdam, now in actual possession of sd Jesse Scrugs; granted to John Clark by Gov Wm Bull 18 May 1773 and by John Clark conveyed 14 & 15 Nov 1774 unto William Minter decd; by will of Wm Minter descended unto Anne Maria Minter daughter to sd Wm Minter decd and now wife to sd Peter Morgan. Wit Wm Coursey, Constant Oglesby, Allen Coursey. /s/ Peter (x) Morgan, /s/ Jesse (H) Scrugs. Release signed by Peter (x) Morgan, /s/ Anne M Morgan. Proven 11 April 1791 by Wm Coursey; Aquilla Miles J P. Recorded 10 October 1798.

p.44-47   John Abney to William Abney Senr. Deed, 14 May 1798, $100, 1750 acres, part of 3500 acres originally granted to sd John Abney upon head of Tarepin Creek of Great Saluda River and head of Persimon lick Creek a branch of Big Creek of Little Saluda river, joining lands of Thos Curls, Sansom, Augusta road, Joseph Culbreath, Wm Taylor, Nathaniel Abney; wit Isabella Abney, Azariah Abney. /s/ John Abney. Proven 14 May 1798 by Azariah Abney;

3

Nathl Abney J.P. Rec 10 October 1798.

p.48-50   James Quarles to Samuel Quarles. Deed, 6 December 1797, £100 sterling, 200 acres adj lands of Dudley Carter, David Quarles, John Clackler, Goodin, David Siglar, Freeman Hardy; wit Benjamin Roper, David Roper, Mary (x) Burnett. /s/ James Quarles. Proven 2 Dec 1798 by David Roper; Chas Old JP. Rec 10 Oct 1798.

p.50-53   John Cheatham to Gutridge Cheatham, planter. Deed, 10 October 1798, 57 acres on branches of Beaverdam of Turky Creek, part of 200 acres formerly granted unto Chapman Taylor & by Taylor conveyed unto Peter Cheatham, and by decease of sd Peter Cheatham, sd 200 acres descended unto sd John Cheatham son and heir unto Peter Cheatham decd; plat by Wm Coursey D.S. Wit W Coursey, John Terry. /s/ John Cheatham. Proven 10 Oct 1798 by John Terry; Rd Tutt JP. Rec 10 October 1798.

p.53-56   Samuel Mays to Nathan Trotter. Deed, 9 March 1798, £100 sterling, 150 acres being part of two tracts originally granted to John Chiney, one of 200 acres granted 29 April 1768 and conveyed by sd John Chiney to sd Samuel Mays; the other 50 being part of a tract granted to John Chiney and conveyed to William Deen, and from sd Wm Deen to Samuel Mays, on big creek of Saluda river, adj lands of Gideon Christon, Samuel Mays, Thomas Berry, William White. Wit Jeremiah (x) Trotter, John (x) Carter. /s/ S Mays. Judge William Anderson certifies relinquishment of dower by Nancy Mays wife of Samuel Mays, 29 Sept 1798; /s/ Nancy Mays. Proven 29 Sept 1798 by Jeremiah (x) Trotter; W Anderson JCE. Rec 10 Oct 1798.

p.56-59   Samuel Mays to Jeremiah Trotter. Deed, 9 March 1798, £41 sterling, 80 acres originally granted to John Chiney and conveyed by sd Chiney unto William Deen; conveyed by sd Deen unto sd Samuel Mays, on branch of Big Creek of Saluda River, adj lands of Nathan Trotter, Gideon Christon. Wit John (x) Carter, Nathan Trotter; /s/ S Mays. Judge Wm Anderson certifies relinquishment of dower by Nancy Mays wife of Samuel Mays, 29 Sept 1798; /s/ Nancy Mays. Proven 29 Sept 1798 by Nathan Trotter; W Anderson JCE. Rec 10 Oct 1798.

p.60-61   Sarah Adams to Susannah Adams. Bill/Sale, 10 January 1798, for love & affection toward granddaughter Susannah Adams, bed & furniture. Wit Little Bery Adams, Benj Adams. /s/ Sary (x) Adams. Proven 10 Oct 1798 by Benj Adams; Rd Tutt JP. Rec 10 Oct 1798.

p.61-64   Samuel Carter to Daniel Rush. Deed, 25 May 1798, £50 207 acres being part of 962 acres originally granted to sd Samuel Carter 3 June 1793 lying on Little Creek of Cuffeetown Creek of Stephens Creek adj lands of Baker, Stephen Mantz, Elizabeth Audulph; wit Davis Williams, David Rush. /s/ Samuel (x) Carter. Proven 25 May 1798 by Davis Williams; Jas Harrison JP. Rec 11 October 1798.

p.64-65   Sally Burton to Samuel Jinkins. Renunciation of Dower. Judge Joseph Hightower certifies that Salley Burton wife of R Burton relinquished dower unto Samuel Jinkins, 9 October 1798; /s/ Sally (x) Burton.   Recorded 11 October 1798.

p.65-66   Davis Moore to James Bullock. Bill of Sale, 6 November 1797, $350, Negro boy Stepney. Wit John Cowbrey, Thos Butler. /s/ Davis Moore. Proven 11 October 1798 by Thomas Butler; Russell Wilson JP. Rec 11th Oct 1798.

p.66-74   Thomas Lawson to William Corley. L&R, 18 December 1791/19 December 1791, £60 Sterling, 100 acres on Savannah River bounded at original survey by lands of William Teddors, being part of 150 acres granted 23 December 1771 by George III to Charles Williams decd. Wit Barnard Caffery, Joseph Tucker, Mordecai McKinney. /s/ Thomas (T) Lawson. Proven 4 Nov 1797 by Barnard Caffery; Russell Wilson JP. Rec 11 Oct 1798.

p.74-82   William Corley to Clement Cargill. L&R, 18 February 1794/17 February 1794, £100, 153 acres being part of original grant to Charles Williams situate on Savannah River, bounded by William Tuddor at time of original survey, granted 23 Dec 1771 by George III to Charles Williams decd. Wit Joseph Tucker, Catlett (x) Corley, William (x) Corley. /s/ William Corley. Proven 4 November 1797 by Catlett Corley; Russell Wilson JP. Rec 11 Oct 1798.

p.82-84   John Lewis Gervais of Charleston, SC, to Richard McCary. Release, 9 February 1798, for 25,000 pounds merchantable inspected tobacco, 550 acres on Birds Creek. Wit Sinclair David Gervais, Thomas Martin. /s/ John Lewis Gervais. Proven 14 July 1798 by Thomas Martin; Henry Key JP. Rec 11 Oct 1798.

p.84-87   Richard Bush Senr to Joseph Walker. Deed, 14 February 1798, 100 silver Dollars,   part of a tract granted 1 May 1773 to Jacob Holley by Gov Wm Bull on Breaces Creek below the Littel mill. Wit

Nathan Godwin, John Bush. /s/ Richard Bush. Proven 11 October 1798 by John Bush; Van Swearingen J.P. Rec 11 Oct 1798.

p.87-94   Anne Maria Williams widow of Major John Williams to the exrs heirs & Legatees of sd John Williams, decd.   Renunciation of Dower & General Release;   John Williams by will signed 24 Sept last past did lend to me during my widowhood land which John Williams in lifetime purchased from Mr Yarborough 276 acres whereon sd John Williams lived at time of his death, on express condition that in case I the sd Ann Maria Williams did not choose to live on sd plantation after decease of sd husband that I should not have any power or authority to dispose of same or to rent sd plantation, but same was to remain to Joseph Williams son & one of the devisees and legatees of sd John Williams; also sd John Williams by will bequeathed to me sd Ann Maria Williams land containing 200 acres lying below Martin Twower joining Joseph Colliers land and Wiers Road together with six Negroes Rose Amy Pleasant Luce Easter and a negro wench at present in possession of my brother Joseph Gouge in North Carolina; also three horses [other livestock and household furniture] one hogshead of merchantable tobacco to be delivered at Augusta to weigh 1000 pounds [other items] sd John Williams made provision that I sd Ann Meria Williams should within six months after decease of testator renounce forever my right or claim of dower in real & personal estate, and give discharge against same and accept the legacies in full satisfaction thereof; and if I sd Ann Meria Williams did not comply, testator by will absolutely revoked sd devise to me; did by will devise same amongst his sons and daughters share & share alike and made no other provisions for me sd Ann Meria Williams. I sd Ann Meria Williams in consideration of sd devise in sd will, and in pursuance of sd will of my late husband do hereby declare myself fully satisfyed therewith and do hereby demise forever quit claim unto the heirs, devisees & executors named in sd will. Discharge the estate both real and personal of sd John Williams and also William Caldwell Esqr and Joseph Williams executors of will of sd John Williams, also sons and daughters heirs devisees and legatees named in will. Wit John Hamilton, Dan Bullock. /s/ Ann Maria (x) Williams. Received 28 October 1794 from William Caldwell & Joseph Williams the executors, the within named legacies bequeathed me by last will and testament of my late husband John Williams deceased. /s/ Ann Meria (x) Williams. Proven 11 October 1798 by Dan Bullock; Richard Tutt JP.   Rec 11 Oct 1798.

p.94-96   Sheriff William Tennent to George Latham. Sheriff

Titles, 2 October 1797, at suit of Christian Inabnet against estate of
Peter Buffington decd, Sheriff to seize and sell at Cambridge to highest
bidder the land whereon Peter Buffington in his lifetime formerly
resided containing 400 acres; struck off to George Latham for £61. Wit
Wm Salton White, P B W Waters. /s/ Wm Tennent. Proven Newberry
County 26 April 1798 by William Salton White Esqr; Frederick Nance
JP. Recorded 11 October 1798.

p.97-99   Thomas Handshaw, Nicholas Woods, and Isham Bivens
to Rachel Morris coheirs of John Morris Junr, decd. Deed, 31 March
1797, £10 sterling, 25 acres on Buckhalters Creek of Stephens Creek of
Savannah River being part of 200 acres originally granted to William
Anderson on 11 February 1773 and conveyed by William Anderson to
William Murphrey and by sd William Murfey conveyed to John Morris
Junr now deceased, and now conveyed by us the coheirs of sd John
Morris Junr decd to Rachel Morris, bounded by lands of James Butler,
Peter Carns. Wit Wm Doby, David Shaw. /s/ Thomas (x) Hanshaw,
Nicholas (N) Woods, Isham (S) Bivens. Proven 2 June 1798 by David
Shaw; Van Swearingen J.P. Rec 11 Oct 1798.

p.99-102   Benjamin McKinney & wife Mary to Buckner Blaylock.
Deed, 13 March 1797, £15 sterling, 100 acres on Beach Creek of
Edisto River adj lands of Mathew Melton, Big Sister pond, Buckner
Blaylock, Samuel Jefcoats line, being 100 acres granted to James Rowe
3 August 1792 by Gov Charles Pinckney; wit John (E) Blalock, Josiah
Gray. /s/ Benjamin McKinney. Judge Joseph Hightower certifies that
Mary McKinney wife of Benjamin McKinney relinquished dower, 11
October 1798; /s/ Mary McKinney. Proven 12 October 1797 by John
(P) Blalock; John Blocker JP. Rec 12 October 1798.

p.102-105   Hezekiah Oden to Mackness Goode. Deed, 2 September
1798, £100, 116 acres on Lawds Creek of Stephens Creek adj lands of
Peter Robertson, John Bayley, Amasa Baugh, John Oden, Samuel
Dagney; Wit Roger Williams, Moses (x) Riley. /s/ Hezekiah Oden.
Plat shows land bequeathed unto Thomas Oden from the original, land
sold to John Baley from the original, land bequeathed unto Peter Oden
from the original grant, land bequeathed unto John Oden from the
original, and old grant line. Pursuant to will of Hezekiah Oden decd as
also the request of Hezekaih Oden Junr, laid out to Hezekiah Oden Junr
116 acres on Loyds Creek a branch of Stephens Creek, part of 300
acres granted to Hezekiah Oden decd by Gov Chas Granville Montague
14 August 1772; W Coursey Dep Survr, 21 January 1798. Proven 12

Oct 1798 by Roger Williams; Henry Key JP. Rec 12 Oct 1798.

p.105-107   Hugh Middleton to his daughter Philadelphia Middleton. Deed Gift, 29 April 1795, for love & affection, also for £30 paid by Edward Prince for sd Philadelphia Middleton, two Negroes, girl named Biddy, boy named Nick, and one mare branded HM. Wit Hugh Middleton Junr, Humphrey Evans. /s/ Hugh Middleton. Proven 28 June 1796 by Hugh Middleton Junr; Henry Key JP. Rec 15 Oct 1798.

p.107-110   Jemimah Garner widow of Archy Garner to her children: sons Lewis and John; daughters Patcy, Elizabeth, Nancy, Joanna Garner. Deed of Gift, 23 April 1798, for love & affection, also for better maintenance of sd Jemimah Garner, to Lewis and John Garner land where I now live joining lands of Mr Coursey, Mr Blaikley, when they come of age; unto daughters a Negro girl named Pat and her increase to be equally divided amongst them when the youngest daughter Joanna Garner arrives to age eighteen, also each of them beds, furniture, a cow and calf to each, also Patcy is to have a mare. Wit Henry Capehart, William Strom. /s/ Jemima (x) Garner. Proven 25 Sept 1798 by William Strom; John Blocker JP. Rec 15 Oct 1798.

p.110-112   Wheaten Pines to Jeremiah Kish. Deed, 4 September 1798, £25, 365 acres granted unto sd Wheaten Pines 2 June 1794 by Gov Wm Moultree, bounding lands of Jeremiah Jones. Wit James Johnston, John (x) Stone. /s/ Wheaten Pines. Proven 28 July 1798 by John Stone; William Calk JP. Rec 20 Oct 1798.

p.112-115   Moses Harris to Briton Mims. Deed, 5 November 1798, £75, half of a half acre lott near Edgefield County Court house. Wit Matthew Mims, James (x) Van. /s/ Moses Harris. Plat shows land of Jno Harris, of original grant, and Jinkin Harris. Proven 5 Nov 1798 by Matthew Mims; Rd Tutt JP. Rec 5 Nov 1798.

p.115-116   William Harden to John Harden. Bill of Sale, 25 August 1798, $126, Negro girl Pegg. Wit Stephen Norris /s/ W Harden. Proven 5 Nov 1798 by Stephen Norris; Rd Tutt JP. Rec 5 Nov 1798.

p.116-118   Philip Lamar to Lucy Cannon. Bill of Sale, 16 May 1798, $170, Negro woman Jude and her boy child Moses. Condition, if above named Philip Lamar or Robert Lamar pay unto Lucy Cannon $170 in specie on or before 16 July next, bill of sale is of no effect. If sd Negroes should die before expiration of the time, it shall not be the less of sd Lucy Cannon or her heirs. Wit Benj Hatcher, George Wallace. /s/ Philip Lamar, Robert Lamar. Proven 16 Nov 1798 by Benj Hatcher; Rd Tutt JP. Rec 16th Nov 1798.

p.118-121   Charity Kirkland to trusty friend John Federick, planter. Power of Attorney, 17 October 1798, to recover from all persons indebted to me in any county or state, to take legal courses for obtaining same, also to pay all persons having lawful demands against me. Wit Lewis Federick, Mary (x) Federick. /s/ Charity (x) Kirkland. Proven 23 Oct 1798 by Lewis Federick; Wm Daniel JP. Rec 21 Oct 1798.

p.121-123   Thomas McGinnis to Reuben Landrum. Deed, 4 June 1798, $300, 100 acres on Log Creek, being land granted to William Cockran in 1771. Wit Benjamin Reeks, Elizabeth (x) McCoy. /s/ Thomas (x) McGinnis. Proven 1 Nov 1798 by Benjamin Reeks; Rd Tutt. Rec 21 Nov 1798.

p.123-126   Henry Key and wife Phebe to Lazarus Chadowick. Deed, 27 June 1798, 100 acres on Stephens Creek of Savannah River, bounded on North by land of Charles Yancey; plat endorsed by Wm Coursey D.S., being part of 250 acres granted unto sd Henry Key by Lt Gov Wm Bull 16 Sept 1774. Wit Edmd Franklin, Charles (x) Findley. /s/ Henry Key, /s/ Phebe (x) Key. Proven 6 Nov 1798 by Edmond Franklin; H Middleton, JP. Rec 1 Dec 1798.

p.126-129   Phil May Junr to William Griffin. Deed, 6 June 1798, £100 sterling, 175 acres originally granted unto James Harris 15 May 1771; to John Spencer 19 June 1772 on Chaves Creek above Mr John Foxes mill, Spencers corner; wit Robert Samuel, John (IB) Buckhalter. /s/ Phill May. Judge Joseph Hightower certifies relinquishment of dower by Sarah May wife of Phill May; /s/ Sarah (x) May. Proven 20 Sept 1798 by John Buckhalter; Chas Old JP. Rec 3 Dec 1798.

p.130-135   Elisha Knight to Mary Young. L&R, 25 March 1796, £50 sterling, 100 acres on Wilsons Branch, Richland Creek, Little Saluda River, being part of 450 acres laid out for James Allen 23 April 1788 by Gov Chas Pinckney; wit Mary (M) Wilson, Abbegail (x) Knight, Jane (J) Buzby. /s/ Elisha (x) Knight. Proven 5 April 1796 by Jane Buzby; Russell Wilson JP. Rec 4 Dec 1798.

p.135-137   Jacob Smith to John Salter. Deed, 28 February 1797, $60, 275 acres on Richland Creek of Little Saluda River, being part of

500 acres granted to sd Smith 7 March 1796 by Gov Arnoldust Vanderhorst, adjoining lands of sd Salter, Powells line, Gillen path; Wit Henry King, Saffie Smith. /s/ Jacob Smith. Proven 27 May 1797 by Henry King; Russell Wilson JP. Rec 4 Dec 1798.

p.137-140   Absalom Williams to Charles Williams. Deed, 20 September 1798, $500, 450 acres on Stephens Creek of Savannah R. Wit John Lyon, Jas Sanders, John Wallace. /s/ Abs Williams. Plat: lands of James Frazier granted to Gibar, of Absalom Williams. Proven 14 November 1798 by John Lyon; James Harrison JP. Rec 12 Dec 1798.

p.140-144   Arthur Watson to Arthur Rice Watson. Deed, 16 December 1795, one pound two shillings fourpence of SC money, 125 acres on dreans of Fowl Creek of Clouds Creek being part of tract originally granted unto Robert Pringle Esqr decd about 26 July 1774 adj John Eidsons corner, Richmond Watsons corner, Hezekiah Watson; Wit Richmond Watson, Bently Stokes, Sarah (x) Watson. /s/ Arthur (x) Watson. Proven 16 August 1796 by Richmond Watson; Russell Wilson JP. Rec 12 Dec 1798.

p.144-146   Martha Laremore to Adam Effort. Deed, 3 November 1798, $40, 50 acres, also part of two tracts containing 100 acres, the plantation where Edward Laremore formerly lived, the land that he willed to his wife Martha Laremore the 17 March 1785, bounded by lands of James McCartey, Simon Tootewine, William Marrin .   Wit Edward McCartey, Arthur (x) Watson. /s/ Martha (o) Laremore. Proven 12 Dec 1798 by Arthur Watson; Rd Tutt JP. Rec 12 Dec 1798.

p.146-149   Arthur Watson to Absalom Watson. Deed, 12 September 1798, $10, 374 acres being part of three tracts all granted to sd Arthur Watson, one tract of 150 acres granted 10 July 1766, one of 250 acres granted 3 April 1772, one of 300 acres granted 21 January 1785, lying on Fall Creek and dreans of Indian Creek waters of Clouds Creek bounded by lands granted to John Person, held by Abner Watson, by Terry Colly, granted to Thomas Kirkland, Hezekiah Watson, Richmond Watson; unto sd Absalom Watson after my death. Wit William Bell, Hezekiah Watson, Nancy (x) Partin. /s/ Arthur (A) Watson. Proven 12 Dec 1798 by Hezekiah Watson; Richard Tutt JP. Rec 12 Dec 1798.

p.149-151   Jesse Harben to Zacheriah Stedham. Deed, 5 December 1794, £17.10 sterling, 50 acres, part of 100 acres granted by Gov Thos Pinckney 1 Dec 1788, conveyed from Joseph Warre to Jesse Harben 21

Oct 1793, lying on Mores Creek. Wit Samuel Messer, Richard (RO) Odum, William (x) McCartey. /s/ Jesse (x) Harben. Proven 9 Feb 1798 by William McCarty; Elkh Sawyer JP. Recorded 17 Dec 1798.

p.152-153 John Hancock to Thomas Hancock. Deed, 9 June 1798, £100 sterling, 221 acres bounded on lands of Cain Gentry, John Hancock Junr, Simon Hancock, William Hancock. Wit George Hancock, Peter Hancock. /s/ John Hancock, /s/ Ann Hancock. Proven 7 Dec 1798 by George Hancock; Chas Old JP. Rec 18 Dec 1798.

p.154-159 William Robertson to William Martin. L&R, 20/21 November 1795, £100 sterling, 539 acres on Mine Creek of Little Saluda granted unto sd Wm Robertson 5 March 1787 by Gov Thomas Pinckney, adj land laid out for Shiles Marsh and on Adam Stalnaker. Wit Reuben Roberts, James Hoge. /s/ William Robertson. Proven 14 Sept 1797 by James Hoge; Van Swearingen JP. Rec 19 Dec 1798.

p.160-161 Zilphia Jack to Buckner Blaylock. Bill of Sale, 2 October 1796, £500 five Negroes named Dick, Milley, Tom, Rose, and Boson, livestock, household goods. Wit J Spann, Henry Spann. /s/ Zilphia (x) Jack. Proven 1 Jan 1799 by John Spann; Van Swearingen JP. Rec 1 January 1799.

p.162-163 William Roper to son Samuel Roper. Bill of Sale, 21 December 1798, love & goodwill, mare, household goods; wit William Wash, Little Berry Adams. /s/ William Roper. Proven 3 January 1799 by Little Berry Adams; Rd Tutt JP. Rec 3 Jany 1799.

p.163-165 John Spann, Deposition; before John Blocker, John Span swears that about seven years past he was in company with James Spann and heard him say that himself and Francis Spann had a Bill of Sale for four Negroes belonging to his father meaning Dick Hannah and two of Hannah's children, and sd James Span said that the way they got the Bill of Sale was that Francis went to his father and told him he had lost the writing that he had given him swimming his beast in the water with the writing in his pocket for the two Negroes he gave him before and that the writing was not on the record and he hoped he would give him a Bill of Sale for them again, his father agreed and in Stead of them two took a Bill of Sale for the above four Negroes; deponant further sayeth he saw Frances after he saw James & Francis told him near or quite the same. Sworn 7 January 1799. John Blocker JP. /s/ J Spann. Rec 7 Jany 1799. Before John Blocker appeared John Spann

11

Senior and made oath that the Bill of Sale he signed was intended by him for two Negroes he had given his son Francis Span before, to wit, a boy named Sam and a girl named Lues, and not intended for the Negroes they now claim on that Bill of Sale if he had known it had been for them negroes he never should have signed it. Jan 7, 1799; John Blocker, JP. John (x) Spann Senr. Rec 7 January 1799.

p.165-167   Vachel Clary to Mary Beal, spinster. Deed, 10 October 1798, £32.10 sterling, 100 acres on Little Stephens Creek divided off from remaining part of Vachel Clary's land by afsd creek, being the westward part of two tracts of land adj land of George Buckelow, James Eddins, John Mainor. Wit James Eddins, Joseph Eddins. /s/ Vachel Clary. Proven 22 October 1798 by Joseph Eddins; John Blocker, JP. Rec 5 Jan 1799.

p.167-169   Willis Whatley to Haley Johnson. Deed, 18 July 1798, $400, 110 acres on Dry Creek bounding on land of Abraham Holsonback, Benjamin Tutt, Moses Kirkland. Wit Ephraim Ferril, Joseph Hightower. /s/ Willis Whatley. Judge Joseph Hightower certifies release of dower by Rebeckah Whatley wife of Willis Whatley, 18 July 1798. /s/ Rebekah (R) Whatley. Rec 5th Jan 1799.

p.169-171   Joannah Ogylvie to her brother Gayle Hampton. Power of attorney for disposing of my part of a tract of land lying in Matterson County, Virginia, containing 365 acres which was willed to me by George Nevel decd of Fauquier County, Virginia. Wit Lucy Exum, Mary Pardue. /s/ Joannah Ogylvie. Proven 4 Jan 1799 by Lucy Exum; Joseph Hightower JCE. Rec Jan 10, 1799.

p.171-174   James Rogers son and heir at Law of William Rogers decd and Agnes Surginer widow of William Rogers and John Surginer husband of sd Agnes Surginer, to William Harden. Deed, 24 December 1798, £25 sterling, 150 acres in Granville at the time of original survey, then binding on land of David Locker, John Con, certified 23 May 1768 by John Fairchild D.S.; granted to sd William Rogers by Lt Gov William Bull 12 Sept 1768, examined pr Saml Hopkins pro Secretary March 1769. Wit Jacob Gallman, Randolph Gallman. /s/ James Rogers, John Surginar, Agness (x) Surginar. Proven 24 December 1798 by Jacob Gallman: Harris Turner JP. Rec 7th Jan 1799.

p.174-180   Samuel Etheredge to Benjamin Etheredge. L&R, 29 March 1791, 5 shillings, 100 acres bounded by land claimed by

William West, originally granted to Lott Etheredge and conveyed to Samuel Etheredge. Wit Sarah (+) Etheredge, Lott Etheredge. /s/ Samuel (x) Etheredge. Proven by Lott Etheredge; James Spann JP. /s/ Lott (x) Etheredge. Rec 7 January 1799.

p.180-182   Zacheus Tharp & wife Catey to James Prichard, planter. Deed, 18 November 1797, £40 sterling, 100 acres on Crucod Run of Turkey Creek of Savannah R, adj lands of Evely, Taylor, being part of 200 acres granted to Ward Taylor by Lt Gov Wm Bull 9 Sept 1774, convaid by Ward Taylor to Leroy Taylor and by Leroy Taylor unto sd Coll Collens 5 Jan 1787. Wit Moses Taylor, William Prichard. /s/ Zacheus Tharp, /s/ Caty (+) Tharp. Proven 14 July 1798 by Moses Taylor; John Blocker JP. Rec 7 Jan 1799.

p.183-185   Roger Williams and wife Catherine to David & William Moore. Deed, 7 January 1799, $500, 100 acres bounded by lands of Thomas Beckam Senr, Thomas Mosely, Jno Purves. Wit Joseph Fuller, Abel Keyes. /s/ Roger Williams, /s/ Caty Williams. Judge Arthur Simkins certifies relinquishment of dower by Catherine Williams wife of Roger Williams. /s/ Caty Williams. Proven 7 January 1799 by Joseph Fuller; Chas Old JP. Rec 7 Jan 1799.

p.185-188   Eleazor Tharp, planter, and wife Elizabeth to Charles James, planter. Deed, 9 March 1798, £25 sterling, 25 acres on Court House Road and Richland and part of tract now held by James Prichard originally granted to Ward Taylor by Lt Gov Wm Bull 9 Sept 1774, bound by dividing line between sd James Prichard and Charles James. Wit Saml Jefcoat, James Prichard. /s/ Eleazor Tharp, Elizabeth Tharp. Proven 14 July 1798 by Jas Prichard; Jno Blocker JP. Rec 7 Jan 1799.

p.188-190   James Hoge to Jacan Robinson. Deed of Sale, 20 December 1798, $100, cattle, hoggs, tools, household furniture, &c. Wit Van Swearingen, Thos Swearingen, Milley (x) Burnet. /s/ James Hoge. Proven 7 Jan 1799 by Thomas Swearingen; Van Swearingen JP. Rec 7 Jan 1799.

p.190-193   Benjamin Etheredge to John Raben. Deed, 21 June 1797, £10 sterling, 215 acres on Cedar Creek. Wit James Calk Sr, Drury Allen. /s/ Benjamin Etheredge. Proven 5 January 1799 by Drury Allen; Russell Wilson JP. Rec 7 Jan 1799.

p.193-198   Sheriff Joseph Culpeper to Richard Bolan, merchant of

Columbia, Richland County, Camden District. Sheriffs Titles, 24
February 1797, Jacob Richman in his lifetime of Orangeburgh District
seized of land containing by original survey 100 acres on Flat Spring
branch of Clouds Creek, originally granted to James Cummings and by
him conveyed to John McCartey; from him to Jacob Richman. Jacob
Richman in his lifetime being indebted to Llewellen Threewitts in sum
of £22.18, sd Llewellen Threewitts for recovery of sd sum commenced
action against Richard Bolan admr of sd Jacob Richman in which action
Llewellen Threewitts in November Term 1791 at Orangeburg recovered
against sd Richard Bolan admr the sum and damages sustained by
reason of nonperformance. Judgment at Orangeburgh 13 May 1791
directed Sheriffs to sell goods chattels and real estate of sd Richard
Bolan admr of sd Jacob Richman. Sheriff Joseph Culpeper sold sd 100
acres 1 January 1792 unto Richard Bolan for £4.10 sterling. Wit
Charles Williamson, William Smart. /s/ Joseph Culpeper Late Shff.
Proven Camden District, Richland County, 5 December 1798 by
Charles Williamson; J Goodwyn JRC. Recorded 8 Jan 1799.

p.198-201   Richard Bolan, merchant of Richland County, to Adam
Efurt. Deed, 5 December 1798, $100, 100 acres on flat spring branch
of Clouds Creek originally granted to James Cummings; by him conveyed to John McCartey; from McCartey to Jacob Richman; by a writ
of Fire Facias, Llewellen Threewits vs Richard Bolan admr of Jacob
Richman was sold by Sheriff Joseph Culpeper of Orangeburgh District
1 Jan 1792 unto afsd Richard Bolan he being highest & last bidder. Wit
J Bostick, Andrew Heatley, Conrad Lowry. /s/ Richard Bolan. Judge
John Goodwyn of Richland County, Camden Dist, certifies relinquishment of dower by Edith B Bolan wife of Richard Bolan, 5 December
1798. /s/ Edith Bolan. Proven, Camden District, Richland County, 5
December 1798 by Conrad Lowry; J Goodwyn JRC. Rec 8 Jan 1799.

p.201-208   James Daniel of Fairfield County, planter, to Wats Man.
L&R, 9/10 May 1787, £200 old SC currency, 150 acres on a branch
of Clouds Creek of Little Saluda River granted 16 Jan 1761 by Lt Gov
Wm Bull unto Linerd Summott 150 acres, by Linerd Summott to Moses
Kirkland and by sd Kirkland to James Daniel. Wit Wm Daniel, John
May, John Daniel. /s/ James Daniel. Proven 25 October 1798 by John
Daniel; Russell Wilson JP.   Rec 8 January 1799.

p.208-210   Thomas Man of Orangeburgh District to Elizabeth Man
of Edgefield. Deed, 1 June 1797, $100, 35 acres part of 250 acres in
Edgefield County on branch of Clouds Creek bounding on lands of

William Johnson, Jno Watts Man, granted to John Watts Man 1 March 1775, sd 35 acres to be taken off joining sd Elizabeth Man's land and lands of Elizah Martin, Butler, Stephen Williams land; sd Thomas Man being the eldest son and heir of John Wats Man decd doth convey the same to Elizabeth Man. Wit John McCreless, Wm Messer. /s/ Thomas (x) Man. Proven 10 March 1798 by William Messer; John P Bond JP. Rec 8 Jan 1799.

p.211-217   James Harkins to James Gouedy. L&R, 10/11 March 1794, £60 sterling, 93.5 acres, which is one third of a tract which fell to sd James Harkins Junr, Roger Harkins, and William Harkins by James Harkins Senr deceased, being one third of land originally granted to James Harkins decd, on Suters Creek of Henleys Creek bounded by lands formerly the property of Robert Gouedy decd, and by William Harkins, John Carew, Roger Harkins. Wit John Carew, Henry White, Timothy Haver. /s/ James Harkins. Proven 3 Jan 1799 by Henry White; Julius Nichols JP.   Rec 12 Jan 1799.

p.218-228   James Gouedy, planter, to Matilda Smyth, widow of Doctor Andrew Smyth, deceased. Titles, 27 May 1797, £150 sterling, 93.5 acres surveyed by David Cunningham decd & delivered to William Shaw Esqr by sd James Gouedy, bounding on lands of Roger Harkins, Robert Gouedy, William Harkins, Hamiltons great survey, contains dwelling house of sd James Gouedy whereon sd James Gouedy now and for several years past resided, being one third of a tract originally granted to James Arkins alias Harkins decd con-taining at original survey 250 acres at time of original survey adj lands of John Hamilton and Robert Gouedy decd. Witness Allen Glover, T Bostick. /s/ James Gouedy.   Judge William Anderson certifies relin-quishment of dower by Susannah Carew formerly widow and relict of James Arkins alias Harkins decd and now the wife of John Carew, 7 May 1797. /s/ Susannah Carew. Judge William Anderson certifies relinquishment of dower by Betcy Gouedy wife of James Gouedy, 27 May 1797. /s/ Betcy Gouedy. Proven 29 August 1798 by Tolever Bostick; Julius Nichols JP.   Rec 12 January 1799.

p.229-236   James Gouedy, planter, to Matilda Smyth, widow of Doctor Andrew Smyth decd. Deed or Titles, 27 May 1797, £150 sterling, 300 acres land originally granted to William Dargan on Henleys Creek bounded by lands surveyed for William Lewiston & his associates, & by Robert Gouedy decd. Tract sold by sd William Dargan to Robert Gouedy, and by Robert Gouedy sold at auction at

Court order and bought by afsd James Gouedy highest & last bidder. Wit Allen Glover, T Bostick. /s/ James Gouedy. Judge William Anderson certifies relinquishment of dower by Betcy Gouedy wife of within named James Gouedy, 27 May 1797. /s/ Betcy Gouedy. Proven 29 Aug 1798 by Tolover Bostick; Julius Nichols JP. Rec 12 Jan 1799.

p.237-238   William Shaw to his sister Matilda Smyth, widow, and niece Betsy Wybeigh Smyth. Deed of Gift, 19 September 1797, for love & affection, Negro girl Rose age about fifteen and her future increase, to my niece Betsy Wybeigh Smyth in case of survival if not to my niece Mary Anne Smyth but the increase of sd Negro girl Rose born in the lifetime of my sister Matilda Smyth to be equally divided between my two nieces Mary Anne Smythe and Betsy Wybeigh Smyth if they are both living, if not the whole to go to the survivor. Wit Jacob Norrill. /s/ Wm Shaw. Proven 25 Sept 1797 by Jacob Norrill; Julius Nichols JP. Rec 12 Jan 1799.

p.239   Samuel Thompson. Certificate, 19 Nov, 1798, State of Tenecy, Blunt County. Samuel Thompson certifies that by virtue of a licence, he married Robert Thompson and Ester Derham about 1787. Edgefield County, 28 January 1799, John Bush swears he was present and saw the within Samuel Thompson sign the within certificate; Van Swearingen JP. Recorded 28 January 1798.

p.239-241   Benjamin Wages to William Smith. Power of Attorney, 28 January 1799, for good causes appoint trusty friend William Smith of Kentucky attorney in my name to recover from Willis Watkins a sum owed for a sorrel mare valued at £30 sterling, appraisement certifyed by William McDowall JP on oaths of David Forester and John Nelson. Wit Mathew Mims, Leroy Pardue. /s/ Benjamin (x) Wages. Proven 28 January 1799 by Mathew Mims; Rd Tutt JP. Rec 29 Jan 1799.

p.242-244   James Thomas to Jesse Stone. Deed, 24 January 1799, $215, 100 acres granted to James Thomas 26 July 1774 on Middle Creek adj lands of C Cox, Desausure, J Tucker, Rutledge. Wit William Key, Joseph Robinson, John Boyd. /s/ James Thomas. Proven 24 January 1799 by John Boyd; Henry Key JP. Rec 31 Jan 1799.

p.245-247   John Griffis Senr, shoemaker, to son Nicholas Griffis. Deed of Gift, 28 January 1799, love & goodwill, 100 acres being part of 400 acres granted to sd Griffis 19 August 1774 by Hon Wm Bull on Bird Creek adj land of John Tolbert. Wit Augustin Bryan, John Key.

/s/ John Griffis Senr. Proven 19(sic) Jan 1799 by Augustin Bryan; Henry Key JP. Recorded 31 January 1799.

p.247-251   John Boyd to John Morris. Deed, 11 January 1799, $180, 180 acres part of tract granted to William Tolbert on Swift Creek branch of Savannah River bounded by Mr Lawly, Butler, Deliho. Wit Jesse Stone, Landon Tucker, Grissim (x) Morris. /s/ John Boyd. Acknowledgment by John Morris of form of within deed; if land is recovered by an older right than William Tolberts grant, Morris is not to bring suit against John Boyd for sum or damage; wit Jesse Stone, Landon Tucker, Grissim (x) Morris. ./s/ John (x) Morris. Proven 24 January 1799 by Jesse Stone; Henry Key JP. Rec 31 Jan 1799.

p.251-254   William Donoho to James Whitehead. Deed, 2 February 1797, $100, 100 acres on the dreans of Beach Creek & Long Branch of Edisto River, adj Brushey Pond, Donohos land, James Tomlin, assigned by Chas Pinckney 1792. Wit James Tomlin, John Walker. /s/ William Donoho. Proven 8 February 1797 by James Tomlin; Van Swearingen JP. Recorded 31 Jan 1799.

p.254-256   John M Dooly son & heir to John Dooly deceased to Robert Kilcrease. Deed, 14 March 1797, $10 [$20?] in compliance with contract executed between himself and Benjamin Kilcrease in lifetime of both, have granted unto Robert Kilcrease son of afsd Benj Kilcrease, 100 acres on Turkey Creek. Wit Edward Holmes, Robert (x) Brooks. /s/ John M Dooly. Proven 26 May 1797 by Edward Holmes; Henry Key JP. Recorded 2 Feb 1799.

p.256[second page of this number]-258   John M Dooly brother & heir to Thomas Dooly deceased to Edward Holmes. Deed, 13 March 1797, $60, 200 acres on Turkey Creek adjoining lands of Alexander. Wit Jonas Holmes, John White. /s/ John M Dooly. Proven 13 March 1797 by Jonas Holmes; Henry Key, JP. Rec 2 Feb 1799.

p.258-260   Charles J Colcock to Abraham Taylor. Deed, 2 February 1799, 142 acres on Rockey Creek bounded on lands late property of Moses Kirkland, Adam Summers same being sold by Sheriff at suit of Commissioners of Treasury against Joseph Decosster & Samuel Decosster and purchased by sd Charles Jones Colocks. Wit Elisha Stevens, A Eskridge. /s/ Charles J Colcock by my attorney S Mays. Proven 2 Feb 1799 by Elisha Stevens; John Blocker JP. Recorded 2 February 1799.

p.260-263   William Eddins to Benjamin Eddins Senr. Deed, 28 December 1798, £64.15 sterling, 133¾ acres in Abbeville on Hard Labour Creek, being part or half of the tract that James Mayson acting as agent for John Rutledge sold to above William Eddins and said Benjamin Edding as going Halfs in the land at that time as the whole tract contains 277½ acres. Wit Joseph Eddins, John Eddins. /s/ William Eddins. Proven 12 Jan 1799 by Joseph Eddins; John Blocker JP.   Rec 2 Feb 1799.

p.263-271   James Hart, yeoman, of Colleton County to John Smedley. L&R, 23 and 24 November 1774, £100 SC money, 100 acres (Bounty) in Colleton County on Red Bank branch of Little Saluda, granted by Gov Charles Montague 1773. Wit Thomas Deloach, Richd Williams, James Scott. /s/ James Hart. Proven 11 March 1775 by Thomas Deloach; Moses Kirkland JP.   Rec 4 Feb 1799.

p.271-278   Thomas Smedley of Green County, Georgia, yeoman, to Lewis Clark. L&R, 4 & 5 December 1790, £17 sterling, 100 acres on Red Bank Creek of Little Saluda, granted by Gov Charles Montague unto James Hart 6 Feb 1773 and conveyed unto John Smedley 1774. Wit Samuel Deloach, Aaron Clark, John Smedley. /s/ Thomas Smedley, Henry King, Averilla (x) King. Proven 2 February 1799 by John Smedley; William Daniel JP.   Rec 4 Feb 1799.

p.279-286   Lewis Clark, yeoman, to William Burdett. L&R, 23/24 February 1791, £40, 100 acres (Bounty) granted by Governor Montague unto James Hart 6 Feb 1773, on Red Bank Creek of Little Saludy River, conveyed from sd James to John Smedley decd 1774; sd land fell to sd Thomas Smedley eldest son ands heir at law by death of his father and was conveyed from sd Thomas Smedley to sd Lewis Clark 1790. Wit Henry King, Thomas Dozer, Aaron Clark. /s/ Lewis Clark. Proven 4 Feb 1799 by Henry King; Rd Tutt JP. Rec 4 Feb 1799.

p.287-289   Benjamin Wages and wife Mary to John Beckham. Deed, 13 December 1796, £30 sterling, 100 acres on Little Saluda River being part of 650 acres originally granted to Jesse Pitts 1792 by Gov Chas Pinckney adj Browns line. Wit Henry King, Wm (x) Burdet. /s/ Benjamin Wages, /s/ Mary (x) Wages. Proven 23 Jan 1799 by William Burdet; William Daniel JP.   Rec 7 Feb 1799.

p.289-291   John Joachim Bulow & Charles William Bulow to Thomas Largant. Deed, 7 June 1798, £40, 150 acres Indian Creek of

18

Little Saludy River originally granted to Michael Bates 5 June 1786 by Gov Wm Moultree, and conveyed from sd Michael Bates unto Joachim Bulow of the City of Charleston; left to us the said John J & Charles W Bulow by will of Joachim Bulow decd. Wit Robt Geddes, Sam Robertson, George Robertson. /s/ John J Bulow, Chas Wm Bulow. Proven 7 June 1798 by Robert Gaddes; John Johnson JP. Rec 14 Feb 1799.

p.292-293   Mark Stephens of Cashaw County, SC, to David Shockley and wife Martha of Edgefield. Deed, 6 January 1799; Stephens agrees to keep David Shockley and wife in comfortable manner during their natural lifetime, for which Shockley and wife grant unto Mark Stephens for his trouble and kind care 100 acres on Long Cane Road, waters of Turkey Creek in Edgefield, livestock, household furniture. Wit Jacob Smith, Absalom (x) Littelfield, George (x) Kizer. /s/ Mark (x) Stephens, /s/ David (x) Shockley. Proven 10 Jan 1799 by Jacob Smith; Russell Wilson JP. Rec 18 Feb 1799.

p.294-300   Ann Vaun to Wilson & John Lee. Deed of Gift, My late husband, Andrew Lee of Edgefield, decd, by will dated 13 December 1795 bequeathed unto his sons John Lee and Wilson Lee all his claim into and out of a bridge ferry passage over Saluda River commonly known as Lees Bridge, and whereas this State passed an act to establish roads & ferrys, further enacted that the ferry commonly called Lees on Saludy River be reestablished and vested in Nancy Lee for fourteen years, and whereas by deed of Nicholas Vaughn, my present husband, previous to our marriage and of myself, Nancy Vaughn late Nancy Lee dated 20 Jan 1798, it was agreed that sd Anne Lee now Nancy Vaughn shall retain for her sole use notwithstanding marriage all estate real or personal, and whereas Mr Horry from Committee on roads & bridges reported on petition of sd Nancy Vaun to vest the Ferry & Bridge afsd in her sons John Lee & Wilson Lee agreeable to will of her late husband Andrew Lee decd, report read and agreed to by the legislature, Now Nancy Vaun, late Nancy Lee, carries into effect the intent of my late husband, and for love & affection unto my beloved sons, also in consideration of $100 silver, grant to sons agreeable to will of Andrew Lee decd all right title &c of the bridge ferry passage & way afsd over Saludy River known as Lees Bridge. Wit Humphrey Williamson, Thos G Harbirt. /s/ Nancy (A) Vaun late Nancy Lee. Proven 15 Jan 1799 by H Williamson; Wm Nibbs JQ. Rec 18 Feb 1799.

p.300-302   Nancy Vaughn to son Gershom Lee. Bill of Sale, 25 December 1798, love & affection to Gershom, Negro boy Stephen. Wit

Abbigail Williamson. /s/ Nancy (x) Vaughan. Proven 15 Jan 1799 by Abbigail Williamson; Wm Nibbs JQ. Rec 18 Feb 1799.

p.302-303   Nancy Vaughan to son John Lee. Deed of Gift, 2 December 1798, love & affection, Negro girl Philles. Wit Higdon Borroum, John Cunningham, Abigail Williamson. /s/ Nancy (A) Vaughan. Proven 15 Jan 1799 by Abbigail Williamson; Wm Nibbs JQ. Rec 18 Feb 1799.

p.304-306   William Todd to William Rice Clark. Deed, 12 January 1799, $193, 667 acres, being upper part of 1000 acres on Mounty Creek granted to William Todd 17 October 1793. Witness John Blocker Junr, John Hunter. /s/ William Todd. Judge Arthur Simkins certifies relinquishment of dower by Jean Todd wife of William Todd, 20 Feby 1799; /s/ Jean (x) Todd. Proven 12 Jan 1799 by John Blocker Junr; John Blocker JP. Rec 20 Feb 1799.

p.307-313   Samuel Fley to Andrew Gamillan[Gamalan]. L&R, 28 & 29 September 1792, £10 SC money, 449 acres granted to him 17 Nov 1791 bounding on lands of Samuel Whitney, Messer Smith, Wm Coursey. Wit B Waring, Geo Joor. /s/ Samuel Fley. Proven 1 October 1792 county of [blank] by Benjamin Waring; Peter Bremar F.R.C. Rec 23 Feb 1799.

p.313-320   James Rowe to Christian Gamilan. L&R, 1 & 2 November 1791, £20 SC money, 100 acres below the ancient boundary line, on Dry fork of Mine Creek of Saludy river, part of 769 acres granted 1787 by Gov Wm Moultree unto Rolan Williams, conveyed by Rolan Williams to James Rowe. Wit Edward Couch, Rolan Williams, Andrew Gamalan. /s/ James Row. Proven 23 Feb 1799 by Andrew Gamelin; Rd Tutt JP. Rec 23 Feb 1799.

p.320-323   John Anderson to John Harkins. Deed, 14 August 1798, $171.43, 150 acres originally granted to John Anderson 1768 on Hard Labor and Cuffeetown Creeks of Stephens Creek. Wit Jas Harrison, Samuel Hall. /s/ John (x) Anderson. Affirmed 14 August 1798 by Samuel Hall; James Harrison JP. Rec 2 March 1799.

p.323-324   James Frazier to William Crane. Deed, 10 October 1798, £50, 340 acres [or 370 acres] on Beaverdam Creek adj lands of sd Crane, John Simkins, Pressly Bland, [blank] Logan, Aaron Carter. Wit Benjamin Frazier, Levi Jester. /s/ James Frazier. Proven 2

February 1799 by Levi Jester; John Blocker JP. Rec 2 March 1799.

p.325-326   John Davis indorsee of Elisha Rogers and Wife to John Street. Bond, 29 November 1792, in penal sum £300. Elijah Rogers, carpenter & wife Jean Rogers, sell unto John Davis, millwright, such land as came to us by earship of allicksander Wilson deceased. Test Benj Clark, Nehemiah Posey. /s/ Elijah Rogers, Jean (x) Rogers.
        I do hereby indorse the within bond unto Joseph Street, 1 Jan 1793. /s/ John Davis. Proven 1 March 1799 by Margret (x) Reeks who saw John Davis indorse Elisha Rogers & wifes bond; Wm Robinson, JP. Proven 5 March 1799 by Nehemiah (x) Posey who saw Elisah Rogers assign above obligation and his wife Jeane (x) Rogers make her mark; John Spann JP. Rec 6 March 1799.

p.326-330   John Sawyer and wife Lidda of Orangeburgh District, SC, to Uriah Collum of Edgefield. Deed, 14 February 1799, £30, 150 acres on West Creek of Clouds Creek of Saluda River, part being land granted to Elisha Nite 7 June 1790, transfered from Elisha Nite to Jno Sawyer; other part being part of tract where Lewis Deshazo now lives granted to Thomas Butler 7 Jan 1788, transfered from Thomas Butler to Heartwell Hart and from Hartwell Hart to John Sawyer; also part on Johns Branch that was granted to afsd Thomas Butler, 30 acres now John Sawyers. Wit Wm Norris, Nathan Norris, Lewis Deshazo. /s/ John Sawyer, /s/ Lydia Sawyer. Judge Arthur Simkins certifies relinquishment of dower by Lydia wife of John Sawyer; /s/ Lydia (x) Sawyer. Proven 1 March 1799 by William Norris; Jos Williams JP. Rec 7 March 1799.

p.331-333   James Courtney and wife Alishabah to Charles Hicks. Deed, 22 November 1798, $128.50, 150 acres on Big Creek of Little Saludy river, being part of 350 acres originally granted to Wm Bolan 5 Jan 1789 by Gov Thos Pinckney, bounded by lands of Joseph Moseley, John Moseley, John Coy, John Cocker, Spencer Bowling. Wit John S Gorman, Richard Buffington. /s/ Jas Courtney. /s/ Elishabah (x) Courtney. Proven 29 December 1798 by Richard Buffington; Nathl Abney JP. Rec 11 March 1799.

p.333-336   Thomas Baker, planter, to Mary Scurrey of Newberry County, SC. Deed, [no date], full sum of £80 sterling, condition Thos Baker make good title to 150 acres, the lower part of 300 surveyed by William Toney on Indian Creek within eight years from within date to Mary Scurry, or repay sd Mary Scurry £40 being purchase money [edge of this page has been cut off] above tract of land if titles cannot be [made] from heirs of Tonsey [or Toxsey?] when the heirs [come] of age. Wit Peter Felbach, P Waters. /s/ Thomas Baker. Be it remembered the wheat on plantation [word cut off] is divided. Wit P Waters. /s/ Thomas B[cut off], /s/ Mary Scur[cut off]. Proven, Newberry Co, [edge of page cut off] 7 March 1799 P B Waters identifies handwriting of Philemon B Waters; Fred Nance JP. Rec 11 March 1799.

p.336-399 [Edge of page is cut off]   David Benton to Allen Body. Deed, 7 October 1797, £10 SC money, [cut off] hundred and fifty acres being part of land [cut off] Jan 1788 by Gov Thos Pinckney, surveyed 28 August 1787 by Samuel Mayes; sd land bounding lands of Allen Body, Moses Prescoats, Ephraim Prescoatts, Thomas Harris. Wit James Wilson, Frances Pepin. /s/ David Benton. Proven [blank] 1797 by Frances Pepin; Elkanah Sawyer JP. Rec 11 March 1799.

p.339-340   Rebecca Watson to Daniel Bullock. Receipt, 18 [month] 1796, received of Daniel Bullock admr, one young Negro woman Phillis, being in full of all debts due of my fathers estates Artimas Watson decd. Wit Benj Watson. Proven 4 December 1797 by Benjamin Watson; Wm Daniel JP. Rec 11 March 1799.

p.340-343   Sheriff William Tennent to Edward Johnson. Sheriff Titles, 14 January 1799; at suit of William Parker agt Robert Stark, court ordered sale of land to highest bidder at Cambridge; struck off to Edward Johnson for $26.50, 300 acres adj lands of David Andress, Benjamin Sims, Herod Thompson; granted to Daniel Hartley, and which sd Robert Stark had at time of the sale. Wit Edward Prince, Hugh Middleton Junr. /s/ Wm Tennent. Proven 16 Feb 1799 by Hugh Middleton Junr; Hugh Middleton JP. Rec 11 March 1799.

p.343-346   Henry Strum[Sturm?] to John Pittman. Deed, 14 October 1796, £55 [p.344 is unreadable] Wit William Wagner, Memoah (x) Mather. /s/ Handra (x) Strum. Proven 9 March 1799 by William Whymer; Jas Harrison JP. /s/ Wm Wagner. Rec 11 Mar 1799.

p.346-350   Allen Body to Mary Prescott. Deed, 4 January 1799, £11.13.4 SC money, 100 acres, being part of a tract formerly granted unto Thomas Butler 17 Jan 1788 by Gov Thos Pinckney, surveyed 28 Aug 1787 by Samuel Mays, bounding on lands held by Wm Mobbley, Mathew Dinkins, land Allen Body had of David Benton. Wit Elkanah Powell, John Powell. /s/ Allen (x) Body, Penny (x) Body. Proven 9

Feb 1799 by Elkanah Powell who saw Allen Body and his wife Penny
Body sign; Elkanah Sawyer JP. Recorded 11 Mar 1799.

p.350-355   Joseph Wood and brothers Daniel and Jeremiah Wood
executors & heirs of will of Daniel Wolecon to Edward Rowell of
Richmond County, Georgia, Esquire. Deed, 2 August 1798; Daniel
Wolecon on 14 October 1782 for £800 sold unto Joseph Moore the
parcel of land hereinafter mentioned; Moore on 7 April 1793(sic)
assigned sd land unto Nathaniel Cocke who on 31 July 1784 assigned
same unto sd Edward Rowell, party hereto who hath fully complied
with the terms of sale. Now Joseph Wood, Danl Wood & Jeremiah
Wood in consideration of $100, sell unto Edward Rowell who is in
possession thereof, all that parcel of land, 400 acres, on Beach Island,
New Windsor township on Savannah river, originally granted unto
Samuel Lamar, bounded at original survey by Thomas Lamar, Michael
Meyers, Thomas Goodale, Sarah Lamar. Wit Isaac Wingate, John
Savage, John Vaughan. /s/ Jos Wood exr, /s/ Danl Wood exr, /s/
Jeremiah Wood exr. Proven 26 December 1798 by John Savage; John
Clark JP. Rec 11 March 1799.

p.355-358   Ephraim Prescoat to Allen Body. Deed, 1797 [no day
or month], £29 sterling, 84 acres on Dry Creek of Clouds Creek of Big
Saluda bounded by lands of Moses Prescott, Samuel Mays, Major
Mees, Fra Williams, it being land granted to Phillemon Waters Esqr by
Gov Chas Pinckney 1790. Wit Francis Pepin, David (x) Meghees. /s/
Ephraim Prescott. Proven 16 June 1798 by Francis Pepin; Elkanah
Sawyer JP. Rec 11 March 1799.

p.359-361   James McMillan to James Perry. Deed, 12 January
1797, £2 SC money, 50 acres, part of land granted unto Daniel Craw-
ford, bounded by lands of Ezekiel Perry Senr, Isaac Foreman, James
Perry, Walker. Wit Ezekiel Perry, John Wimberley. /s/ James
McMilan. Proven 12 March 1798 by John Wimberley; John Blocker
JP. Rec 11 March 1799.

p.361-364   Jacob Fudge of Georgia to Phill May. Deed, 21 September 1798, £100, 325 acres whereof 150 acres lie on Chaves's Creek
part of 300 acres originally granted to Richard Kirkland, and part of a
tract granted to Phill May Senr; 75 acres part of tract of 299 acres
originally granted to Elizabeth Reynolds; the remaining 100 acres, part
of above 300 acres originally granted to Richard Kirkland by Gov
Montague 20 July 1772, adjoining William Coggins spring branch,

Zacheriah James. Wit John G Cooke, Isaac Hopkins. /s/ Jacob Fudge.
Proven 3 January 1799 by Isaac Hopkins; Van Swearingen JP. /s/
Jacob(sic) Hopkins.   Rec 11 March 1799.

p.364-367   John Adams to William Cox.   Deed, 14 January 1799,
£30, 100 acres, part of grant to Peter Loger on Stephens Creek bounded by lands of Moses Findley and John Garrett. Wit Edward Harrison, Moses (x) Findley. /s/ John Adams. Judge Arthur Simkins certifies relinquishment of dower by Sarah Adams wife of John Adams, 11
March 1799. /s/ Sarah (x) Adams. Proven 14 January 1799 by Moses
Findley; Jas Harrison JP.   Rec 11 March 1799.

p.368-370   John McDaniel of Newberry County, SC, to Hardy Keel.
Deed, Orangeburgh, 96 District, 2 June 1798, $150, 150 acres on
Edisto River being part of 300 acres originally granted to William Drew
23 June 1774 by Gov Wm Bull. Wit Martin Witt, John Mowrey. /s/
John McDaniel, /s/ Layah (x) McDaniel. Proven 28 July 1798 by
Martin Witt; Wm Calk, JP.   Rec 11 March 1799.

p.370-371   Samuel Hammond of Chatham County, Georgia, planter,
to David Bowers. Deed/Sale, 6 June 1798, $400 paid or secured, two
Negro men named Lewis and Doctor. Wit Jeremiah Wood. Proven 9
March 1799 by Jeremiah Wood; John Clarke JP.   Rec 11 Mar 1799.

p.372-375   John Adams to Moses Findley. Deed, 14 January 1799,
$130, 100 acres being half of 200 acres on a branch of Stephens Creek
originally granted to Peter Leger 3 April 1775. Wit Edward Harrison,
William Cox. /s/ John Adams. Plat shows Mr. Glantons land. Judge
Arthur Simkins certifies relinquishment of dower by Sarah Adams wife
of John Adams, 11 March 1799. /s/ Sarah (x) Adams. Proven 14 Jan
1799 by William Cox; Jas Harrison JP. Rec 11 March 1799.

p.375-378   Clement Cargill to Cary Morgan. Deed, 14 January
1799, $100, 150 acres being part of tract originally granted to Charles
Williams on Savannah River bounded by land of William Tidders at
original survey. Wit Barnard Caffery, Nancy (x) Cafrey. /s/ Clement
Cargill. Judge Joseph Hightower certifies relinquishment of dower by
Patsey Cargill wife of Clement Cargill, 11 March 1799. /s/ Patsey (x)
Cargill. Proven 7 March 1799 by Barnard Caffery; Henry Key JP.
Rec 11 March 1799.

p.379   Barrott Travis, planter, to John Glanton, planter. Deed,

9 October 1798, $100, 100 acres being part of 312 acres originally
granted to William Humphreys on Mine Creek and the road from 96 to
Charleston, bounding William Daniel's land. Wit Mumford Perryman,
Jonathan Glanton. /s/ Barrott (x) Travis. Proven 2 March 1799 by
Jonathan Glanton; Wm Daniel JP. Rec 11 Mar 1799.

p.381-384   John Miller of Charleston to Isaac Lewis, planter. Deed,
1 November 1797, £54 sterling, 300 acres on Halfway Swamp of Saluda River bounded by lands of Bushead Thomas, Peter McDole[?]. Wit
Abel McDowall, Patrk McDowall. /s/ For my Papa John Miller, Elizabeth Miller, /s/ John (x) Miller. Judge John Sandford certifies that
Catherine Miller wife of John Miller appeared and relinquished dower,
8 Nov 1797. /s/ Catherine (x) Miller. Proven 21 April 1798 by Patrick
McDowall; Wm Robertson JP. Rec 11 March 1799.

p.385   Benjamin Kirkland's Oath. 11 March 1799 Description
of Marks & Brands for his granddaughter Ester Kirkland and his son
William Kirkland; Van Swearingen JP. Rec 11 Mar 1799

p.385-387   John Douglass to Rachel Mobley. Deed, 15 December
1798, $100, 100 acres on Penn Creek of Little Saluda River, 50 acres
thereof conveyed by Thomas Deloach to Moses Brown; from Moses
Brown to John Douglass, the other 50 acres was part of 90 acres granted to sd Brown, 50 whereof was conveyed from Moses Brown to John
Douglass. Wit Henry King, Jean Weaver. /s/ John (I) Douglass. Prov-
en 2 Jan 1799 by Jehu Weaver; Wm Daniel JP. Rec 11 Mar 1799.

p.388-389   John Douglass to Rachel Mobbley, widow. Bill of Sale,
8 December 1798, $100, Negro boy Charles. Wit Henry King, Jehu
Weaver. /s/ John (x) Douglass. Proven 2 January 1799 by Jehu
Weaver; William Daniel JP.   Rec 11 Mar 1799.

p.389-392   Moses Jones and wife Elizabeth to Joseph Eaten. Deed,
19 September 1798, £20 sterling, 140 acres on Mountain Creek of
Turkey Creek being part of 364 acres originally granted to James Harrison 3 April 1786.   Wit R McCoombs, John (x) Sloan, John (x) Hamilton. /s/ Moses (x) Jones, /s/ Elizabeth (x) Jones.   Proven 9 March
1799 by Robert McCombs; Julius Nichols JP.   Rec 11 Mar 1799.

p.392-395   Daniel Barksdale and Robert Ware to James Thomas.
Bond, 9 March 1799, penal sum $5000 to be paid to James Thomas;
Daniel Barksdale purchased of James Thomas two tracts, the first

contains 500 acres on Stephens Creek adj land granted to Wm Wainer and granted to James Simpson; the second of 50 acres & granted to Joseph Chalwin; bond conditions. Wit Saml Crafton, Martin Goza. /s/ Daniel Barksdale, /s/ Robt Ware. Proven 11 March 1799 by Martin Goza; Rd Tutt JP. Rec 11 Mar 1799.

p.395-398   Manoah Weatherton & wife Susanna to Levi Wetherton. Deed, [blank] March 1799, £20 sterling, 100 acres on Horse pen Creek of Cuffeetown Creek being part of 234 acres originally granted to Menoah Wetherton 23 November 1793. Wit John Todd, Thomas (x) Wetherton, Gools B (x) Garner. /s/ Manoah (x) Wetherton, Susanna (x) Wetherton. Proven 11 March 1799 by Thomas Wetherton; William Robertson JP.   Rec 11 Mar 1799.

p.398-400   John Douglass to Bartlett Bledsoe. Bill of Sale, 19 November 1798, $300, Negro man Joe, Negro boy Landy; Wit George Mason, Elizabeth Mason. /s/ John (x) Douglass. Proven 11 Mar 1799 by Elizabeth (x) Mason; John Spann JP.   Rec 11 Mar 1799.

p.400-404   John Arledge to John Hall. Deed, 9 February 1799, $300, SC money, 100 acres being part of 370 acres on Turkey Creek granted to Jacob Youngblood, and 185 acres conveyed to us by Jacob Youngblood, of sd 185 there is laid off about 75 acres to Thomas Landrum and about 25 acres that I bought from Joel Chandler (&c), mouth of Haw Branch. Wit Thomas Hall, Sam (x) Jinkins, Edward (x) Hatcher. /s/ John (x) Arledge, /s/ Ann (x) Arledge. Judge Arthur Simkins certifies relinquishment of dower by Ann Arledge wife of John Arledge, 9 Mar 1799. /s/ Ann (x) Arledge. Proven 11 Mar 1799 by Thomas Hall; John Blocker JP.   Rec 11 Mar 1799.

p.404-407   George Abarnathy of Newberry County to James Blaylock. Deed, 1 March 1799, $250, 250 acres on Indian Creek of Little Saluda granted to Thomas Appleton 25 April 1774 by Gov Wm Bull to Wm Appleton ; by heirship to his daughter Martha Appleton, the same now the wife of sd George Abarnathy. Wit Penington King, William Tinney. /s/ George Abernathy. Judge Le Casey certifies relinquishment of dower by Martha Abarnathy wife of George Abarnathy, 4 Mar 1799; /s/ Martha Abarnathy. Proven Newberry County, 4 Mar 1799 by Pennington King; Levi Casey JNC. Rec 11 Mar 1799.

p.408-411   Lewis Etheredge to Harmon Coleburn. Deed, 11 September 1797, $7, 50 acres on Two Mile Branch of Saludy River adj

land land of Abel Etheredge, being part of tract surveyed 9 Feb 1773
for Mary Thomas. Wit Isaac Stephens, William (x) Etheredge. /s/
Lewis (L) Etheredge. Proven 1 July 1798 by William Etheredge;
Elkanah Sawyer JP. Rec 11 Mar 1799.

p.411-415   Alexander Paterson and wife Susanna to John Adams.
Deed, 5 March 1796, £30 SC money, 75 acres being part of 300 acres
on Red Bank of Little Saluda granted to James Hughston in 1774, the
75 acres bounded by land of William Adams, Paterson, Wm Adams
Junr, being half of a tract conveyed from James Hughston to Alexr
Paterson. Wit James Adams, William (mark) Adams. /s/ Alexr Pater-
son, Susanna (x) Paterson. Proven 31 December 1796 by James
Adams; Julius Nichols JP.   Rec 11 Mar 1799.

p.415-419   James Hughston to William Adams. Deed, 3 August
1796, £30 sterling, 75 acres being part of 300 acres on head of Red
Bank Creek of Little Saluda granted to James Hughston by Lt Gov Wm
Bull 16 Sept 1774 & adj lands of Benjamin Row, Starks, John Adams,
James Adams, Amos Adams. Wit James Adams, Mary Huston. /s/
James Huston. Receipt wit by James Adams, Mary Adams. /s/ James
Huston. Proven 21 Apr 1798 by James Adams; Wm Robertson JP.
Rec 11 March 1799.

p.419-422   Benjamin Melton to John Fortner. Deed, 2 August
1798, £30, 150 acres being part of land granted to sd Benja Melton by
patent 3 Oct 1796. Wit James Wolf, P Bland, John Hearn. /s/ Benjamin
(B) Melton.   Proven 6 Aug 1798 by John Hearn; William Daniel JP.
Rec 4 Mar 1799.

p.422-424   Edward Rutledge to Joseph Morris. Deed, 17 January
1799, $350, 500 acres on Little Stephens Creek bounding on Richd
Buckelow and Garret Buckelow, original grant to Robert Pringle Esqr.
Wit M Rutledge, W Drayton. /s/ Edward Rutledge. Proven [no date] by
William Drayton who with Mary Rutledge saw Edward Rutledge deliver
within instrument; Wm M Parker JP.   Rec 11 Mar 1799.

p.424-426   William Abney to William Laney. Deed, 2 December
1798, $100, 134 acres on Half Way Swamp adj lands of Joseph Cul-
breath, Rufus Inman, Luis Boatner, John Low, Joel Pardue, originally
granted to sd Abney 3 Dec 1787. Wit Walter Abney, Benj Taylor. /s/
W Abney.   Proven 9 March 1799 by Benjamin Taylor; Nathl Abney
JP.   Rec 11 Mar 1799.

p.426-428   John Douglass to daughter Jean Weaver, widow. Deed of Gift, 8 December 1798, for love, Negro woman Princess[?]. Wit Henry King, John Weaver. /s/ John (I) Douglass. Proven 2 January 1799 by Jehu Weaver; Wm Daniel JP.   Rec 11 Mar 1799.

428-436   James Warren of Colleton County, Ninety Six District, to Henley(Henly) Webb of Colleton County, planter. L&R, 29/20(sic) May 1785, £300 SC money, 140 acres on Clouds Creek, Saluda River bounded by lands of John Williams, Capt Benjamin Tutt. Wit William Odum, John Vardell, Mary (x) Odum. /s/ James (I) Warren. Proven 11 June 1785 by Wm Odom; George Mee JP.   Rec 11 Mar 1799.

p.436-438   Nicholas Ware Senr, gent, to Robert Ware. Deed, 1 January 1799, fifty cents, 500 acres bounded by lands of Mouldon, Colcock, sd Robert Ware, Jones. Wit Samuel Crafton, John Prince, Nicholas Ware. /s/ Nicholas (x) Ware. Proven 11 Feb 1799 by Saml Crafton; Hugh Middleton JP.   Rec 12 Mar 1799.

p.438-441   Elventon Squires, yeoman, to Nehemiah Posey, yeoman, of Orangeburgh. Deed, 1 February 1797, £25 sterling, 887 acres on Rockey Creek of Edisto River. Wit Laban Shepherd, Zacheriah Posey. /s/ Elvenon Squyars, /s/ Ann (x) Squyars.   Proven 4 March 1797 by Laban Sheppard; James Wells JP.   Rec 12 March 1799.

p.441-444   Richard Bush Junr, planter, to John Wimberley, planter. Deed, 22 July 1797, £60 sterling, 143 acres on Clouds Creek bounded by lands of estate of Michael Watson decd, Col Robert Stark, Jacob Odom, and land sold by Late Sheriff Thomas Farrar as property of Colonel Robert Stark and was bought by sd Richard Bush and was conveyed by sd Thos Farrar to sd Richard Bush 4 July 1796. Wit Bibby Bush, William Squyars. /s/ Richard Bush Junr. Judge Arthur Simkins certifies relinquishment of dower by Sarah Bush wife of Richard Bush, 12 March 1799; /s/ Sarah (x) Bush. Proven 22 July 1799 by Bibby Bush; S Mays JP.   Rec 12 Mar 1799.

p.444-447   Elventon Squires, yeoman, to Nehemiah Posey, Orange-burgh District. Deed, 1 February 1797, £25 sterling, 400 acres on line between sd Squires, Wm Donohoo, on Rockey & Back Creeks, head branches of Edisto River. Wit Laban Sheppard, Zacheriah Posey. /s/ Elventon Squires, /s/ Ann (+) Squires. Proven Orangeburgh Dist, 4 March 1797 by Laban Sheppard; James Wells JP. Rec 12 Mar 1799.

p.448-454   William Swift, Newberry County, to William Caison of Lawrence County. L&R, 25/26 November 1795, £30 SC money, 176¾ acres on Brushey fork of Halfway Swamp granted 5 February 1787. Wit John Rowe, Joseph Cason, Wm Caison. /s/ William Swift, /s/ Elizabeth Swift. Proven 22 March 1799 by Wm Cason; Nathaniel Abney JP. Rec 22 Mar 1799.

p.454-456   David Coulter of Orangeburgh District to James Leslie and Margaret Leslie, admr & admx of George Leslie decd of Campbellton. Bill/Sale, 20 February 1799, $900, Negro woman named Press with her three children Salley, Polley, Sam and future increase of the females. Wit Wm F Taylor, S Savage Junr. /s/ David Coulter. Proven 8 Mar 1799 by Samuel Savage Junr; Wm Garrett. Rec 12 Mar 1799.

p.456-459   Sheriff William Tennent to Briton Mims. Sheriffs Titles. At suit of William Stevens against Moore & Chastain, the sheriff was directed to expose to sale at Cambridge sd land which was struck off to Briton Mimms highest bidder for £29, half of a town lott near the Court house formerly occupied by Moore & Chastain. Wit J Hall, Tal. Lovingston. /s/ Wm Tennent, Sheriff 96 Dst. Proven 12 Mar 1799 by John Hall; Richard Tutt JP. 12 Mar 1799.

p.459-462   John Bolger to William Coleman. Deed, 12 May 1798, £50 sterling, 200 acres late property of Matthew Wills decd being laid off to his widow, now wife of John Bolger, as part of her dower; upon Berrys Creek of Saluda River adj land of Richard Coleman and lands belonging to children of Matthew Wills decd. Wit Richard Coleman, James Carson, Isabella Abney. /s/ John Bolger. Proven 12 May 1798 by Richard Coleman; Nathaniel Abney JP. Rec 12 Mar 1799.

p.462   Samuel Crafton to Thomas Key. Receipt. Received the 10th April 1797 of Samuel Crafton full satisfaction for the within mortgage. Wit James Cobbs. /s/ Thomas Key. Rec 12 Mar 1799.

p.462-464   Federick Cullens to John Wimberley. Bill/Sale, 7 March 1798, $230 silver, Negro woman Ada about 22 years old. Wit James Barefield, Thomas Trotman. /s/ Frederick Cullens. Proven 16 Aug 1798 by James Barefield; Russell Wilson JP. Rec 12 Mar 1799.

p.464-469   Jeremiah Youngblood, planter, and wife Susannah to John Palattey, planter, 25 November 1794, £25 sterling, 50 acres on Rockey Creek of Little Stephens of Turkey Creek of Big Stephens

Creek of Savannah River, adj James Barker, Henry Middleton Esqr, surveyed by William Coursey DS being part of 200 acres granted unto Wm Blakely by Gov Chs Montague 13 April 1769, by Blakely transfered 1769 unto Peter Mehl, by Mehl conveyed 1772 unto Silvanus Stephens, by Stephens conveyed 1787 unto James Youngblood; by will unto his son sd Jeremiah Youngblood. Wit Jonathan Clegg, Samuel (x) Clegg. /s/ Jeremiah (x) Youngblood, /s/ Susannah (x) Youngblood. Survey made 24 November 1794 at request of Jeremiah Youngblood and John Palattey, 50 acres on Rockey Creek; /s/ Wm Coursey D.S. Proven 11 June 1798 by Cammell (x) Clegg(Claigg); John Blocker JP. Rec 12 Mar 1799.

p.469-472   Keziah Cottney to John Cotney, planter. Deed, 23 March 1798, £5, 108 acres on Beaverdam Creek of Little Saluda River, part of a tract of 216 acres formerly granted to Phillemon Waters by Gov Wm Multeer 15 Feb 1787, conveyed to James Durham, from him conveyed to Keziah Cotney 1790. Wit Wm Cotney, Danl Cotney, John (x) Pike. /s/ Keziah (x) Cottney. Proven 14 June 1798 by William Cotney; Elkanah Sawyer JP. Rec 12 Mar 1799.

p.473-475   Keziah Cotney, widow, to Daniel Cottney, planter. Deed, 23 March 1798, £5, 150 acres being part of 762 acres on Beaverdam branch of Little Saluda bounding when surveyed on Samuel Johnston and Thomas Snowden, granted by Gov Chas Pinckney unto sd Keziah Cotney 14 Nov 1792. Wit John Cotney, Wm Cotney, John (x) Pike. /s/ Keziah (K) Cotney. Proven 14 June 1798 by John Cotney; Elkanah Sawyer, JP. Rec 12 Mar 1799.

p.475-477   James Leslie & Margaret Leslie of Campbellton to David Coulter of Orangeburgh District. Bill of Sale, 20 February 1799, $480, Negro woman Estther and future issue, and her son Jack. Wit Wm F Taylor, S Savage Junr. /s/ James Leslie, /s/ Margaret Leslie. Proven 8 Mar 1799 by S Savage Junr; Wm Garrett JP. Rec 12 Mar 1799.

p.477-484   Daniel Laremon to William Warren. L&R, 8/7 September 1792, £15, 100 acres part of two tracts of land patented 1763 unto Elias Daniel, 100 acres on branch of Clouds Creek of Little Saluda River; also 100 acres granted unto Edward Laremon joining the old tract. Wit Jacob Tomlin, John (x) Pike, Thos Walker. /s/ Daniel Laremon. Proven 15 Feb 1798 by Thomas Walker; Henry King JP. Rec 12 Mar 1799.

p.484-487   Thomas Warren to William Warren. Deed, 5 May 1796,
£2 SC money, 149 acres formerly granted unto Thomas Warren 1796
by Gov Thos Pinckney, on a branch of Clouds Creek called Mores Crk
of Little Saluda. Wit William Wright, Adam Efurt, Sarah (x) Warren.
/s/ Thos Warren. Proven 18 June 1796 by Adam Efurt; Russell
Wilson, JP. Rec 12 Mar 1799.

p.487-488   Federick Williams to John Wimberley. Bill of Sale, 3
April 1795, £65 sterling, Negro man Cuff. Wit John Vardell, William
Bell. /s/ Fredk Williams. Proven 4 Jan 1796 by Wm Bell; Nathaniel
Abney JP. Rec 12 Mar 1799.

p.489-491   Daniel Nail Senr, planter, to Casper Nail. Deed, 9
March 1799, $143 SC money, 47.5 acres bounding on lands of George
Benderneith[?], John Clark, William Evans, sd Casper Nail. Wit John
Clarke, Daniel Nail. /s/ Daniel Nail. Proven 12 March 1799 by John
Clarke; Rd Tutt JP. Rec 12 Mar 1799.

p.491-494   Alexander Oden executor of will of Hezekiah Oden decd
and his wife Lewrany Oden to John Bayly, planter. Deed, 20 February
1798, $100 paid to Hezekiah Oden decd, 65 acres on Loyds Creek of
Stephens Creek of Savannah River, bounding on land sold from the
original grant unto Jesse Baley, bequeathed from original grant unto
Peter Oden, Hezekiah Oden Junr, Thomas Oden. Certifyed 14 Jan
1798 by Wm Coursey DS being part of 300 acres granted unto afsd
Hezekiah Oden decd by Gov Chs Montague at Charleston 14 December
1772. Wit Thomas Oden, Zacheriah Lunday. /s/ Alexr Oden, /s/
Lewrany (x) Oden.   Proven 12 Mar 1799 by Zacheriah Lunday; John
Blocker JP. Rec 12 Mar 1799.

p.494-497   Alexander Oden exr/will of Hezekiah Oden decd, & his
wife Lewrany Oden, to Jesse Bayly, planter. Deed, 20 February 1798,
$100, 67 acres on branches of Loyds Creek of Stephens Cr of Savan-
nah River bounding on land bequeathed from Old Grant unto Peter
Oden, sold from old grant to John Bayly, certifyed 12 Jan 1798 by Wm
Coursey D.S. being part of 300 acres granted by Gov Chs Montague
1772, and 37 acres granted 1789 by Gov Chs Pinckney to afsd Hezekiah decd. Wit Thos Oden, Zacheriah Lunday. /a/ Alexr Oden, /s/
Lewrany (O) Oden. Proven 12 Mar 1799 by Zacheriah Lunday; John
Blocker JP. Rec 12 Mar 1799.

P.498-501   James Thomas to Daniel Barksdale. Deed, 9 January

1799, $1650, 500 acres on Stephens Creek of Savannah river bounding
on land granted to Wm Mainer, granted to James Simpson 12 July
1771; also 50 acres on Stephens Creek granted 3 Sept, 1754 to Joseph
Chatwin. Wit Robert Ware, Samuel Crafton, Martin Goza. /s/ James
Thomas. Judge Joseph Hightower certifies relinquishment of dower by
Elizabeth Thomas wife of James Thomas, 12 March 1799. /s/ Eliza-
beth Thomas. Proven 12 March 1799 by Samuel Crafton; Matt Martin
JP. Rec 12 Mar 1799.

p.502-505   David Cornelius Neal of Augusta, Richmond County,
Georgia, merchant, to Casper Neal, gentleman. Deed, 14 November
1798, $620 SC money, 106 acres in Beech Island, Edgefield County,
bounding on land of Michael Rogers, and Daniel Neal. Wit John
Clarke, Wm Shenholser. /s/ David C Neal. Proven 12 March 1799 by
John Clarke; Rd Tutt JP. Rec 12 Mar 1799.

p.505-508   Robert Collins to Edward Day. Deed, 1 February 1799,
50 acres granted to Alexander Oden 1 Sept 1785, it being part of 220
acres granted to David Chadwick, adj branch of Stephens Creek, sd
David Chadwick. Wit Charles (x) Franklin, Dennis Collins. /s/ Robert
(R) Collins. Judge Joseph Hightower certifies relinquishment of dower
by Anne Collins wife of within Robert Collins, 4 March 1799; /s/ Anne
(x) Collins. Receipt, 1 Feb 1799, for $60 in full for within debt. /s/
Robert (R) Collins. Proven 12 Mar 1799 by Charles Franklin; Matt
Martin JP. Rec 12 Mar 1799.

p.508-510   Wm Holley Junr to His Children. Deed Gift, 15
September 1798, love & affection, to my beloved children namely
Pleasant Holley, Frederick Holley, Nathaniel Holley, Polley Holley,
Phereby Holley and William Holley, 100 acres originally granted to
John Dooly on Stephens Creek, and my Negros namely Peter Cate Jack
West Molley Joseph and Lotty, two horses, cattle, hoggs. Also a
Negro namely Letty about five years old. Wit Mackss Goode, John
Gardner. /s/ William (x) Holley. Proven 11 Mar 1799 by John
Gardner; Charles Old JP. Rec 12 Mar 1799.

p.511-514   Robert Collins to Edward Day. Deed, 20 December
1798, 90 acres Gunnels Creek of Stephens Creek, Matthew Caps Spring
Branch, being part of land granted to David Chadwick 1785. Wit Chas
Franklin, Dennis Collins. /s/ Robert (R) Collins. Judge Joseph High-
tower certifies relinquishment of dower by Anne Collins wife of Robert
Collins, 4 March 1799; /s/ Anne (x) Collins. Receipt, 2 Dec 1798,

$150 in full for within debt. /s/ Robert (R) Collins. Proven 12 March 1799 by Charles (x) Franklin; Matt Martin JP. Rec 12 Mar 1799.

p.514-516   James Butler to son John Butler. Deed Gift, 2 February 1799, love & good will and $2, 72 acres Chaveses Creek of Savannah River. Wit James (x) Butler, Wm Coursey. /s/ James Butler. Proven 12 Mar 1799 by James (x) Butler; Matt Martin JP. Rec 12 Mar 1799.

p.516-519   Keziah Cotney, widow, to William Cotney, planter. Deed, 23 March 1798, £5 sterling, 108 acres on Beaverdam of Little Saluda River being part of 206 acres formerly granted to Phillemon Waters by Gov Wm Moultrie 15 Feb 1787, conveyed 1788 to Thomas Snowden, and by Snowden 1794 to Kizier Cotney. Wit John Cotney, Daniel Cotney, John (x) Pike. /s/ Keziah (K) Cotney. Proven 14 June 1798 by John Cotney; Elkanah Sawyer JP. Rec 12 Mar 1799.

p.519-520   Nicholas Ware Senr to Nicholas Ware Junr. Deed/Gift, natural love for nephew Nicholas Ware Jr son of Robert Ware, Negro boy Reuben son of Charity a yellow woman slave. Wit Samuel Crafton, John Prince. /s/ Nicholas (x) Ware. Proven 11 Feb 1799 by Samuel Crafton; Hugh Middleton JP. Rec 12 Mar 1799.

p.521-523   Daniel & John Whitehead(sic) to Peter Utz. Deed, 28 Janu-ary 1799, $74, unto sd Peter Outs 100 acres on Sleepy Creek adj John Tom[?]'s land, granted to Christian Catharine Classer 1773. Wit James Blocker, John Forgee. /s/ Daniel Whiteman, /s/ John (x) Whiteman. Proven 28 January 1799 by James Blocker; John Blocker JP. Rec 12 March 1799.

p.523-527   Rowling Cortney of Winton County, SC, to Joshua Deen. Deed, 10 December 1790, £150 sterling, now in actual posses-sion by virtue of a bargain for one year, 280 acres on Big Creek of Saluda River bounded by lands of Isaac Crouther at time of survey and originally granted to sd Rowling Coatney 21 Jan 1785. Wit Thomas Dozer, Thomas Scott, Wm (x) Green. /s/ Rowlan (x) Coatney. Receipt for £150 in full consideration. /s/ Rowling (x) Coatney. Proven 6 Jan 1794 by Thos Dozer; Russell Wilson JP. Rec 13 Mar 1799.

p.527-528   Benjamin Breedlove to David Boswell. Bill of Sale, 17 December 1798, $350, Negro boy Peregrin. Wit Robert Hatcher, John Covington. /s/ B W Breadlove. Proven 12 Mar 1799 by Robt Hatcher; James Cobb JP. Rec 13 Mar 1799.

p.529-532   James Hargroves to John Power. Deed, 8 April 1797, £70 sterling, 265 acres on Horns and Dry Creeks bounding on John Cogbern, Lewis Noble, James Cobb, Fielding Reynolds, Little Berry Adams, Reedy branch, and William Washer. Wit Ephraim Ferril, John Fox. /s/ James Haregrove. Judge Arthur Simkins certifies relinquishment of dower by Mary Haregrove wife of James Haregrove; /s/ Mary (x) Haregrove.   Proven 8 April 1797 by Ephraim Ferril; Rd Tutt, JP. Recorded 13 March 1799.

p.532-536   Jeremiah Roberts to William Miller. Deed, 8 October 1798, £100 sterling, 100 acres being part of land originally granted unto Thomas Roberts decd bounded by Horns Creek, Samuel Dolittle, Drury Adams, Thomas Palmer. Wit Daniel Marques, Joshua Marques. /s/ Jeremiah Roberts. Judge Arthur Simkins certifies relinquishment of dower by Anne Roberts wife of within named Jeremiah Roberts; /s/ Anne (x) Roberts. Proven 8 March 1799 by Daniel Marques and Joshua Marques; Matt Martin JP.   Rec 13 Mar 1799.

p.536-537   Thomas Davis of Burke County, Georgia, to Luke Smith. Bill of Sale, 18 February 1799, $1, Negro girl about thirteen years of age called Ame in trust of Mrs Ann Lamar (senior). Wit Melines C Leavenworth. /s/ Thomas Davis. Proven 14 March 1799 by Melines C Leavenworth; Rd Tutt JP. Rec 14 Mar 1799.

p.537-539   Absalom Williams to John Smith. Deed, 2 February 1799, $10, land on Hard Labour Creek adj John Holleys corner, Benjamin Blacks land. Wit John Vardell, Alexander McMillion, Edward Harrison. /s/ Abs Williams. Proven 14 Mar 1799 by John Vardell; Richard Tutt JP.   Rec 14 Mar 1799.

p.540-541   Jeremiah Hatcher to J Zinn & W Taylor. Receipt, 14 March 1799.   Barbara Tutt vs Thomas Lamar sale by execution first Saturday in July last, received of Jacob Zinn & Walter Taylor $401.50 for the purchase of Negro man named Jacob. Wit Melines C Leavenworth.. /s/ J Hatcher, Shff EC. Proven 14 Mar 1799 by Melines C Leavenworth; Rd Tutt JP.   Rec 14 Mar 1799.

p.541-543   Charles James to Nathaniel Taunton. Deed, 22 October 1798, $102.50, 34.5 acres being part of tract granted to Ward Taylor 9 Sept 1774 on Crooked Run of Turkey Creek of Stephens Creek of Savannah River and on the Charleston Road and on the road for Allens ford on Turkey Creek to Edgefield Court House, bounded at present by

lands of Wm Sturms, Moses Taylor. Wit Shadk Stokes, James
Prichard, Wm Blackley. /s/ Charles James. Plat. Proven 14 Mar 1799
by James Prichard; James Cobb JP. Rec 14 Mar 1799.

p.543-545   Wm Smith of Cambridge Town, SC, to Mary Beal. Bill
of Sale, 14 September 1798, $400, Negro woman named Frank about
twenty years old. Wit Davis Moore. /s/ Wm Smith. Proven 14 Mar
1799 by Davis Moore; Russell Wilson JP. Rec 14 Mar 1799.

p.545-547   William Smith to Briton Mims. Deposition, 14 March
1799, a note concerning a parcel of Negroes purchased by Briton Mims
of deponant and John Bostick given to sd Smith and John Bostick or to
sd William Smith alone about 1 September 1798 in which note Briton
Mims was bound to pay at different periods certain sums of money
therein specifyed and to which sd Briton Mims did sign his name is lost
and cannot be obtained to deliver up to Mims who has fully complied
with terms of sd note, the parties having rescinded sd bargain and sd
Briton Mims having redelivered back the Negroes for which he gave the
afsd instrument of writing. /s/ W Smith. Davis Moore further makes
oath that a paper of above description was put in his hands by Smith &
Mims which he cannot lay his hands upon, which from the acknow-
ledgement of the parties and his knowledge of the contract knows to be
void. /s/ Davis Moore. Received 14 March 1799 of Briton Mims five
shillings, same being in full for a purchase of Negroes made by him of
myself & John Bostick on 1 Sept 1798. Test Russell Wilson Senr. /s/
W Smith. Rec 14 Mar 1799.

p.547-548   William Smith to Briton Mims. Bond, Smith bound in
sum $3000 to sd Mims, condition Mims assigned to sd Smith in North
Carolina about 4 or 5 Sept last a note of hand for Negroes, which note
is lost; if sd note is ever found I bind myself under above penaltie to
deliver it to sd Mims. Wit Lewis Mathews, Davis Moore. /s/ William
Smith. Proven 14 Mar 1799 by Davis Moore; Russell Wilson JP. Rec
14 Mar 1799.

p.548-550   Absalom Williams to John Smith. Quit claim, 2 February 1799, $10, release unto John Smith land on Hard Labour Creek
on John Kenedays line. Wit John Vardell, Alexander McMillan,
Edward Harrison. /s/ Abs Williams. Proven by John Vardell; Rd Tutt
JP. Rec 14 Mar 1799.

p.550-551   Jeremiah Hatcher to Luke Smith. Receipt. Sale by

Execution, Andrew Pickens & Co vs Thomas Lamar. Defendant's plantation on 6 January 1798 by order of Judges. Received of Luke Smith $160 full amt for purchase of Negro wench named Hana & her two children Phillis and Bet and their increase, which Negroes to sd Luke Smith in trust for use of Mrs Ann Lamar. Wit Melines C Leavenworth. /s/ J Hatcher, Shff E C. Proven 14 Mar 1799 by Melines C Leavenworth; Rd Tutt JP. Rec 14 Mar 1799.

p.552-554   Susannah Parker, widow, to her Grand Children James Stewart, William Stewart, Ann Stewart. Deed Gift, 11 March 1799, love & goodwill, livestock (descriptions here omitted). Wit David Ardis, Jno Sturzenegger. /s/ Susannah (H) Parker. Proven 15 Mar 1799 by David Ardis; Rd Tutt JP. Rec 15 Mar 1799.

p.554-557   James Smith, planter, to William Ogle, planter. Deed, 6 December 1798, $200, 140 acres being part of 257 acres granted to Isaac Huskey 5 December 1796 on Stephens Creek bounded by Wm Rowan, Obediah Henderson, Spring branch. Wit Joab Blackwell, Isaac Huskey. /s/ James Smith. Proven 4 Mar 1799 by Isaac Huskey; Henry Key JP. /s/ Isaac (x) Huskey.   Rec 16 Mar 1799.

p.557-560   Isaac Huskey, planter, to James Smith, planter. Deed, 6 December 1798, $200, 140 acres being part of 257 acres granted to me 5 Dec 1796 on Stephens Creek bounded by Wm Rowan, Obediah Henderson, Spring branch. Wit Joab Blackwell, Wm (x) Ogle. /s/ Isaac (x) Huskey. Proven 4 March 1799 by William Ogle; Henry Key JP. Rec 16 Mar 1799.

p.560-564   Moses Brafford and wife Fanny to Isaac Huskey. Release, 27 July 1798, £60 sterling, 100 acres on Rockey Creek of Savannah River bounding on Jonathan Huskey, Joseph Able, Viott Morriss. Wit Ezekiel Hudnall, Jonathan (x) Huskey, Thomas (x) Ogle. /s/ Moses Brafford, /s/ Fanny (x) Brafford. Proven 4 Mar 1799 by Thomas Ogle; Henry Key JP. Rec 16 Mar 1799.

p.564-566   Evan Morgan to Enos Morgan. Deed, 4 February 1799, $10, 150 acres being part of two tracts; one granted to Solom Newsom of 300 acres 11 Feb 1773; the other to Evan Morgan 250 acres 11 Aug 1774; bounding on lands of Ozias Morgan, James Carson. Wit Ozias Morgan, Robert Cason. /s/ Evan Morgan. Proven 6 Feb 1799 by Ozias Morgan; Charles Old JP.   Rec 25 Mar 1799.

p.566-568   Evan Morgan to Enos Morgan. Deed, 4 February 1799, $10, 50 acres being part of two tracts; one granted to Solomon Newsom of 300 acres 11 Feb 1773; other to Evan Morgan 250 acres on 11 Aug 1774, bounding on William Stringers, Ozias Morgan. Wit Ozias Morgan, Robert Carson. /s/ Evan Morgan. Proven 6 Feb 1799 by Robt Carson; Chas Old JP.   Rec 25 Mar 1799.

p.569-571   Evan Morgan to Ozias Morgan. Deed, 5 February 1799, $100, 200 acres being part of two tracts; one granted to Solomon Newsom of 300 acres on 11 Feb 1773; other to Evan Morgan for 250 acres on 11 Aug 1774, adj Stephens Creek, Eli Morgan, William Stringer, Enos Morgan, James Carson.   Wit Enos Morgan, John Stringer. /s/ Evan Morgan. Proven 6 Feb 1799 by Evan Morgan; Chs Old JP. Rec 25 Mar 1799.

p.571-575   Jacob Hibbler to William Bobbett. Deed, 12 February 1799, £70 sterling, 107 acres on Stevens Creek and Savannah River being part of tract originally granted to Benjamin Bell bounding lands of Howley, Samuel Stalnaker, Richard Tutt Senr, Hiram McDaniel, other half of sd old survey and sold by Wm McDanolds to Jacob Hibbler. Wit Abner Perrin, Thomas (x) Wilburn. /s/ Jacob Hibbler. Judge Arthur Simkins certifies relinquishment of dower by Jincey Hibbler wife of Jacob Hibbler; /s/ Jincy Hibbler.   Proven 12 Feb 1799 by Abner Perrin; James Harrison JP.   Rec 25 Mar 1799.

p.576-578   Samuel Melton of Columbia County, Georgia, to John Stringer. Deed, 1 December 1798, $5, 150 acres on Stephens Creek. Wit John (x) Lee, Ely Stringer. /s/ Samuel Melton. Proven 23 Mar 1799 by John Lee; Wm Garrett JP.   Rec 25 Mar 1799.

p.578-582   George Abney and wife Salley to David Griffeths of Newberry County SC. Deed, 12 December 1798, £74.13.4 sterling, 100 acres being part of 150 acres conveyed from Dannett Abney to sd George Abney and originally granted to sd Dannett Abney, upon Persimon Lick Creek of Little Saluda river, bound by Joseph Griffeths, Samuel Abney. Wit William Boulware, Joseph Griffeths, John Gwyn. /s/ George (x) Abney, /s/ Sally (x) Abney. Judge William Anderson certifies relinquishment of dower by Salley Abney; /s/ Salley (x) Abney. Proven 18 Mar 1799 by Joseph Griffeths; Nathl Abney JP. Rec 16 Mar 1799.

p.582-585   George B Moore to William Moore. Deed, 22 January

1799, £46.13.4 sterling, 199 acres Horns Creek joining lands claimed by Capt John Ryan, Benj Darbey, and Benjamin Ryan Junr, provided sd William Moore pay £46.10.4 sterling with legal interest from first January next ensuing without deduction or abatement. Wit Thos Butler, Gilson Yarbrough. /s/ George B Moore. Receipt for £46.13.4 sterling full consideration. /s/ George B Moore. Proven 7 March 1799 by Gilson Yarbrough; Nathaniel Abney JP. Rec 19 Mar 1799.

p.585-588 George Abney to William Chapman, Newberry County. Deed, 20 August 1798, $100, 90 acres on Persimon Lick creek, part of original grant to John Abney, also the land on which William Crow once lived, bounded by Peter Buffington, John Roe, reserving one square acre near the center for a meeting House. Wit Joseph Griffeth(sic), Gibion Burton, Isaac Abney. /s/ George (x) Abney, /s/ Sarah (x) Abney. Judge William Anderson certifies relinquishment of dower by Sally Abney wife of George Abney, 12 December 1798; /s/ Salley (x) Abney. Proven 7 March 1799 by Joseph Griffin; Nathl Abney JP. Rec 27 Mar 1799.

p.588-592 Elkanah Sawyer to Robert Atkins. Deed, 14 January 1797, £46, 125 acres on Clouds Creek of Saluda River, east part of 325 acres originally granted to Wm Stent[?] 3 April 1775, bounded by land surveyed by John Fairchild, Silas Carter, Wm Staut, Moses Prescott, sd land transfered unto John Wells 1776 and from John Wells conveyed to Nathaniel Powel 1789, from Powel unto Isom Brooks 1793, and from Brooks unto Elkanah Sawyer 1795. Wit William Pickel, Nat (x) Powell. /s/ Elkanah Sawyer, /s/ Mariam (x) Sawyer. Proven 15 April 1799 by William Pickel; Elkanah Sawyer JP. Rec 15 April 1799.

p.592-605 John Carter to Andrew Pickens, Mary Moore, Thomas Bacon, Exrs & Exrx of James Moore deceased. L&R by way of a Mortgage, 7 & 8 January 1799, John Carter's bond 7 Jan in penal sum $6850, condition the payment of $3425 with interest, 400 acres in fork of Horse Creek and Savannah river joining Thomas Lamar. Wit Jno Trotter, Jas Scott. /s/ John Carter. Proven, Charleston District, 3 April 1799 by James Scott; Wm Nibbs JQ. Rec 5 Apr 1799. [Marginal note: "This Deed of Release is satisfied in full by the payment of money required, 5 Decr 1800 Geo Bowie[?] for A Pickens"]

p.605-607 Charles Jones Colcock of Prince William Parish, SC, by my attorney Samuel Mays of Edgefield County, to Tyre Moulding of Abbeville County, SC. Deed, 13 January 1799, $450, 200 acres adj

Savannah river & Samuel Crafton, being part of 640 acres sold at
Sheriff sale at Cambridge as property of Major Benjamin Tutt decd and
bought by Charles Jones Colcock. Wit William Hill, Archy Moulden.
/s/ Charles J Colcock by his attorney S Mays. Proven 5 April 1799 by
Archabel Moulden; Hugh Middleton JP. Rec 8 Apr 1799.

p.608-611   George Abney & wife Salley to Joseph Griffeths. Deed,
12 December 1798, £37.6.8 sterling, 50 acres being part of 150 acres
conveyed from Dannett Abney to sd George Abney, originally granted
to sd Dannett Abney upon Persimon Lick creek of Little Saluda river,
sd 50 acres between Joseph & David Griffeth, adj Simon Brooks, James
Reed. Wit William Boulware, David Griffeths, John Gwinn. /s/
George (x) Abney, /s/ Salley (x) Abney. Judge William Anderson
certifies the relinquishment of dower by Salley Abney wife of George
Abney 12 December 1798; /s/ Salley (x) Abney. Proven 13 March
1799 by David Griffeths; Nathl Abney JP.   Rec 15 Apr 1799.

p.611-614   Sheriff Jeremiah Hatcher to Joseph Cunningham. Sheriffs
Titles, 5 September 1795. At suit of James Hagood against Reuben
Frazier, sheriff directed to sell three tracts of land to highest bidder for
ready money; sd land struck off to Joseph Cunningham for £20 sterling
he being highest & last bidder. Jeremiah Hatcher to Joseph Cunning-
ham 241 acres originally granted to Reuben Frazier by Gov William
Moultree by grants dated 1786 and 1793. Wit Eugene Brenan, S
Butler. /s/ J Hatcher S.E.C. Proven 17 Apr 1799 by Sampson Butler;
Rd Tutt JP. Rec 17 Apr 1799.

p.614-617   Sheriff Jeremiah Hatcher to John Howard. Sheriff Titles,
5 March 1796, at suit of Phill May Junr against John Fudge, sheriff to
sell to highest bidder for ready money at Edgefield Court House; struck
off to John Howard for £7.12. Jeremiah Hatcher to John Howard,
Little Horse creek of Savannah River. Wit Eugene Brenan, S Butler.
/s/ J Hatcher Sheff E.C.   Proven 17 Apr 1799 by Sampson Butler; Rd
Tutt JP.   Rec 17 Apl 1799.

p.617-621   Roger Smith of Charleston to Jourdan Brooks. Deed,
Charleston District, 10 April 1799, $140, 72 acres on Log creek of
Turkey creek of Savannah River, being part of a larger tract held by sd
Smith, bounding on lines of Simkins, Ellenbegers, Simkins. Wit
Daniel Baugh, Peter (x) Morgan. /s/ Roger Smith. Plat by William
Coursey D.S. 28 March 1798. Proven 17 April 1799 by Daniel Baugh;
Rd Tutt JP. Rec 17 April 1799.

p.622-624   Lazarus Phillips & Abner Essary to John Hargrove.
Deed, 15 November 1798, $260, 220 acres on Mountain Creek of
Turkey Creek of Stephens Creek and Savannah River granted to sd
Lazarus Phillips by governor of State and bounded by lines of King,
Nicallas, and unknown. Wit John Stewart, Thomas Henderson. /s/
Lazarus (x) Phillips, Abner Essary. Proven 19 April 1799 by John
Stewart; Richard Tutt JP.   Rec 19 April 1799.

p.624-627   Shadrack Henderson to Samuel Cartledge. Deed, 22
April 1799, £130 sterling, 500 acres whereon sd Cartledge now lives on
Bird Creek of Stephens Creek originally granted unto James Simson
Esqr, surveyed 20 Nov 1771. W it John Boyd, Robt McComb.   /s/
Shadrack Henderson. Justice William Nibbs certifies relinquishment of
dower by Helena Henderson wife of Shadrack Henderson.   /s/ Helena
(x) Henderson. Proven 22 April 1799 by John Boyd; Rd Tutt JP.   Rec
22 Apl 1799.

p.628-631   Phill May to James May.   Deed, 28 January 1799,
$1000,   275 acres as followeth: 150 acres whereof on Chaveses Creek
of Savannah River being part of 300 acres originally granted to Richard
Kirkland and part of a tract granted to Phill May Senr; also 50 acres of
granted to sd Kirkland on North side Chaveses Creek; also 75 acres on
same waters being part of 299 acres originally granted to Elizabeth Reynolds adj land of Phill May Sr, land of William Griffin.   Wit Clement
Cargill, Solomon (x) Lucas. /s/ Phill May.   Proven 9 February 1799
by Clement Cargill; Russell Wilson JP.   Rec 22 April 1799.

p.631-634   Sheriff Sampson Butler to William Moore son of John.
Deed, 2 March 1799. At suit Green Moore against John Moore; sheriff
sells land to highest bidder for ready money at Edgefield Court House;
struck off to William Moore for £40, 142 acres on Ninety Six Creek.
Wit Timothy K Johnson, Jas McMillan. /s/ S Butler S.E.C.   Proven 23
April 1799 by James McMillan; Rd Tutt JP.   Rec 23 Apr 1799.

p.634-636   William H Hayne(sic) to Samuel Mays. Power Attorney,
11 January 1799, Wm Hayne heir by will of Isaac Hayne of St. Bartholomews Parish decd, appoints Colonel Samuel Mays of Edgefield his
attorney to sell or lease several tracts of land. Wit Wm Ed Hayne, Robt
Hill. /s/ John H Hayne. Proven York County, SC, 11 Feb 1799 by
Wm Ed Hayne who deposes that he was present and saw within named
John H Hayne sign within instrument and that Robt Hill was a
subscribing witness thereto; Wm Hill J.C.C. Rec 24 Apr 1799.

p.636-637   Joseph Lewis to Jonathan Weaver. Bill of Sale, 6 February 1799, $400, Negro boy Jacob, Jennys son. Wit John Permenter, Willis Federick. /s/ Joseph Lewis. Proven 6 Apr 1799 by Willis Federick; Wm Daniel JP. Rec 24 Apr 1799.

p.638-641   Isaac Lewis of Effingham County, Georgia, to Jonathan Weaver. Deed, 23 January 1799, $200, 200 acres on Rockey Creek of Stephens Creek of Savannah River beginning at the Cedar Branch adj John Rowe, one John Rowes line to John Threewitts line, to Jonathan Weavers line, thence of Talton Roltons[?] line, being part of 446 acres granted to sd Isaac Lewis by Gov Wm Moultrie at Charleston 1786. Wit John Roe, Willis Federick, Joseph Lewis. /s/ Isaac Lewis. Proven 6 Apr 1799 by Willis Federick; Wm Dannel JP. Rec 24 Apr 1799.

p.641-643   William Robinson to John Buckelow. Deed, 5 March 1799, £18 sterling, 103 acres Mountain Creek of Savannah River bounded by lines of William Robinson. Wit David Harkens, John Thiel. /s/ William Robinson. Proven 25 April 1799 by David Harkens; Rd Tutt, JP. Rec 25 Apr 1799.

The following fragmentary pages are without numbers.
p.--   8 October 1798. Wit David Thomson, Edward Fowler, Mary (x) Fowler. /s/ Willis (x) Johnson. Receipt; received of Ce-- 8 Oct -- 20--. Witnesses and signature as above.
p.--   Proven by David Thomson, 9 Oct 1798, Rd Tutt. Rec 9 Oct 1798.

pp.--   Henry Jones Senr to Michael Bruner. Deed, 19 March 1794 between Henry Jones Senr of Richmond County, Georgia and Michael Bruner of Edgefield, in consideration of --, -- hundred and 50 acres near Town Creek-- adj George Benders originally granted unto Gasper Strowell. Wit --hn Evans, --ry Jones Junr. /s/ Henry Jones Senr. Proven by Henry Jones Junr before---.

pp.--   -- and John Gossett Senr of county -- SC, £30 SC money, sd William Desha--, --actual possession now being by vir--, -- branch of Clouds Creek--, originally granted --siah Cotney by Gov Charles --kney 4 June 1792, ...said William Deshazo to sd Jno --tt. Wit Isaac (x) Gossett, John Gossett, John Watkins. /s/ William Desha--, /s/ Barbary (V) Desh--. Proven 8 Aug 1795 by John Watkins; Elkanah Sawyer JP.

End of Edgefield County Conveyance Book 16

p.1-3   Lazarus Phillips to David Harkins.   Deed, 16 February 1799, £25 sterling, 150 acres on Mountain Creek of Turkey Creek, Stephens Creek. Wit John M Moore, John Crabtree. /s/ Lazarus (x) Phillips. Proven 16 Feb 1799 by John Crabtree; William Robinson JP. Rec 25 April 1799.

p.3-6   John Stewart to Micajah Drake of Union County, SC. Deed, 16 November 1798, $300, 100 acres Turkey Creek of Stephens, part of 400 acres originally granted unto John Stewart decd. Wit James Brown, Reuben Landrum. /s/ John Stewart. Judge Arthur Simkins certifies relinquishment of dower by Candace Stewart wife of John Stewart. /s/ Candace (x) Stewart. Proven 3 May 1799 by James Brown; Arthur Simkins J.C.E.   Rec 3 May 1799.

p.6-9   Richard McCary, planter, to John Loughton. Deed, 3 January 1799, $100 paid by John Lofton, planter, unto sd John Lough ton 15 acres Bird Creek of Stephens Creek of Savannah River, being part of 550 acres bought of Colonel Gervis. Wit Edmond Truwit, Wm Coursey. /s/ Richard McCary. Proven 8 April 1799 by Edmond Truwitt; John Blocker JP. Rec 4 May 1799.

p.9-11   James Van Senr to youngest children William and Elizabeth Van. Deed Gift, 3 May 1799, love & affection, 100 acres originally granted to Joseph Jones lying on Turkey Creek, also 200 acres part of original survey granted to Robert Burton, also two cows & calves, household furniture. Wit Edward Van Senr, Joseph Van. /s/ James (I) Van. Proven 4 May 1799 by Joseph Van; Van Swearingen JP. Rec 4 May 1799.

p.11-14   Robert Burton to James Vann. Deed, [blank] 1798, $100, 200 acres on Turkey Creek of Savannah River, being part of land granted sd Robert Burton by Gov Chas Pinckney 5 Dec 1791, joining land granted to Joseph Jones. Wit Josiah Van, Richard Bush. /s/ Robert Burton. Proven 13 April 1799 by Josiah Van; Van Swearingen JP. Rec 4 May 1799.

p.14-16   Widow Mary Johnson of the Natchez to John Blocker. Deed, 9 March 1797, $50, 150 acres granted to George Shaws[Shaur?] 21 Oct 1765 on Log Creek bounded by land granted to John Gruber & conveyed unto John Savage and descended from sd Savage by heirship to Mary Savage now Mary Johnson. Wit William Prichard, James Blocker. /s/ Mary Johnson. Proven 14 March 1797 by Jas Blocker;

Van Swearingen JP.   Rec 4 May 1799.

p.16-19   Nathaniel Abney to Joel Abney.   Deed, 12 April 1799,
$300,   160 acres on Saluda River being part of three tracts; 200 acres
originally granted to sd Nathaniel Abney; 100 acres granted to John
Caldwell; 375 acres granted to William Spragins; sd 160 acres begin at
road to Higgins Ferry at head of Nathaniel Abney's lane, thence to line
of Azariah Abney, estate of Clabourn German.   Wit John Abney, A
Eskridge. /s/ Nathaniel Abney.   Proven 12 Apr 1799 by John Abney
and Austen Eskridge; Nathl Abney JP.   Rec 10 May 11799.

p.20-23   Nathaniel Abney to Azariah Abney.   Release, 12 April
1799, $300, 150 acres on Saluda River being part of three grants: 200
acres granted to sd Nathaniel Abney; 400 acres granted to Henry Medcalfe; 375 acres granted to William Spragins; sd 150 acres adj Nathl
Abney's lane and road from Higgins ferry upon Joel Abneys land then
to John Abneys land, Medcalfs line.   Wit John Abney, A Eskridge. /s/
Nathl Abney.   Proven 12 Apr 1799 by John Abney and Austen
Eskridge; Nathl Abney JP.   Rec 10 May 1799.

p.23-35   William Moore, planter, and wife Isbal of Granville
County, S.C., to Thomas Butler, planter.   L&R, 17 & 18 March 1774,
£500 SC money, 300 acres in Granville County on both sides Stephens
Creek granted to sd William Moore by Gov Chas Montague, 14 Aug
1772, examined pr Daniel Mazyck, Memorial entered 16 Oct 1772 pr
Rd Lambton Dy.Audr., certifyed 18 Mar 1772 pr John Bremar D.S.
Genl., William Goode D.S.   Wit Robert Moore, James (x) Moore,
Agness (x) Moore. /s/ William Moore, /s/ Isbal (x) Moore.   Proven 18
Mar 1774 by Robert Moore; John Johnston JP.   Rec 11 May 1799.

p.36-38   John Norwood to Tolover Bostick.   Deed, 20 April 1799,
5 shillings, love & affection, Negroes Molly Liddy Lockey Jack and the
increase of the females under limitation upon trust hereinafter mentioned: expressly declared that before mentioned Negroes shall remain
exempt from being sold or in any manner disposed of by sd Tolover
Bostick but shall be kept for use & behoof of Nancy Norwood the now
wife of John Norwood and shall not dispose of sd Negroes on any
pretence whatsoever; further understood that the increase arising from
sd Negroes shall be for the use and under the directions of sd Nancy
Norwood forever, to her and to her heirs forever.   Sd Negroes shall be
the absolute property of sd Nancy Norwood and her heirs.   Wit Jacob
Fannin, Wm Burton, Douglas Burton. /s/ John Norwood.   Proven 10

43

May 1799 by William Burton; Wm Robinson JP. Rec 12 May 1799.

p.39-43   James Hargrove to William Welsh. Deed, 4 January
1797, $400 SC money, 91¾ acres on Dry creek adj William Moseleys
line, Widow Alexanders land, Samuel Doolittles land, William Mosley
and Benjamin Joiners lines. Wit Charles P Jeter, John Welsh.   /s/ Jas
Hargrove. Judge Arthur Simkins certifies relinquishment of dower by
Mary Hargrove wife of James Hargrove, 8 April 1797; /s/ Mary (x)
Hargrove. Proven 11 March 1797 by Charles P Jeter; John Blocker JP.
Rec 13 May 1799.

p.43-46   Talton Brown to William Welsh. Deed, 27February
1799, $192.85, 185 acres on Crooked branch of Terky Creek of Sav-
annah River, granted unto Benjamin Godfrey 11 Aug 1774 by Gov Wm
Moultrie. Wit Joseph Hogh, John Welsh. /s/ Talton Brown. Proven 13
May 1799 by Joseph Hogh; Rd Tutt JP. Rec 12 May 1799.

p.46-47   Nancy Vaughn to Susannah Lee. Receipt. Received
$600 in full satisfaction for two Negroes; fellow Jeff and wench Juda
and her increase. Wit Higdon Borroum, John Cunningham. /s/ Nancy
(A) Vaughan.   Proven 15 May 1799 by Higdon Borroum; Russell
Wilson JP. Rec 17 May 1799.

p.47-51   Joseph Trotter of Newberry County to George Lewis
Patrick. Deed, 14 November 1797, $325, 180 acres, 115 acres being
a part of 300 acres originally granted to John Gormon 5 June 1786 on
head of Mill creek of Saluda River, sd 115 acres conveyed by John
Gormon to Joseph Trotter 26 Oct 1792, 180 acres hereby sold is part of
150 acres originally granted to Charles Carson 25 June 1771; by him
conveyed to James Carson; by sd Carson to John Webb; by Webb to
Joseph Trotter 18 Aug 1785; sd ballance above mentioned containing 65
acres beginning at Mill Creek, bounding on Thos Berrys land. Wit John
Abney, John Bolger, Thomas Berry. /s/ Joseph (T) Trotter.   Proven 3
January 1798 by John Abney; Nathl Abney JP.   Rec 17 May 1799.

p.51-54   Amos Adams and wife Elizabeth to James Adams.
Deed, 1 February 1799, £20 sterling, 25 acres being part of 54 acres
surveyed for Amos Adams on the head of Red Bank of Little Saluda;
Gov Chas Pinckney at Columbia 5 Feb 1798, bounding on lands of
Charles Adams, James Adams. Wit Benj Rowe, Gabriel Jones. /s/
Amos Adams, /s/ Elizabeth (x) Adams.   Proven 25 Apr 1799 by Benj
Rowe; Wm Robinson JP.   Rec 18 May 1799.

p.55-58   James Huston to James Adams, planter. Deed, [blank] 1796, £30 SC money, 75 acres it being part of 75 acres on head of Red bank of Little Saluda river; Lt Gov Wm Bull 16 Sept 1774 and 75 acres on the head of Red Bank on south prong joining Chas Adams, Carson, Paterson, Wm Adams, it being part of land granted to James Huston. Wit William (x) Adams, Benjamin Rowe, Mary Huston, William (x) Adams, Gabriel Jones. /s/ James Huston. Proven 21 April 1798 by Benj Rowe; Wm Robertson JP. Rec 18 May 1799.

p.58-59   Elenor Cowan to William Holley. Bill of Sale, 22 December 1798, Negro girl named Let. Wit James Quarles. /s/ Elenor (I) Cowan. Proven 25 Mar 1799 by James Quarles; Chas Old JP. Rec 18 May 1799.

p.59-62   William Murphey[Murphy] to William Ellis. Deed, 23 November 1798, $295, 90 acres, beginning at James Butlers corner on Old Ridge path that leads to sd Murpheys old plantation, line surveyed by Moses Kirkland, Marget Morrises land, crossing Five Notched Road. Wit Hicks Ellis. John Dobey. /s/ Wm Murphey. Proven 21 May 1799 by John Dobey; James Cobb JP. Rec 20 May 1799.

p.62-65   Amacy Wade to Richard Johnson. Deed, 12 January 1799, $500, 140 acres being part of 150 acres on Dry Creek granted to John Wade, bounding then on land held by Rambo now held by Richd Gantt, John Lucas, Lewis Nobles, Isaac Randolph. Wit Thomas Marbury, William Watson. /s/ Amasy (A) Wade. Proven 11 May 1799 by Thos Marbury; James Cobbs, JP. Rec 23 May 1799.

p.65-67   Henry Ray[Wray] to Edward Holmes. Bill of Sale, 15 April 1799, $300, Negro boy named Wilson. Wit Mumford Perryman, Federick Holmes. /s/ Henry Ray. Proven 25 May 1799 by Federick Holmes; William Daniel JP. Rec 26 May 1799.

p.67-69   Zepheniah Harvey to George Grizzell. Deed, 30 December 1798, $400, 135¼ acres granted to Job Red and by him conveyed to William [no surname] bounded by Savannah river, the original grant was 150 acres, part taken of the upper end, beginning about the mouth of Reedy Branch. Wit James McDaniell Senr, James McDaniell. /s/ Zepheniah Harvey. Proven 23 May 1799 by James McDaniell Senr; H Middleton JP. Rec 27 May 1799.

p.69-73   Daniel Gill and wife Susannah of Abbeville to William

Whitlock of Edgefield. Deed, 29 December 1798, $170, 170 acres near mouth of Stephenses Creek of Savannah River bounded by lands of Samuel Crafton, Peter Morgan, William Anderson Esqr. Wit Wm Nichols, Chs Covington. /s/ Daniel Gill, /s/ Susanna (x) Gill. Judge Andrew Hamilton, Abbeville County, certifies relinquishment of dower by Susanna Gill wife of Daniel Gill, 21 December 1798. /s/ Susanna (x) Gill. Proven 16 May 1799 by Charles Covington; Wm Garrett JP EC. Rec 27 May 1799.

p.73-75   Zepheniah Harvey to George Grizzel. Deed, 30 December 1798, $400, 110 acres on William Harveys line and the estate of Field and Savannah river. Wit James McDaniel Senr, James McDaniel. /s/ Zepheniah Harvey. Proven 23 May 1799 by James McDaniel Senr; Hugh Middleton JP. Rec 27 May 1799.

p.75-79   Anthoney Cooper of Richmond County, Georgia, to Federick Slappey. Deed, 3 December 1798, £150 SC money, three tracts: 250 acres on Cuffeytown Creek originally granted to Michael Kise bounding on sd creek; 50 acres joining above tract also on Cuffey-town Creek originally granted to Anna Elizabeth Kise August 1765; also 100 acres on north side of above 50 acres adj land laid out to Adam Hen the sd originally granted to Peter Henby by grant 23 Aug 1795. Wit John Shibley, William Waggoner, William Watson. /s/ Anthony Cooper "Wrote in the German Language." Proven 18 May 1799 by John Shible; Jas Harrison JP. Rec 28 May 1799.

p.79-82   John Strother to John Robertson. Deed, 1 December 1798, £80 Sterling, 110 acres on Little Stephenses Creek adj land of Joseph Stephens when surveyed, now joining John Bridgers, Edward Burt, Dionysius Oliver. Wit Dionysius Oliver, William Robertson. /s/ John Strother. Judge Arthur Simkins certifies relinquishment of dower by Temperance Strother wife of John Strother, 11 March 1799. /s/ Temperance (x) Strother. Proven 1 June 1799 by William Robertson; Rd Tutt JP. Rec 1 June 1799.

p.82-86   John Caldwell Burns son and heir at law of Patrick Burns decd of Laurens County to Rebeccah Cotton. Release, Laurens County, 16 March 1799, £35 Sterling paid by John Cotton of Edgefield, grant unto Rebeckah Cotton administratrix of sd John Cotton decd for use of heirs of sd John Cotton: Salley, Didamia, Jemimah & John Allenson [Allison] Cotton, 150 acres surveyed for Patrick Burns 2 Dec 1772 on Beaverdam Creek of Turkey Creek of Savannah River bounding on

James Robertson at time of survey, granted 1774 by Gov Wm Bull. Wit Cornelius Craddock, John Bowlan. /s/ Jno Caldwell Burns. Judge William Mitchell of Laurens County certifies relinquishment of dower by Mary Burns wife of John Caldwell Burns, 16 March 1799. /s/ Mary (x) Burns. Proven Laurens County 16 March 1799 by Cornelius Craddock; Wm Mitchell JLC. Rec 1 June 1799.

p.86-88   Thomas Reynolds, planter, to James Monday, planter. Deed Bill Sale, 25 February 1799, $350, a mulatto girl named Jude about 18 or 19 years of age together with her future increase. Wit William Ingrom, Richard (x) Johnson. /s/ Thos (x) Reynolds. Proven 3 June 1799 by William Ingrom; James Cobb JP.   Rec 3 June 1799.

p.89-92   John Sullivan and wife Sarah Sullivan to John Williams Hendrick, 13 February 1799, $400, 224 acres on Stephens Creek of Savannah River on ridge road leading from Fort Charles to Augusta, joining land of Amon Roberts. Wit Edward Prince, Delilah (+) Williams. /s/ John Sullivan, /s/ Sarah (x) Sullivan. Judge Arthur Simkins certifies relinquishment of dower by Sarah Sullivan wife of John Sullivan, 3 June 1799; /s/ Sarah (x) Sullivan. Proven 14 February 1799 by Edward Prince; H Middleton JP. Rec 3 June 1799.

p.93-95   Hezekiah Salmon counter Executor of will of Joseph Fortune decd to Mary Hargrove widow of William Hargrove deceased in trust for children and representatives of sd William Hargrove. Deed, 20 Oct 1796, 250 acres originally granted to John Cockburn surveyed 8 July 1791 lying on Dry Creek otherwise called Nobles Creek bounding at time of survey on Benjamin Tutts land. Wit Geo Miller, Briton Mims. /s/ Hezekiah Salmon, executor for estate of Jos Fortune decd. Proven 5 June 1799 by Briton Mims; Rd Tutt JEC. Rec 5 Jun 1799.

p.96-100   Samuel Stalnaker to John Lyon & Wm Evans. Deed, 17 January 1799, $1000, 200 acres, 100 acres being part of a survey near a branch of Stephens Creek called Haw, now Cuffeytown Creek, granted to Allen Addison 7 May 1762; the other 100 acres bounding on sd Allen Addison, Benjamin Bell and granted to Daniel Rodgers 4 July 1769. Wit Alexander (x) McDonald, Thomas Evans. /s/ Sa Stalnaker. Justice William Nibbs certifies relinquishment of dower by Drusilla Stalnaker wife of Samuel Stalnaker, 13 February 1799; /s/ Drusilla (x) Stalnaker. Proven 4 March 1799 by Thomas Evans; Jas Harrison JP.   Rec 8 June 1799.

p.100-105   Thomas Bacon Esqr pf Beaufort District SC to John Anderson. Deed, 6 February 1799, $645, 431 acres on Cuffeytown Creek called North & South fork of Bee tree on sd Creek, of Stephens Creek & Savannah river. Wit Allen Williams, Mary (x) Bryant. /s/ Thos Bacon Senr. Plat shows lands of Lawleys, Thomas Bacon, Matthew Barrott, Tutts old road. Justice Charles J Brown certifies relinquishment of dower by Martha Bacon wife of Thomas Bacon, 6 February 1799; /s/ Martha Bacon. Proven 6 Feb 1799 by Allen Williams; Chas J Brown JQ. Rec 8 June 1799.

p.105-107   Julius Alford & Wm Mapp of Green County, Georgia, to Isaac Bush of Edgefield. Bill of Sale, 4 May 1799, $175, Negro girl Jenney about seven years of age. Wit Eugene Brenan, S Butler. /s/ Julius Alford for self & Wm Mapp. Proven 11 May 1799 by Eugene Brenan; Rd Tutt JP. Rec 11 May 1799.

p.107-112   William Martin and wife Margaret to John Terry. Deed, 2 May 1799, $200, 194 acres on Rockey Creek of Turkey of Savannah River as shown on a plat by Wm Coursey DS, being part of 250 acres granted unto James Rowan and by decease of sd Rowan sd land descended unto above Margaret daughter of sd Rowan decd and wife to William Martin. Wit Stephen Terry, Abraham (x) Martin. /s/ Wm (x) Martin, /s/ Margaret (x) Martin. Judge Arthur Simkins certifies relinquishment of dower by Margaret Martin wife of William Martin, 10 June 1799; /s/ Margaret (x) Martin. Proven 29 May 1799 by Stephen Terry; Jas Harrison JP. Rec 10 June 1799.

p.112-115   Van Swearingen to Stephen Medlock. Deed, 23 August 1797, $10, 150 acres being part of 1084 acres granted to sd Van Swearingen 5 Feb 1787, joining lands of Thomas Swearingen, Morris, Little huckleberry pond, Thomas Swearingen, waggon road from Pine woods house to Granbee. Wit Isaac Kirkland, Wm (x) Nobles, Ambrous Ripley. /s/ Van Swearingen.   Proven 11 June 1799 by Isaac Kirkland; Rd Tutt JP. Rec 11 June 1799.

p.116-118   William Carson to Paul Williams. Deed, 1 January 1799, $400, 100 acres on Cuffeetown Creek of Savannah River, being part of 300 acres laid out for William Rowan and bounded in original survey by McDaniel now held by Richard Tutt Senr. Wit Jno Anderson, John Kenady. /s/ William (S) Carson. Proven 1 Jan 1799 by Jno Anderson; Rd Tutt JP.   Rec 1 Jan 1799.

p.118-121   George Randolph to Benjamin Reynolds of Georgia.
Deed, 8 December 1798, £100 Sterling, 277 acres surveyed for John
Herndon 19 Feb 1788 and granted to Benjamin Reynolds 4 Feb 1793 by
Gov Wm Moultree, situated on Coins fork bounded by Jacob Forten-
burgh, Joab Wootan, and vacant land. Wit Daniel Bullock, Dan Ritchy.
/s/ George (x) Randal. Proven 25 May 1799 by Dan Ritchy; Henry
Key JP.   Rec 22 June 1799.

p.122-125   John Hancock Senr to Agness Bozeman. Deed, 29
December 1798, £50, 85¼ acres on Slash Branch being part of 500
acres originally granted unto Benjamin Wareing 8 July 1774. Wit
Freeman Hardy, Thomas Carter. /s/ John Hancock. Judge Joseph
Hightower certifies relinquishment of dower by Ann Hancock wife of
John Hancock, 15 June 1799. /s/ Ann Hancock. Proven 22 May 1799
by Freeman Hardy; Wm Garrett JP. Rec 24 June 1799.

p.125-128   Elijah Bond, planter, to William Pitman. Deed, 21 Janu-
ary 1799, $100, 75 acres whereon I now live which I purchased of sd
Wm Pitman, on Bird Creek. Wit Wm Key, James Blackwell. /s/ Elijah
(S) Bond. Proven by William Key; Henry Key JP. Rec 28 June 1799.

p.128-132   John Mayes to Austen Whitten of Abbeville County, SC.
Deed, 14 November 1791, £5, 200 acres on Beddingsfields Creek of
Savannah River. Wit John McCoy, Jno Trice. /s/ John Mayes. Proven
14 February 1799 by Jno Trice; Jas Harrison JP.   Rec 1 July 1799.

p.132-135   James Cason to George Delaughter. Deed, 28 January
1799, $300, 100 acres on Stephens Creek [originally] granted to Solo-
mon Newsom. Wit Ludbrook Lee, Daniel Hardy. /s/ Jas Carson.
Proven 28 May 1799 by Daniel Hardy who saw James Carson sign and
acknowledge within deed; Chas Old JP.   Rec 1 July 1799.

p.135-137   John Douglass to daughter Elizabeth Mason and grand
Children Celah Benjamin Nancy Susannah Mary and Elizabeth Mason
and as many Children as shall be born of my sd Daughter lawfully be-
gotten. Deed Gift, 24 November 1798, love & goodwill, two Negroes,
wench named Phillis and boy named Joe, they and their increase to my
daughter during her natural life and then to my sd grand children. Wit
Bartlett Bledsoe, Lydia (x) Bledsoe.   /s/ Jno (I) Douglass.   Proven 11
March 1799 by Bartlett Bledsoe; J Spann JP.   Rec 1 July 1799.

p.137-140   James Baker to Alexander Stewart. Deed, 13 April

49

1799, $500, 93 acres known as Poverty Hill; bounded by lands of John Pierce, Col Leroy Hammond, William Morgan, Wm Covington now held by Charles Colcock Esqr, being near the mouth of Stephens Creek. Wit John R Bartee, Jos Glover, Mary (+) Glover. /s/ James Baker. Judge Joseph Hightower certifies relinquishment of dower by Elizabeth Baker wife of James Baker, 13 April 1799. /s/ Elizabeth (x) Baker. Proven 1 July 1799 by John R Bartee; Chas Old JP. Rec 1 July 1799.

p.141   Mary Vann to Robert Mosely. Renunciation of Dower, 1 July 1799, Judge Arthur Simkins certifies Mary Van wife of Edward Vann examined separately declared she freely released unto Robert Mosely her right of dower. /s/ Mary (x) Vann. Rec 1 July 1799.

p.142   Ulysses Rogers & David Walker to John Pounds. Bond, 7 January 1788; Ulysses Rogers bound in penal sum £1000, condition he make unto John Pounds full title to 185 acres known as Rodes land adjoining Mr Coody & Burrell Johnsons land. /s/ Ulysses Rogers, /s/ David Walker. Marshall Martin proves handwriting of Ulysses Rogers, 1 July 1799; Rd Tutt JP. /s/ Marshall Martin. Rec 1 July 1799.

p.143-145   Benjamin King of Charleston to William Crabtree. Deed, 11 March 1799, $200, 300 acres granted 1 August 1785 to my father Benjamin King and by my sd Father willed to me. Wit Julius Nichols Junr, John Crabtree. /s/ Benj King. Proven 11 March 1799 by Julius Nichols Junr; Wm Nibbs JQ. Rec 1 July 1799.

p.145-147   Leroy Roberts to Lewis Holliway. Deed, 25 June 1799, £300, 200 acres Horns Creek, adj lands of Sherrod Whatley, Thomas Traylor, David Glover, Shurley Whatley Senr, legatees of John Pursell decd. Wit Roger Williams, William Pursell, William Miller. /s/ Leroy Roberts. Proven 1 July 1799 by William Miller; John Blocker JP. Rec 1 July 1799.

p.148-151   Thomas Jones to William Terry. Deed, 3 April 1799, $625, 140 acres part of 200 acres granted to John Mayson in 1772 on Beaverdam Creek bounding land of Jesse Scruggs, Charles Jones, Wm Terry and others. Wit Wm Longmire, John Terry Junr, Betsey Jones. /s/ Thos Jones, /s/ Leanna Jones. Judge Arthur Simkins certifies the relinquishment of dower by Elana Jones wife of Thomas Jones, 1 July 1799. /s/ Leanna Jones. Proven 21 June 1799 by John Terry; James Cobb JP. Rec 1 July 1799.

p.151-153   Will Johnson to Davis Williams, farmer. Deed, 6 December 1798, Will Johnson with approbation of James Harrison Esqr hath bound himself to be an apprentice with Davis Williams to dwell with him untill sd Will Johnson shall come to age twenty one or day of marriage during which time Will Johnson shall faithefully serve his master Davis Williams honestly & obediently. Sd Davis Williams doth covenant to teach Will Johnson the art mistry and occupation of a farmer, allow sufficient meet Drink apparel washing lodging meet for an apprentice. Wit   John Spratt, Richard Lewis. /s/ Will (+) Johnson. Acknowledgment above indenture made with consent of Will Johnson; Jas Harrison JP.   Proven 1 July 1799 by Richard Lewis; Jas Harrison JP. Rec 1 July 1799.

p.154-159   Thomas Green to Catlett Corley. L&R, 10/11 December 1784, £8 sterling, 350 acres on Clouds Creek of Little Saluda bounding land of Mary Thomas. Wit Francis Jones, Wm Davis, John Abney. /s/ Thomas Green. Proven 20 May 1796 by John Abney; Nathl Abney JP.   Rec 1 July 1799.

p.159-160   Benjamin King, house carpenter of Charleston, to John Crabtree. Deed, 9 February 1799, 275 acres below antient boundary on Mountain Creek of Turkey Creek. Wit John Hamilton, Jesse Paine. /s/ Benjamin King. Proven 9 March 1799 by Jesse Paine; Wm Robinson JP. Rec 1 July 1799.

p.160-167   William Donoho of Rockey Creek, planter, and Mary his wife to Samuel Williams.   L&R, 1 & 2 December 1791, £38 sterling, 150 acres on branches of Rockey Creek being part of 250 acres on Rockey Creek of Stephens Creek of Savannah River granted to sd Wm Donoho by Gov Thos Pinckney 6 Aug 1787; adj lands of Moses Smith, Messer Smith, Frasers line.   Wit. John (x) Williams, James Scott. /s/ Wm Donoho.   Proven 9 Feb 1792 by John (x) Williams; Henry King JP. Rec 1 July 1799.

p.168-173   James Fleming, planter, of Newberry County, SC, to William Robertson, planter. Release, 14 May 1787, £45 SC money ackd by sd James Flemmons, 100 acres on Beaverdam Creek of Saluda River bounding on land of John Porter, Elisha Brooks, William Robertson, Robert McCutchens, Thomas Right, Thomas Wright, originally granted unto William Flemmons 16 June 1768.   Wit D Clary, John Wilson. /s/ James (x) Flemmon.   Proven 14 May 1787 by Daniel Clary; P Waters JP. Rec 1 July 1799.

p.174-176   Gilliam Rainey to Daniel Tillman. Deed, 8 May 1799, 5000 lbs good inspected tobacco, 190 acres except 5 acres taken off by an old survey being originally granted to William Rhodes by Gov Wm Moultre 5 June 1786 on Cedar Creek of Horns Creek. Wit Daniel Huff, Douglass Huff, Lewis Tillman. /s/ Gilliam Rainey. Judge Arthur Simkins certifies relinquishment of dower by Nancy Rainey wife of Gilliam Rainey, 1 July 1799; /s/ Nancy (x) Rainey. Proven 1 July 1799 by Lewis Tillman; Rd Tutt JP. Rec 1 July 1799.

p.177-179   William Robertson of Charleston SC to James McMillan. Deed, 13 December 1796, £100 sterling, 500 acres on branch of Little Saluda near branches of Edisto River originally granted to Daniel Crawford bounding on lands of Jacob Smither, unknown persons. Wit Robert McDougall, J Spann. /s/ William Robertson. Justice Jacob Drayton, Charleston District, certifies relinquishment of dower by Susan Robertson wife of Wm Robertson, 3 April 1799. /s/ Susan B Robertson. Proven 8 June 1799 by John Spann; Wm Daniel JP. Rec 1 July 1799.

p.180-182   Isaac Coe to Edward McCartey. Deed, 22 February 1799, $160, [acreage not stated] land which was run for Jacob Smith & William Slurring and is bounded by Jacob Smith, Zion Davis, Roger Smith, Jas Gillian, Wm Burges. Wit Joseph Warren, John Warren. /s/ Isaac Coe. Judge Arthur Simkins certifies relinquishment of dower by Nancy Coe wife of Isaac Coe, 1 July 1799; /s/ Nancy (x) Coe. Proven 28 June 1799 by Joseph Warren; Wm Daniel JP. Rec 1 July 1799.

p.182-184   Wm Floren, Prince Edward County, Virginia, and Phebe Childress to William Butler. Deposition by William Floren before magistrate Richard Bibb, Prince Edward County: about thirty years of age he well remembers that he saw joined in matrimony William Butler and Phebe Childress by Parson Gardner of Prince Edward County, VA. Prince Edward County, VA, 22 Sept 1794, before magistrate Richard Bibb: Ann Childress made oath: about thirty years ago her daughter Phebe Childress and William Butler set off from her house to go to parson Gardner to be married and they returned and lived together as man & wife for a number of years in this part of the country. Francis Watkins, clerk of Prince Edward County, VA, certifies that Richard Bibb who signed within affadavits was qualified and acting Justice of the Peace for the county afsd, 14 October 1798. Thomas Scott, presiding Justice/Peace, Prince Edward County, certifies on 1 Nov 1798 that Francis Watkins was on the date thereof and on the day of within certificate Clerk of the Court of Prince Edward County. Rec 1 July 1799.

p.184-187   Thomas Levingston, Abbeville County, SC, planter, to Major William Robertson. Deed, 20 December 1797, £57 sterling, 96 acres three rods and thirty two perch on Beaverdam branch being part of a tract originally granted to Robert McCutchen 13 July 1762 bounded by lands of sd Wm Robertson, Robert McCutchen. Wit G Burns, John Hoard, James Gowdey. /s/ Thomas Levingston. Proven 10 June 1799 by George Burns; W Anderson JCE. Rec 1 July 1799. Plat surveyed 25 Dec 1797, W Anderson D.S., shows road to Cambridge, land of Dan Bullock and Wm Robinson. Rec 1 July 1799.

p.188-195   Samuel Lewis, planter, to John McCreless, planter. L&R, 7 & 8 September 1792, £50 SC money, 262 acres on branches of Little Stephens Creek of Saluda River, being part of 1462 acres granted to sd Samuel Lewis by Gov Wm Moultre 5 June 1786; sd 262 acres bounded by lands of William Bryant, Widow Robinets, William Dean. Wit Thomas Pulley, David Richardson. /s/ Samuel Lewis. Proven 5 October 1792 by David Richardson; Henry King JP. Rec 1 July 1799.

p.195-197   William Deen to Samuel Mays. Deed, 17 January 1799, $180, 100 acres on Halfway Swamp Creek of Saluda River, bounded by lands of estate of Luke Macmahan, other sides by sd Samuel Mays land, and was originally granted to Richard Allison 2 August 1757 and left by will of Richard Allison to his son James Allison, and by sd Jas Allison conveyed to sd Wm Deen.   Wit Gilson Yarbrough, William Hill. /s/ William (W) Deen. Proven 19 Jany 1799 by William Hill; Nathaniel Abney JP. Rec 2 July 1799.

p.198   Phillis Whatley to Alexander Edmonds. Renunciation of dower. Judge Arthur Simkins certifies relinquishment of dower by Phillis Whatley wife of Edmond Whatley, 2 July 1799. /s/ Phillis (x) Whatley.   Rec 2 July 1799.

p.199-201   Sheriff William Tennent to Charles J Colcock Esqr. Sheriffs Titles, 5 October 1795, at suit of Peter Bosquet and James Mitchell commissioners of the Treasury of SC against Joseph Decoster & Samuel Decoster; sheriff seized land for sale to highest bidder for ready money at Cambridge; struck off to Charles J Colcock for £5.13; 268 acres both sides Edisto River bounding land of Robert Rowbuck. Wit Chas Tennent, Robt Smith. /s/ Wm Tennent. Proven 23 May 1799 by Robert Smith; Wm Nibbs JQ.   Rec 2 July 1799.

p.202-204   John Martin to Luke Smith Williams. Deed, 24 October

1798, $500, 140 acres on Haw branch being part of a grant to James Harrison, bounded by lines of John Rainsford, Edward Mosely, Butler Williams, Browten, land surveyed by Daniel Huff, and remainder of the original grant. Wit Abel Keyes, Daniel Tillman. /s/ Jno Martin. Judge Arthur Simkins certifies relinquishment of dower by Elizabeth D Martin wife of John Martin, 2 July 1799; /s/ Elizabeth D Martin. Proven 11 March 1799 by Daniel Tillman; James Cobbs JP. Rec 2 July 1799.

p.204-206   John and Jacob Harlin to Samuel Jinkins. Deed, 13 November 1798, $150, 100 acres granted to Margaret Brannan 1 Oct 1765 on Little Turkey Creek a branch of Big Turkey Creek of Savannah River, bounding on land of Barbary Michals and vacant land when surveyed, descended by heirship to John Harlen and Jacob Harlen his brother. Wit William Crabtree, W Davis. /s/ John (x) Harlen, /s/ Jacob (x) Harlen. Test: Arthur Simkins as to sd Jacob. Proven 11 March 1799 by William Crabtree; John Blocker JP. Rec 2 July 1799.

p.207   Phillis Whatley to Charles Martin. Renunciation of Dower, Judge Arthur Simkins certifies that Phillis Whatley wife of Edmond Whatley privately examined freely released dower right, 2 July 1799; /s/ Phillis (x) Whatley. Rec 2 July 1799.

p.208-210   Peter & Conrad Migler sole legatees of Joseph Meagler of Amelia Township, planters, to Thomas Farquhar, planter. Deed, 26 October 1798, $140, 300 acres on small branch of Wilsons Creek of Saluda River bounded on Thomas Anderson, Joseph Pain, Thomas Farquhar, and vacant, originally granted to Joseph Meagler 12 July 1771. Wit Rebeccah Anderson, Thomas Anderson. /s/ Peter Migler, /s/ Conrad Migler. Proven 1 July 1799 by Thomas Anderson; W Anderson JCE. Rec 2 July 1799.

p.210-213   Sheriff William Tennent to Samuel Mays. Sheriffs Titles, 7 August 1797; at suit of Christopher Fitzsimmons against estate of Andrew Williamson decd, to sell three tracts of land to highest bidder for ready money at Cambridge; struck off to Samuel Mays for £43.1.8. Forty acres in Granville County, Ninety Six Dist, on Rocky Creek of Stephens Creek bounding on Jno Hearst, James Miscampbell. Also 250 acres near Cuffeetown on Stephens Creek adj Daniel Rogers, Charles Williams, Thomas Goode; also 72 acres on Rockey Creek of Stephens Creek adj Margaret Fulton, Samuel Estar, Walter Bell. Wit Thos Levingston, Charles Tennent. /s/ Wm Tennent S 96 Dt. Proven 23 May 1799 by Thos Levingston; Wm Nibbs JQ. Rec 2 July 1799.

p.213-215   Margaret Harlin to Samuel Jinkins. Deed, 24 January 1799, $5, 100 acres granted to sd Margaret 1 Oct 1765 lying on Little Turkey Creek of Big Turkey Creek of Savannah River when known by the name of Margaret Browner, sd lands now in possession of sd Samuel Jinkins. Wit Arthur Simkins, George Youngblood. /s/ Margaret (M) Harlen. Proven 11 March 1799 by George Youngblood; John Blocker JP.   Rec 2 July 1799.

p.216   Elizabeth D Martin to Charles Martin. Renunciation of Dower; Elizabeth wife of John Martin voluntarily released dower right; Arthur Simkins, 2 Jul 1799. /s/ Elizabeth D. Martin. Rec 2 July 1799.

p.217   Joseph Hightower to Benjamin Adams. Receipt. Received 5 January 1799 from Benjn Adams $700 and $14 in full for five negros: Judah Jinney Flora Sampson Lucy with future increase of females. Wit John Hogh, Wm Hogh. /s/ Joseph Hightower. Proven 2 July 1799 by William Hogh; Rd Tutt JP.   Rec 2 July 1799.

p.218-220   James Allison, planter, to William Deen, planter. Deed, 7 October 1796, £50 sterling, 100 acres on Halfway Swamp adj lands of Samuel Mays, estate of Luke Mchan, originally granted to Richard Allison father of James Allison 2 August 1759 and left by will of Richard Allison to sd James Allison. Wit S Mays, John (x) Whitley. /s/ James Allison.   Justice William Nibbs certifies that Sarah Burton late Sarah Allison late wife of within named Richard Allison decd declared she freely renounced her interest and right of dower in the premises mentioned, 16 Jan 1799. /s/ Sarah (x) Burton late Sarah Allison.   Proven by John Whitley 7 October 1796; Samuel Mays JP. Recorded 2 July 1799.

p.221-223   Sheriff William Tennent to Charles J Colcock. Sheriffs Titles, 5 October 1795; at suit of Peter Bosquet and James Mitchell commissioners of the Treasury of SC against Joseph Decoster & Samuel Decoster, Sheriff sold publicly at Cambridge to highest bidder a tract of 142 acres for £13.1 lying on Rockey Creek adj property of Moses Kirkland, Adam Summers. Wit Robt Smith, Chas Tennent. /s/ Wm Tennent S 96 Dist. Proven 23 May 1799 by Robert Smith; Wm Nibbs JQ. Rec 2 July 1799.

p.224-225   George Bussey to Peter Gibert Esqr of Abbeville and Jesse Dabbs late of Virginia, mill wright. Deed, 8 June 1799, land originally granted to Samuel Scott and made over to Joseph Robertson by sd Saml Scott and coveyed by Jos Robertson 20 Oct 1795; also part of a tract originally granted to Joseph Robertson and conveyed to me by same above conveyance, the tracts contiguous, and contain 180 acres, waters of Stephens Creek bounding on lands of Traves Hill, Samuel Scott, Samuel Garner, and road from Capt Paces plantation to the crossroads to Campbellton.

p.226 is misnumbered

p.227-228   Witness: Thomas Oden, George (x) Turner. /s/ George Bussey. Judge Arthur Simkins certifies relinquishment of dower by Lucy Bussey, 2 July 1799; /s/ Lucy (x) Bussey. Proven 10 June 1799 by George Turner; Henry Key JP. Rec 2 July 1799.

p.228-230   Mathew Devour to David Tillman & wife Elizabeth. Deed of Gift, 2 July 1799, love & affection,   Negroes Grace & her future increase and Joe; also goods given to me by Elizabeth Tamer by deed/Gift 8 Oct 1796. Wit G H Perrin, J Hatcher. /s/ M (M) Devore. Proven 2 July 1799 by G H Perrin; Rd Tutt JEC. Rec 2 July 1799.

p.230-232   William Smith to Bowling Deas. Deed, 31 December 1798, $110, 200 acres; sd land granted to Joseph Lewis, surveyed for Samuel Whitney 15 January 1787 on Turkey Creek bounded by land of Reuben Kirkland, Isaac Lewis. Wit Henry Herrin, Dennis Weaver. /s/ William (x) Smith. Proven 13 June 1799 by Henry Herin; Wm Daniel JP. Rec 2 July 1799.

p.232-245   Daniel Rogers to Charles Williams. L&R, 23 & 24 June 1777, £300 SC money,100 acres being part of 200 acres granted by Gov Thos Boone to Allen Addison 2 May 1762, by Allen Addison transfered to Daniel Rogers 1767, land lying in Granville County near Haw Creek of Stephens Creek bounding on land held by Charles Williams; plat endorsed by Wm Coursey 1777. Wit John Frazier, William Coursey. /s/ Daniel (x) Rogers. Proven 20 June 1797 by William Coursey; Henry Key JP. Rec 2 July 1799.

p.245-247   James McMillan, planter, to George Foreman. Deed, 6 July 1797, 250 acres near the old ridge being part of 500 acres original-ly granted to Daniel Crawford, joining land of Thomas Lackey, Snydar, M Wright the surveyor. Wit James Perry, John Wimberley. /s/ James McMillan. Proven 29 June 1799 by James Perry; John Spann JP. Rec 2 July 1799.

p.247-251   Peter Morgan and wife Ann Meriah to William Roberts. Deed, 19 November 1798, $150.57, 150 acres binding on lands of James Carson, Evin Morgan, Moses Lucas, and vacant. Wit Jonathan Taylor, Daniel Roberts, Fanny (x) Talbert. /s/ Peter (x) Morgan, /s/ Ann Meriah (x) Morgan. Judge Arthur Simkins certifies relinquishment of dower by Ann Meriah Morgan wife of Peter Morgan, 11 March 1799; /s/ Ann Meriah (x) Morgan. Proven 19 Nov 1798 by Jonathan Taylor & Daniel Roberts; Henry Key JP. Rec 2 July 1799.

p.251-254   Thomas Bacon Senr of St Peters Parish, Beaufort District, to Thomas Wilburn, 6 February 1799, £200 sterling, 500 acres in three tracts contiguous to each other lying on Cuffeetown Creek of Savannah river, bounding on lands held by Garrett Longmire, Jacob Shibly, Sally Boovey, Matthew Barrett, estate of Joseph Morton, James McMillian, Abner McMillian, William Hall. Wit Allen Williams, Mary (x) Bryant. /s/ Thomas Bacon Senr. Justice Charles Jones Brown of Orangeburgh District certifies relinquishment of dower by Martha Bacon wife of Thos Bacon, 6 Feb 1799; /s/ Martha Bacon. Proven Beaufort District, 6 February 1799 by Allen Williams; Charles J Brown JQ. Rec 22 July 1799.

p.255-257   Thomas Farquhar, planter, to John Hardy, planter. Deed, 20 February 1799, $200, 300 acres on branch of Wilsons Creek of Saluda River bounded by lands of Thomas Anderson, Joseph Pain, Thomas Farquhar, originally granted to Joseph Meagler 12 July 1771. Wit Richd Pollard, James Farquhar, William Farquhar. /s/ Thomas Farquhar. Proven 1 July 1799 by William Farquhar; W Anderson JCE. Recorded 2 July 1799.

p.257-258   William Pittman, planter, to Elijah Bond, planter. Deed, 21 January 1799, $200, 75 acres bounding on lands of Samuel Cartledge Middleton and others, it being where I now live. Wit William Key, James Blackwell. /s/ William (x) Pittman. Proven 25 June 1799 by William Key; Henry Key JP. Rec 2 July 1799.

p.259-261   Matthew Turpin to Hugh Middleton. Deed, 20 May 1796, £30 SC money, 50 acres, part of 300 acres granted to Samuel Scott on Stephens Creek; by Scott transferred to Edward Prince Senr about 1776; by sd Prince 150 acres sold to Mathew Turpin in 1782; lying on the bank above the fish dam against the Island. Wit Hugh Middleton Junr, Eliza Middleton. /s/ Matthew (M) Turpin. Proven 11 June 1799 by Hugh Middleton Jr; James Cobbs JP. Recorded 4 July 1799.

p.261-271   Charity Thomas of Colleton County, SC, spinstress, to
Charles Williams of Granville County, planter.   L&R, 11 & 12 June
1770, £200 SC money, 200 acres in Granville County bounded by lands
granted to Francis Bryce now held by Daniel Rogers and vacant land at
time of survey.   Wit James Findley, William Roberts. /s/ Charity
Thomas.   Proven 12 June 1770 by William Roberts; John Purves JP.
Recorded all that could be seen 2nd July 1799.

p.271-273   Matthew Caps and wife Elizabeth to Hugh Middleton.
Deed, 22 March 1798, £30 SC money, 160 acres being part of 200
acres granted to Nickless Ware--heirs of sd Nickles to Matthew Caps,
bounding on Stephens Creek and joining land of George Cowan now
belonging to estate of Charles Blackwell. Wit John Boyd, John
Kimball, Hugh Middleton Junr. /s/ Matthew Caps, /s/ Elizabeth (#)
Caps. Proven 11 June 1799 by Hugh Middleton Junr; James Cobbs JP.
Rec 4 July 1799.

p.273-275   Richard Johnson Junr to Jesse Roundtree. Deed, 12
October 1798, $1000, 315 acres lands formerly owned by the Chicke-
saw Indians, confiscated by state of South Carolina, sold by the commissioners of the state, and known in the plan of sd lands as #7 & #8
joining on Savannah River.   Not warranted against Thomas Glasscock
Esqr of Georgia.   Wit Eugene Brenan, Wm Burt. /s/ Richard Johnson.
Proven 8 Aug 1799 by Wm Burt; Richard Tutt JP.   Rec 8 Aug 1799.

p.276-277   Jesse Rountree to Richard Johnson Junr. Agreement, 13
October 1798: be it remembered that about 1784 or 1785 I sold Thomas
Glasscock of Georgia two adjoining tracts of land containing 315 acres.
Whereas it doth appear that Glasscock neglected to record the titles in
time and that there is doubt whether his right is good to Jesse Rountree
to whom he has since sold the land, this therefore is to certify that
Richard Johnson Junr this day signed sealed & delivered unto Jesse
Rountree a deed of conveyance from me. In case there be any dispute
before the signing, sealing and delivery of this deed of conveyance the
sd Richd Johnson Jr shall not be liable in any respect whatsoever to sd
Jesse Rountree or his heirs. Wit Eugene Brenan. /s/ Jesse Rountree.
Proven 5 Aug 1799 by Eugene Brenan; Rd Tutt JP.   Rec 5 Aug 1799.

p.277-283   Charles Goodwin, attorney at Law, to William Garrett.
L&R, 6 & 7 March 1795, £72.8, lots 3 & 24 at Campbellton contain-
ing one fourth of an acre each adj lots of Quires, James McQueens,
Thomas Heron, William Covington. Wit Wm Nibbs, Wm Williamson.

/s/ Charles Goodwin. Proven 2 March 1799 by William Williamson; Chas Old JP. Rec 26 July 1799.

p.283-285   Richard Bolan of Columbia, SC, merchant, to James Sanders Guignard of Columbia, SC, gentleman. Deed, 26 July 1799, $100, 240 acres on Tigar Branch of Shaws Creek bounded by Robert Lang, originally granted to Richardson Bartlett 25 Feb 1786 and granted to Richard Bolan by Gov Arnoldus Vanderhorst 1 Feb 1796. Wit Wm Taylor, Jacob Smith. /s/ Richard Bolan. Proven 26 July 1799 by Jacob Smith; Sion Taylor JP. Rec 30 July 1799.

p.286-289   Thomas Bacon Esqr of Saint Peters Parish SC to Matthew Barrett. Deed, 6 February 1799, $150, 179 acres on north fork of Beetree branch of Cuffeetown Creek of Stevens Creek and Savannah River. Wit Allen Williams, Mary (x) Bryant. /s/ Thomas Bacon Senr. Plat shows 179 acres adj Beetree branch, Thomas Bacons land, Thomas Williams land, Matthew Barretts land, John Andersons land.   Charles Jones Brown, Justice of the quorum of SC, certifies that Martha Bacon wife of Thomas Bacon freely relinquished dower rights, 6 Feb 1799; /s/ Martha Bacon. Proven 6 Feb 1799 by Allen Williams; Charles J Brown JQ. Recorded 10 August 1799.

p.290-291   Christian Gamillan to Thomas Swearingen. Deed of sale, 15 January 1799, $175 Spanish mild Dollars, negro boy Moses. Wit Russell Robertson, Joseph Robison. /s/ Christian (x) Gamillan. Proven 2 August 1799 by Joseph Robertson; Van Swearingen JP.   Rec 3 Aug 1799.

p.291-294   Rice Swearingen Senr to Mary Swearingen. Deed, 2 October 1797, £10 sterling, 250 acres, the lower part of land whereon I now live beginning where Charleston Road crosses thence to Ryans Mill path; to Mary Swearingen and at her decease to Rice Swearingen Junr, Jas Swearingen and Larken Swearingen. Wit Thos Swearingen, Benja Hatcher. /s/ Rice Swearingen. Proven August 1799 by Thomas Swearingen; Van Swearingen JP. Rec 3 Aug 1799.

p.294   Marshall Martin to Edmund Holleman. Deed, 1 July 1799, $60, 316 acres on branches of Gunnels Creek of Stephens Creek of Savannah River bounded by lands of Marshall & Matt Martin, James Smith, Edmund Fraklin, John Glanton & Ryles, John Logan, David Thomson, which land was granted to sd Marshall Martin 5 August 1793 by Gov Wm Moultrie. Wit J Hatcher, S Butler. /s/ Marshall Martin.

Judge Arthur Simkins certifies relinquishment of dower by Mary Martin wife of Marshall Martin, 1 July 1799. /s/ Mary (x) Martin. Proven 5 August 1799 by Sampson Butler; Richard Tutt JP. Rec 5 Aug 1799.

p.297-300   Marshall Martin, planter, to William Howle, planter. Deed, 1 July 1799, $90,   206 acres surveyed 1 March 1785; granted 4 July 1785 by Gov Wm Moultrie; on branches of Gunnels of Stephens Creek, adj Matt Martin. Wit J Hatcher, S Butler. /s/ Marshall Martin. Judge Arthur Simkins certifies relinquishment of dower by Mary Martin wife of Marshall Martin, 1 July 1799; /s/ Mary (x) Martin.   Proven 5 August 1799 by Sampson Butler; Richard Tutt JP.   Rec 5 Aug 1799.

p.301-304   John Martin to David Moore. Deed, 2 July 1799, $100, 60 acres on Horns Creek, being part of 400 acres granted to Thomas Beck-um 15 May 1775 & conveyed from him to sd John Martin including the mill seat & pondage. Wit Richard Tutt, Geo H Perrin. /s/ John Martin. Plat shows lands of Sherod Whatley, Roger Williams land & fence, Robert Lang, Aquila Miles, Shugar Bush, Pen Howlet, high water mark, spring branch. Plat certified by Robert Lang D.S. Judge Arthur Simkins JCE certifies relinquishment of dower by Elizabeth D Martin wife of John Martin, 2 July 1799; /s/ Elizabeth D Martin. Proven 5 Aug 1799 by George H Perrin; Rd Tutt JP. Rec 5 Aug 1799.

p.305-308   William Blaikley & wife Proudence and Thomas Ellis & wife Nancy to John Burt. Deed, 9 March 1799, £30; 300 acres, part of original grant to Joseph Tucker 20 March 1775 on Cuffeetown, Bird, & Siper Creeks, bounding on lands held by Samuel Anderson, John Adams, Gray, Edward Wade, which land came to possession of Wm Blaikley and Thomas Ellis by sale from Joseph Tucker. Land conveyed to John Burt is bounded by lands granted to James Gray, John Adams, Samuel Anderson, Yancey Key. Wit Batte Evans, Evans Stokes, Shadk Stokes. /s/ Wm Blaikley, /s/ Thomas Ellis. Proven 3 August 1799 by Batte Evans; Jas Harrison JP.   Rec 7 August 1799.

p.308-309   James Barefield & David Rowland to Philip Ikner. Bill of Sale, 12 March 1799, $500, Negro wench named Clarender about 24 years of age, her boy child about 2 months old named Bolt. Wit Frederick Holmes, James (x) Hitso. /s/ James Barfield, /s/ David Rowland. Proven 15 August 1799 by Frederick Holmes; William Daniel JP.   Rec 16 August 1799.

p.310-311   Philip Ikner to William Daniel. Bill of Sale, 15 August

1799, $400, two Negroes, Clarender and child Bault. Wit John Daniel, William Herin. /s/ Phillip Ikner. Proven 16 Aug 1799 by William Herin; Richard Tutt JP. Rec 16 Aug 1799.

p.311-315   William Bexley to Peter Utz[Outs]. Deed, 6 August 1799, $160, 200 acres on Sleepy Creek of Savannah River bounding lands of Peter Durne[Dume?], granted unto John Jacob Messer Smith by Lt Gov Wm Bull 6 April 1773. Wit Henry (x) Timberman, Peter (x) Timberman. /s/ William Beaxly. Judge Arthur Simkins certifies relinquishment of dower by Barbery Bexley wife of Wm Bexly, 13 August 1799; /s/ Barbara (x) Bexley. Proven 13 August 1799 by Henry Zimmerman; Arthur Simkins JCE. [Zimmerman signed his name as Henry (x) Timberman]. Rec 13 Aug 1799.

p.315-316   Jobe Martin, blacksmith, to Wm Jeter Senr. Bill of Sale, 23 February 1799, $50, my whole set of smith tools, to be delivered to sd Jeter on or before 20 Sept next; if sd Martin pays $50 this instrument is void. Wit William Wash. Proven 13 August 1799 by William Wash; Rd Tutt JP. Rec 13 Aug 1799.

p.316-317   Benjamin Mannen of Washington County, Georgia, to Hightower Thorn[Thorne] of Edgefield. Bill of Sale, 17 April 1799, $350, Negro wench Tiller about 17 yrs old. Wit James Garrett, Jno Wills. /s/ Benjamin Mannen. Proven 27 Jul 1799 by John Wills; William Garrett JP. Rec 14 Aug 1799.

p.318-319   James Barfield and David Rowland to William Herrin. Bill of Sale, 14 June 1799, $200, Negro boy agoing in three years old named Handy. Wit William Nichols, Andrew Gamalan. /s/ James Barefield, /s/ David Rowland. Proven 24 June 1799 by Andrew Gamalan; Wm Daniel JP. Rec 16 Aug 1799.

p.319-320   Nicholas Ware Senr to Joseph Ware. Bill of Sale, 2 June 1795, £50.15 sterling, Negro man Isaac. Wit Lewis Harris, Saml Crafton. /s/ Nicholas (x) Ware. Proven 18 July 1799 by Samuel Crafton; Wm Tennent JQ. Rec 19 Aug 1799.

p.321-322   Nicholas Ware Senr to grandson Nicholas Ware Junr son of son Robert Ware. Deed of Gift, 6 July 1799, love & affection, Negro boy Reuben son of Charity a yellow woman. To rectify a mistaken in a deed given by me to my sd grandson Nicholas Ware Junr bearing date 8 January 1799 and recorded by Richd Tutt Clerk of County Court

12 March 1799 is my intention in making this second deed. It will be found by reference to the record that the word nephew is made use of in the eldest deed whereas it should be grandson. Wit Samuel Crafton, John Prince. /s/ Nicholas (x) Ware Senr. Proven 18 July 1799 by Saml Crafton; Wm Tennent JQ. Rec 19 Aug 1799.

p.322-323   Briton Mims to Drury Mims Senr. Bill of Sale, 3 November 1798, $750, Negroes named Rachel and Tannstan. Wit Livington Mims, Mat Mims. /s/ Briton Mims. Proven 5 Aug 1799 by Matthew Mims; Rd Tutt JP. Rec 5 Aug 1799.

p.324-325   Drury Mims to son Tingnell Mims. Deed of Gift, 3 August 1799, love & affection, six Negroes Rachel, Tunstan, Jenny, Peter, Violet, Joseph with future increase of the females. Wit Eugene Brenan, William Burt. /s/ Drury Mims. Proven 5 August 1799 by William Burt; Rd Tutt JP. Rec 5 Aug 1799.

p.326-328   Abraham Herndon to John G Cook. Deed, 4 February 1799, $150, 170 acres on Chaves's Creek adj lands of James May, John Griffin, sd Herndon, being part of 1000 acres originally granted unto John Herndon 4 Feb 1793, lines of John Griffin, head of a branch "where Lucy Reah brings water[?]", down branch to Mays line. Wit Richard Booth, Henry Barns. /s/ A Herndon. Proven 20 Aug 1799 by Henry Barns, Rd Tutt JP. Rec 20 Aug 1799.

p.328-332   Peter Cassity of High Hills of Santee to Matt Gayle, planter. L&R, 3 & 4 March 1789, 250 guineas, 500 acres granted 2 Aug 1771 by Gov Wm Bull unto Peter Manigault Esq in St Pauls Parish now Edgefield County on Horse Pen branch between Ninety Six and the Ridge bounding on John Brue's land, Thos Fletcher, Henry Shickels land, which tract of 500 acres was conveyed by sd Peter Manigault to Tacitus Gilliard in 1773. Peter Cassity atty in fact for sd Tacitus Gilliard.. Wit Ulyssus Rogers, William Nichols, William Mills. /s/ Peter Cassity. Proven Claremont County, 13 June 1799 by Ulyssus Rogers; William Merrell JPCC. Rec 27 Aug 1799.

p.333-334   Richard Bolan of Richland County SC to Ambrose Ripley, planter. Deed, 10 April 1796, $100, 240 acres on Tigar branch of Shaws Creek bounded by land of Robert Lang, originally surveyed for Richardson Bartlett 25 Feb 1786 & granted to Richard Bolan by Gov Arnoldus Vanderhorst 1 Feb 1796. Wit James Hickey, James Sanders Guignard. /s/ Richard Bolan. Proven Richland County, Camden

District, 18 April 1796, by James Sanders Guignard; Martyn Alken JP. Rec 29 Aug 1799.

p.335-337   James Atcheson, planter, to Bennett Henderson. Deed, 10 April 1799, $146, 137 acres being part of 600 acres granted to John Earnest Poyas 7 April 1770 and lately conveyed to me James Atcheson by Henry Inglesby and Ann his wife daughter and heiress of sd Poyas, being at time of original survey on Rockey Creek of Stephens Creek & bounded by part of sd survey sold to James Fraser, by part sold to Obediah Henderson Junr & Senr. Wit Obediah Henderson, Obediah Henderson Senr. /s/ James Atcheson. Proven 9 May 1799 by Obediah Henderson; Henry Key JP. Rec 3 Sept 1799.

p.337-340   James Atcheson, planter, to Obediah Henderson Senr. Deed, 10 April 1799, $60, 36 acres being part of 600 acres situate at time of original survey in Granville now Edgefield County on Rockey Creek of Stephens Creek granted to John Earnest Poyas 7 April 1770 and since conveyed to me by Henry Inglesby and wife Ann daughter & heiress of sd John Earnest Poyas, bounded by part of sd survey sold by me to Bennett Henderson and by part of same to Obediah Henderson Junr, and by part of same yet in my possession. Wit Bennett Henderson, Obediah Henderson Junr. /s/ James Atcheson. Proven 9 May 1799 by Bennett Henderson; Henry Key JP. Rec 3 Sept 1799.

p.340-342   James Atcheson, planter, to Obediah Henderson Junr. Deed, 10 April 1799, $100, 100 acres being part of 600 acres in Granville now Edgefield County on Rocky Creek of Stephens Creek granted 7 April 1770 to John Earnest Poyas, lately conveyed to me James Atcheson by Henry Inglesby and wife Ann daughter & heiress of sd Poyas; sd 100 acres bound by original line, by part of survey sold to Bennett Henderson, by part sold to Obediah Henderson Senr, and by part sold to William Ogle. Wit Bennett Henderson, Obediah Henderson Senr. /s/ James Atcheson. Proven 9 May 1799 by Bennett Henderson; Henry Key JP. Rec 3 Sept 1799.

p.343-345   Henry Inglesby & wife Ann, before marriage called Ann Poyas, of Charleston, to James Atcheson. Deed, 25 February 1799, $8.57, 600 acres on Rocky Creek of Stephens Creek in Granville bounding on Arnold Russell and vacant land, originally granted to John Ernest Poyas now deceased, late of Charleston, father of Ann Inglesby and left to her by his will as one of his children. Wit John Monk, James Cantey. /s/ W. B. Inglesby, /s/ Ann Inglesby. Justice Edward

Darrell certifies relinquishment of dower by Ann Inglesby wife of Henry Inglesby, 25 Feb 1799. Proven 25 February 1799, City of Charleston, by John Monk; Ed Darnell JP. Rec 3 Sep 1799.

p.346-349   James Atcheson, planter, to William Ogle. Deed, 25 July 1799, $160, 100 acres being part of 600 acres originally granted to John Ernest Poyas 7 April 1770 on Rockey Creek of Stephens Creek. Wit Harkalus (x) Ogal, Obediah Henderson Junr, Henry (H) Gess. /s/ James Atcheson. Justice William Tennent certifies relinquishment of dower by Alizebeth Atcheson wife of James Atcheson, 25 July 1799; /s/ Betcy (x) Atcheson. Proven 2 Aug 1799 by Harkulus (x) Ogal; Henry Key JP. Rec 3 Sept 1799.

p.349-350   Jude Henderson, Deposition, 22 April 1799, before Henry Key JP: Deponant had divers sons, George and others, by her former husband, Jeremiah Cook. Son George Cook took to wife Elizabeth Thomas of Georgia. Sd wife was delivered of a child in dwelling house of Obediah Henderson husband of deponant in Edge-field County, which child, William Cook, was born 6 March 1784. Deponant said her son George requested deponant to take care of his wife, and went from deponant's house September 1783 to Tennessee and there took a second wife and had one child by her after which he deceased by being drowned in Whites Creek of Cumberland River in Davidson County. /s/ Jude (+) Henderson. Rec 3 Sept 1799.

p.350-352   Conrad Merck, planter, and wife Margaret to George Merck, planter. Deed, 29 December 1797, $200, 100 acres on Hardlabour Creek bounded by land of John Swillings, Abraham Martin, and vacant when surveyed, originally granted 25 March 1772 to Rosinah Margret Fritz. Proven 11 September 1799 by Federick Knop; Rd Tutt JP. Rec 11 Sep 1799.

p.353-354   James Crabtree of Green County, Tennessee, to William Crabtree. Deed, 17 August 1799, $200, 220 acres below the antient boundery on Watery branch of Little Stephens Creek. Wit Daniel Peak, Martin Gwyn. /s/ James (x) Crabtree. Proven 17 August 1799 by Daniel Peak and Martin Gwyn; Elisha Baker JP. Rec 14 Sept 1799.

p.355-357   Hugh Middleton Esqr to Richard Quarles. Deed, 11 April 1799, £100, 191 acres, part of 500 acres granted to Abraham Martin on Cuffeytown & Bird Creek. Wit Rebeca Prince, Eliza Middleton, Hugh Middleton Junr. /s/ Hugh Middleton. Justice William Tennent certifies relinquishment of dower by Aggy Middleton wife of Hugh Middleton, 19 August 1799; /s/ A (x) Middleton. Proven 19 August 1799 by Eliza Middleton; Wm Tennent JQ. Rec 16 Sep 1799.

p.357   James Ogylvie to Daniel Bullock. Receipt. Received February 14, 1799, of Daniel Bullock administrator to estate of Artimus Watson decd one likely young Negro for his wife's part of her fathers estate, recd by me in full of all demands. /s/ James Ogylvie. Ackd before Wm Daniel JP. Rec 10 October 1799.

p.358-359   James Beaty of Burk County, Georgia, to Joseph Williams. Deed of Sale, 26 September 1798, Negro man Frank, Negro woman Hannah, for $800 to me paid by Joseph Williams. /s/ Wit William Bell. /s/ James Beaty. Proven 24 April 1799 by William Bell; John Spann JP. Rec 10 October 1799.

p.359-362   Hugh Middleton Esqr to Richard Quarles. Deed, 11 April 1799, $300, 100 acres bounded by James McMillan, George Lamken, and by land formerly held by sd Hugh Middleton, originally granted to Mrs Blake. Wit Rebecca Prince, Eliza Middleton, Hugh Middleton Junr. /s/ Hugh Middleton. Justice William Tennent certifies relinquishment of dower by Aggy Middleton wife of Hugh Middleton, 17 August 1799; /s/ A (X) Middleton. Proven 19 August 1799 by Eliza Middleton; Wm Tennent JQ. Rec 16 Sept 1799.

p.362-363   Jo S Jones & Rd Owens to Jno Olliphant. Receipt, 29 August 1799, $1045 in full for three Negroes: Peter about 20 years of age, Milley, 17, and Nancy about 18 years old. Wit David Burns, John Frazier. /s/ Rd Owens, Jo S Jones. Proven 18 Sept 1799 by John Frazier; Rd Tutt JP. Rec 18 Sep 1799.

p.363-364   Winifred Richardson to David Sandidge. Renunciation off dower, 18 September 1799, by Winefred Richardson the wife of Abraham Richardson certified by Joseph Hightower JCE. /s/ Winifred (x) Richardson. Rec 18 Sept 1799.

p.364-369   Charles B Cochran, Marshal of SC District, to John Scott. Titles, 2 October 1797, Thomas Lamar was seized of inheritance of land. Also James Brown Senr and James Brown Junr about 12 May 1797 before Justices of Federal Circuit Court held at Charleston obtained judgment against Thomas Lamar, Philip Lamar & John Carter for $900.10 for their costs and charges in prosecuting their suit; execution of judgment was issued out of Federal Circuit Court, writ tested by Hon Oliver Ellsworth chief Justice; dated Charleston 12 May 1797, directed to Marshal of goods and lands of sd Thomas Lamar, Philip Lamar and John Carter, convicted as appears by record, to levy sum of $910.10. Walter Taylor lawful deputy of Charles Cochran exposed to public auction for satisfaction of sd sum on 2 October 1797; sold land to John Scott for $910.10 he being high & last bidder. Chas B Cochran, marshal, confirmed unto John Scott 200 acres bounded at time of survey by lands of Thomas Smith & Savannah river. Wit Robt E Cochran, Robt Cochran. /s/ Charles B Cochran marshal Dist of SC. Receipt for $910.10. /s/ Chs B Cochran.

p.370-371   Philip Ikner to Jesse Pitts. Bill of Sale, 1 July 1799, $500, Negro woman about 24 years of age and her child about 6 months old. Wit Simeon Perry. /s/ Philip Ikner. Proven 24 Sept 1799 by Simeon Perry; John Spann JP. Rec 27 Sep 1799.

p.371-374   Sheriff William Tennent to Walter Taylor. Sheriffs Titles, 5 March 1798; at suit of John Smith against William H Gibbs admr of Macartan Campbell decd, Sheriff sold to Walter Taylor, the highest bidder, at Cambridge for $470   800 acres on Beach Island bounded by land of estate of Leonard Meyers decd and by land of Hall Arington decd commonly known as Horse Shoe tract. Wit Oswell Eve, Jno Trotter. /s/ Wm Tennent Shff 96 Dist.   Proven 10 Oct 1799 by Oswell Eve; Richd Tutt JP. Rec 10 Oct 1799.

p.374-375   Sarah Jones to Walter Taylor. Renunciation of dower. Chatham County, GA, before Judge Joseph Clay, Sarah wife of George Jones Esqr who was lately the wife of McCartan Campbell late of Augusta, gentleman, deceased, voluntarily released right of dower to land surveyed for Thomas Goodale containing 800 acres surveyed 19 October 1750 bounded by Robert McMurdy and Savannah River, for which Walter Taylor, planter, received sheriffs title to sd land. Ackd at Savannah in Chatham County, GA 4 May 1798. /s/ Joseph Clay. /s/ Sarah Jones. Recorded 10 October 1799.

p.375-376   James Carson to Paul Abney Senr. Bill of Sale, 8 October 1799, $35, sorrell mare nine years old. Wit William Abney, John Abney. /s/ James Carson. I hereby indorse within Bill of Sale to Nathaniel Abney for value received, 9 October 1799. Wit Azariah Abney. /s/ Paul Abney. Proven 9 October 1799 by John Abney; Nathl Abney JP. Rec 10 Oct 1799.

p.377-379   Alexander Oden to James King. Deed, 10 August 1798, $50, 225 acres on Stephens Creek bounded by lands of John Kimbrel, Saml Scott formerly sd Odens, Jacob Claheld formerly Barnabas Caps; grant made to sd Alexander Oden 1 December 1794. Should land be recovered by any prior grant, sd Oden is not to be liable to damages. Wit Joshua Bussey, Joseph Collier. /s/ Alexander Oden. Proven 13 August 1798 by Joshua Bussey; Hugh Middleton JP. Rec 10 Oct 1799.

p.379-381   Nathaniel Abney to Austen Eskridge. Deed, 14 August 1799, $400, 100 acres on Saluda river adj land originally granted to John Caldwell, Joel Abneys line, William Richardsons land, Andrew Browns land, being part of two tracts one of which was granted to John Caldwell, the other to Nathaniel Abney, together with all rights except the spring that sd Nathaniel Abney now makes use of. Wit Joel Abney, John Abney. /s/ Nathaniel Abney. Proven 14 August 1799 by John Abney; Nathl Abney JP.   Rec 10 Oct 1799.

p.382-383   Simeon Perry to Isaac Funderburg. Bill/Sale,16 July 1799, $335, Negro woman Nancy and her increase. Wit Elijah Martin, William Pike. /s/ Simeon Perry. Proven 24 Sept 1799 by William (x) Pike; John Spann JP.   Rec 10 October 1799.

p.384-385   Simeon Perry to John Wimberley. Bill of Sale, 2 February 1799, $400, two Negroes, Pat and Pol. Wit Ezekiel Perry Senr, James Perry. /s/ Simeon Perry. Proven 8 Oct 1799 by James Perry; John Spann JP. Rec 10 Oct 1799.

p.385-386   Joshua Jones to John Wimberley. Bill/Sale, 25 May 1799, $700, three Negroes: woman Jane, boy Jim, girl Rachel. Wit James Perry, A Yarbrough Junr. /s/ Joshua Jones. Proven 8 Oct 1799 by James Perry; John Spann JP. Rec 10 Oct 1799.

p.386-390   Benjamin Moore to Michael McKie. Deed, 25 December 1789, £100 SC money, 100 acres on Saluda river originally grant- ed to Catharine Miller 6 June 1764 bounded by lands of sd Michael McKie, Samuel Savage. Wit Thomas Anderson, John (x) Gorman. /s/ Benjamin Moore. Proven 26 December 1789 by Thomas Anderson; William Anderson JP.   Rec 10 Oct 1799.

p.390-392   William Doby, planter of Lancaster County, SC, to Demcy Weaver of afsd county. Deed, 8 April 1799, £35 sterling, sold by Power of Attorney given to me by Nathaniel Doby living in Granvill

County, Virginia, unto Demcy Weaver, 100 acres adj lines of Charles Partin on Dry Creek. Wit Jonathan Glanton, William Homes, Charles (CP) Partin. /s/ Wm Doby. Proven 31 August 1799 by William Homes; Wm Daniel JP. Rec 10 Oct 1799.

p.392-394   James Perry to Ezekiel Perry Senr. Deed, 3 December 1796, £100, land on Peters Creek, 100 acres patented to Moses Powell 2 March 1762 near Clouds Creek of Saluda, bounded by lands surveyed for William Watson, Andrew Shipes; also 30 acres part of grant to Wm Doby on branch now called Spring branch, Powells corner & line. Wit S Spann, Ezekiel Perry, Lewis Wimberley. /s/ James Perry. Judge Arthur Simkins certifies that Sarah Perry wife of James Perry freely relinquished dower, 26 March 1798; /s/ Sarah (P) Perry. Proven 10 Oct 1799 by Ezekiel Perry Junr; Rd Tutt. Rec 10 Oct 1799.

p.395-397   Jesse Hopkins to the daughters of Thomas Youngblood: Winnefred Kirksey, Elizabeth Adams, Rebecca Haregrove, Amy Williams, and Isabella Youngblood. Deed of Gift, 17 September 1799, natural affection, all the bonds, notes, open accounts & cash I am possessed of, also livestock and property I may possess at the time of my death; should any donees depart this life without lawful issue, their part to be equally divided among the survivors. Wit James Youngblood, Thomas Youngblood. /s/ Jesse (x) Hopkins. Proven 17 Sept 1799 by James Youngblood; Wm Robertson JP. Rec 10 Oct 1799.

p.397-399   Whitten Pines to Nathan Jones. Deed, 16 February 1796, £2, 52 acres being part of a tract formerly granted unto sd Whitten Pines 29 May 1794 by Gov Wm Moultrie. Wit Wm Right, Watts Man. /s/ Whitten (x) Pines. Plat certified by Wm Wright D.S. shows adjoining McDarnels land, Charleston road. Proven 17 Sept 1796 by Wm Wright; James Webb JP. Rec 10 Oct 1799.

p.399-401   Michael Deloach to Thomas Lee Senr. Deed, 9 October 1799, £50 sterling, 150 acres granted to Ann Jordan 21 Feb 1772 adj Jacob Smith and Russell Wilson. Wit William Case, Grandboy (x) Floyd, Jacob Smith. /s/ Michael Deloach. Proven 9 Oct 1799 by Jacob Smith; Russell Wilson JP. Rec 10 Oct 1799.

p.401-403   Phill May to James Bowding. Deed, 25 December 1798, $250, 50 acres being part of 300 acres originally granted to Richard Kirkland on Chaves Creek to Cogings Spring branch. Wit James May, Mary (M) May. /s/ Phill May. Proven 11 Oct 1799 by James May; Jas

Cobbs JP. Rec 11 Oct 1799.

p.404-407   Samuel Bugg of Richmond County, planter, to Samuel W Jones of Augusta, silversmith. Deed, Georgia, 27 June 1799, $400 GA money, half of a tract of land containing 150 acres in Beach Island, SC, bounding on [blank] Tobler, Neal, Smithers, Benders land, which tract was late the property of John Tobler, sd moiety on 8 June Inst was deeded to sd Saml Bugg by Robert Walton, Robert Watkins, James Pearre, and James Fox commissioners apptd by Superior Court of Richmond County to make destribution of sd Estate. Wit Chas Wynn, Will Robertson Clk. /s/ Samuel Bugg. Will Robertson Clerk of Superior Court certifies relinquishment of dower by Charlotte wife of Samuel Bugg, 27 June 1799; /s/ Charlotte Bugg. Proven 11 Oct 1799 by Will Robertson; Rd Tutt JP. Rec 11 Oct 1799.

p.407-408   David Coalter to John Tarrance. Bill of Sale, 7 August 1799, $700 in full for four Negros: Nanny, Isaac, Glasgow, Moses, and the future issue of females. Wit Smith Milner, Lucy Exum. /s/ David Coalter. Proven 7 August 1799 by Smith Milner; Joseph Hightower JCE. Rec 11 Oct 1799.

p.408-414   Willis Anderson to Matthew Bettis. L&R, 29 & 30 August 1793, £20 SC money, 100 acres on head dreans of Petters Creek of Clouds Creek bounding on vacant and Christian Currey's land. Wit William Bell, Stephen Bettis, Frances Bettis. /s/ Willis Anderson, /s/ Patience (x) Anderson. Proven 9 Jan 1797 by Stephen Bettis; Van Swearingen JP. Rec 11 Oct 1799.

p.414-416   Thomas Berry to Samuel Berry. Deed, 28 June 1799, $100, 85 acres being part of 150 acres originally granted to Charles Carson 25 June 1771 on west side of Mill Creek formerly called Beaver Creek branch of Great Saluda river, adj land of George Lewis Patrick, Thomas Berry, Moses Walton, Tosetys creek, John Carter. Wit Gabriel Berry, Joseph Taylor. /s/ Thos Berry. Proven 7 July 1799 by Joseph Taylor; Nathaniel Abney JP. Rec 11 Oct 1799.

p.417-419   Bibby Bush to John Walker. Deed, 27 July 1799, $100, 256 acres granted to sd Bibby Bush by patent 5 September 1791 on Bog branch of Edisto river bound by lands of Prescoat Bush, Gunnels, Edward Couch when surveyed. Wit Frances Walker, Amos W Stacher. /s/ Bibby Bush. Judge Joseph Hightower certifies that Mary Bush wife of Bibby Bush relinquished dower, 4 October 1799; /s/ Mary (x) Bush.

Proven 17 Sept 1799 by Frances Walker; J Spann JP. Rec 11 Oct 1799.

p.419-423   Thomas Swearingen to Peter Cloud. Deed, 12 September 1799, $50, 100 acres adj land surveyed for Phillip Ships, Fraziers land now hilt by Isaac Kirkland; being the lower part of 671 acres granted to the sd Thomas Swearingen 7 Nov 1798 on Paces branch of Shaws Creek. Wit William Swearingen, Judith Hall. /s/ Thomas Swearingen.   Judge Arthur Simkins certifies relinquishment of dower by Peggy Swearingen wife of Thomas Swearingen, 11 Oct 1799; /s/ Peggy Swearingen. Proven 12 Sept 1799 by William Swearingen; Van Swearingen JP.   Rec 11 Oct 1799.

p.423-426   Samuel Scott to Charles Franklin. Deed, 20 July 1799, $400,   100 acres; also an adjoining tract containing 250 acres on Stevens Creek originally granted to Arthur Gilchrist, sold by Arthur Gilchrist & wife 1791 to James Scott, and by James Scott & wife to Samuel Scott party hereto on 18 Dec 1793. Wit D Burks, Zachariah Lunday. /s/ S Scott. Justice William Tennent certifies relinquishment of dower by Jane Scott wife of Samuel Scott, 5 August 1799; /s/ Jane Scott.   Proven 11 Oct 1799 by Zachariah Lundy; Matt Martin JP. Rec 11 March 1799(sic)

p.426-427   Ezekiel Perry to Moses Holstun. Bill of Sale, 21 April 1798,   £28.6.4 sterling, Negro girl named Cans. Wit Simeon Perry, Wm Holstun, John Wimberley. /s/ Ezekiel Perry. Proven 5 May 1798 by William Holstun; Wm Calk JP.   Rec 11 March 1799.

p.428-431   Wright Nicholson to Caleb Mauldin. Deed, 28 March 1795, £70 sterling, 300 acres being part of 500 acres granted to John Duglas 20 January 1773 by Gov Chas Granville, conveyed to Wright Nicholson by John Douglass; sd 300 acres divided from remainder by a line crossing near Bullocks; also that other tract containing 90 acres granted to sd Wright Nicholson 3 March 1788 by Gov Thos Pinckney. Wit Henry King, James Ogylvie, William Ogylvie. /s/ Wright Nicholson. Proven 12 Oct 1799 by James Ogylvie; Wm Daniel JP. Rec 12 Oct 1799.

p.431-432   Mary Wilson to Shepherd Spencer. Renunciation of dower, Justice William Nibbs certifies that Mary Wilson wife of Russell Wilson freely relinquished her claim of dower, 12 October 1799; /s/ Mary (x) Wilson.   Rec 12 Oct 1799.

p.432-436   Charles Heard to Tolover Bostick. Deed, 12 September
1799, £100 sterling, 200 acres granted to Frederick Glover 12 Oct 1770
on Rockey & Ninety Six Creeks bounding on William Bean, McSalter
White, William Beale as shown on platt annexed to original grant. Wit
John Cowdrey, John Reordan. /s/ Charles Heard. Justice William
Nibbs certifies relinquishment of dower by Mary Heard wife of Charles
Heard, 12 December 1799; /s/ Mary (xi) Heard. Proven 12 September
1799 by John Reordan; Wm Nibbs JQ. Rec 11 Oct 1799.

p.436-439   Charles Jones Colcock of Prince Williams Parish, Beaufort District, SC, to Tolover Bostick. Deed, 13 April 1799, $3000,
400 acres granted to James Mayson Lucas Holt, south side of Santee
river in Birkly County at a place called Ninety Six bounding on lands of
John Murray Esqr, Thomas Brown, Timothy Reordan, Thomas Nightin-
gale, adj Cambridge, on which Charles Jones Colcock lately resided.
Wit John Dunlap, Julius Nichols Junr. /s/ Charles J Colcock. Proven
11 Sept 1799 by John Dunlap; Wm Nibbs JQ. Rec 12 Oct 1799.

p.439-440   John Glover of Abbeville County to Mary Hamilton.
Deed, 29 April 1799, £30 sterling, 186 acres on Mountain and Rockey
Creek of Savannah river bounded by lines of James Morrison &
unknown. Wit Joseph Aiton, John (x) Hamalton, Sarah (x) Aiton. /s/
John Glover. Proven 26 Sept 1799 by Joseph Aiton; James Harrison
JP. Rec 12 Oct 1799.

p.441-443   Jesse Christian to Gideon Christian. Bill of Sale, 12
November 1798, £60 SC money, Negro boy Abraham aged eleven
years; if Gideon Christian pays £60 sterling by first May next, this deed
of sale shall be on none effect. It is agreed that sd Gideon Christian
keep Negro boy in his possession untill end of term mentioned. Wit
Gilson Yarbrough, Wm Moore. /s/ Jesse Christian. Proven 20 Sept
1799 by William Moore; Nathl Abney JP.   Rec 12 Oct 1799.

p.443-445   James Carson to William Moore. Deed, 12 October
1799, £20,   55 acres being part of 288 acres granted to sd James Car-
son on Tosseties Creek bounded by land of Thomas Butler, James and
Salley Carson, Cullen Lark, John Abney. Wit Eugene Brenan, Joseph
Hackney. /s/ James Carson. Proven 12 Oct 1799 by Eugene Brenan;
Wm Nibbs JQ. Rec 12 Oct 1799.

p.445-447   Abraham Yeates to William Anderson. Deed, 27 Nov
1797, $400,   200 acres Wilsons Creek originally granted to Thomas

Bell 17 Mar 1760, bounded when surveyed by vacant land. Wit Godfrey Adams, Stephen Bostick, Thomas Anderson. /s/ Abraham Yeates. Proven 14 Oct 1799 by Thomas Anderson; Rd Tutt JEC. Rec 14 Oct 1799.

p.447-449   Robert Lang to Thomas Trayler. Deed, 20 June 1798, £10, 53 acres on Dry Creek of Chaveses Creek being part of 100 acres originally granted to sd Robt Lang 4 July 1791 bounded by lands of William Glover, road to bridge on Horns Creek, Col Eveleighs line. Wit Robt O Williams, David Burkhalter. /s/ Robt Lang. Judge Joseph Hightower certifies relinquishment of dower by Sary Lang wife of Robert Lang, 17 Oct 1798; /s/ Sarah Lang. Proven 16 Mar 1799 by Robert O Williams; James Cobbs JP. Rec 14 Oct 1799.

p.450-452   Robert Lang to Thomas Trayler. Deed, 16 October 1798, £10, 52 acres on Horns Creek bounding on land of Roger Williams, Sherod Whatley, Roy Roberts, Col Eveleigh; which grant was originally made unto sd Robert Lang 22 July 1798. Wit Robt O Williams, Holley[Hatley?] Lang. /s/ Robt Lang. Judge Joseph Hightower certifies relinquishment of dower by Sary Lang wife of Robert Lang, 17 Oct 1798; /s/ Sarah Lang. Proven 16 Mar 1799 by Robt O Williams; James Cobbs JP. Rec 14 Oct 1799.

p.452-454   William Anderson to Benjamin Burton. Deed, 14 February 1799, $500, 200 acres on Wilsons Creek bounded by vacant land at original survey, originally granted to Thomas Bell on 17 March 1760, by sd Thomas Bell sold to Thomas Yeates, and by his son and heir Abraham Yeates sold to William Anderson. Wit John Findley, Thos Anderson. /s/ W Anderson. Proven Newberry County 13 August 1799 by John Findley; Jas Mayson JNC. Rec 14 Oct 1799.

p.454-460   Darrel Johnson to Elizabeth Young. L&R, 7 & 8 March 1796, £30 sterling, 79 acres situate on Coes Branch, Clouds Creek adj Henley Webb, it being part of tract granted to Darrel Johnson by Gov Arnoldus Vanderhorst 11 Feb 1795. Wit Martha (x) Bell, Abigal (x) Right(Night?), Mary (x) Young. /s/ Darrel (x) Johnson. Proven 1 April 1796 by Martha Bell; Russel Willson JP. Rec 14 Oct 1799.

p.460-467   Arthur Watson to Mary Watson. L&R, 25 & 26 March 1793, pursuant to will of Michael Watson decd between Arthur Watson executor and Mary Watson, £105 SC money, 150 acres originally granted unto John George Grim the father of Laurence Grim and

conveyed to sd Laurence Grim to Michael Watson 1767, on Clouds
Creek of Little Saluda River bounding on John Carlin. Wit Willis
Anderson, Lewis Wimberley, Elijah Watson. /s/ Arthur (x) Watson.
Proven 20 Jan 1797 by Lewis Wimberley; Wm Daniel JP. Rec 14
October 1799.

p.467-470   William Jeter Senr to William Jeter Junr. Deed, 11
January 1796, £100, 139 acres on Horns Creek adj Ferneds(?) line,
John Shaws old line. Wit John Burt Senr, Eleazar Jeter. /s/ William
Jeter. Judge Arthur Simkins certifies relinquishment of dower by
Margaret Jeter widow of W Jeter decd, 1 July 1799; /s/ Margaret (x)
Jeter. Proven 11 October 1799 by Eleazar Jeter; James Cobbs JP. Rec
15 Oct 1799.

p.470-473   William Jeter Senr, planter, to Stephen Mays. Deed, 1
August 1799, 139 guineas, 139 acres on Horns Creek where Turners
line crosses, Furneds corner, John Shaws old line. Wit Charles P Jeter,
Mary Jeter, Salley Jeter. /s/ W Jeter Senr. Judge Arthur Simkins certi-
fies relinquishment of dower by Lucy Jeter wife of William Jeter, 1
August 1799; /s/ Lucy Jeter. Proven 1 August 1799 by Chas P Jeter;
Arthur Simkins JCE. Rec 15 Oct 1799.

p.473-474   Christian Gamalan to Ambrose Ripley. Bill Sale, 28
August 1799, £100, Negro man Primas. Wit William Nichols, Julius
Nichols. /s/ Christian (x) Gamalan. Proven 15 October 1799 by Wm
Nichols; Russell Wilson JP. Rec 15 Oct 1799.

p.474-478   William Coursey, Deputy surveyor, to Constant Ogyls-
by, planter. Deed, 17 June 1799, £50 sterling, 210 acres on Beaverdam Creek of Turkey Creek of Savannah river; bounding on Horse pen
branch, Goodes orphans, Thurmond, being part of 946 acres granted
unto Wm Coursey by Gov Wm Moultrie at Charleston 7 Aug 1786. Wit
Mills Witt, Robert Coursey, Moses (x) Meso. /s/ W Coursey. Proven
15 Oct 1799 by Mozes (S) Mezo; James Cobbs JP. Rec 15 Oct 1799.

p.478-481   Susanna & John Parker to Melines C Leavenworth.
Deed, [no date], $100, 150 acres Town Creek adj Doctor Printrees
land, formerly Zublas, land granted to Thomas Lamar, land of Isaac
Parker, land surveyed for David Zubla. Wit Elizabeth (x) Pance, Richd
Hampton. /s/ Susannah (x) Parker, John (x) Parker. Proven 20 June
1799 by Elizabeth Pence; Joseph Hightower JCE. Rec 15 Oct 1799.

p.481-483   Philip Lamar to James Jones. Deed, 12 January 1799, $15, fifteen acres beginning on original line at John Jones's corner, by Jacob Guyton.Wit Robert Lamar, John Jones. /s/ Philip Lamar. Proven 12 Oct 1799 by Robt Lamar; John Clarke JP.   Rec 15 Oct 1799.

p.483-485   Rufus Inman, Blacksmith, and wife Elizabeth to Delilah Mabry, planter. Deed, 24 October 1798, $100, 150 acres on a branch of Halfway Swamp creek bounded by land of William Taylor and others, which was originally granted to Wm Taylor and conveyed to Rufus Inman 4 Sept 1793. Wit John Mitchell, Mattox Mays, John Inman. /s/ Rufus Inman, /s/ Elizabeth (x) Inman. Proven 16 Oct 1799 by Mattox Mays; Richard Tutt JP. Rec 16 Oct 1799.

p.486   Thomas Oden to Peter Robertson. Receipt, 8 December 1797, $70 in part of payment for land on Loyds Creek containing 100 acres bounded on Hazekiah Odens line, Williams line, Dagneys old path, Colliers line. When balance is paid, rights to be made to sd Robertson. Wit Richd Christmas. /s/ Thos Oden. Proven 16 Oct 1799 by Richard Christmas; Rd Tutt JP. Rec 16 Oct 1799.

p.487-494   Orandatus Watson son of Jacob Watson of Burk county, GA, to Willis Anderson. L&R, 17 & 17(sic) February 1791, £10 SC money, 100 acres Peters Creek of Clouds Creek bounding on land helt by Christian Currey. Wit Moses Harrison, Abner Watson, Arthur (x) Watson. /s/ Orandatus Watson. Proven 3 March 1791 by Arthur (x) Watson; William Anderson JP.   Rec 16 October 1799.

p.494-495   Jeremiah Hatcher to Luke Smith. Bill of Sale, 15 October 1799, Sales of the Court House 3d February 1798. Ephraim Terrel v Thos Lamar entered in Shffs office 6 Novr 1794. Luke Smith to sail Dr To three Negro: Peter Susy & Jim their child. Recd Edge-field Court House of Luke Smith $400 a balance of $600 in full for right & title of Thomas Lamar to above Negroes, which Negroes was levied on by me under Fieri Facias, and sold to highest bidder. Wit S Butler. /s/ J Hatcher Shff EC. Proven 16 Oct 1799 by Sampson Butler; Wm Garrett JP. Recorded 16 October 1799.

p.496-498   Nathan Jourdan to Christopher Cox. Bill Sale, 14 September 1799, cattle [description here omitted], other livestock, household goods and tools, and the lands where I now live, this property to satisfy sd Cox for the sum of $170 to be paid on March the first day the insuing year, sd Jourdan by paying sd Cox above sum is to have the property again; if Jourdan do not pay Cox, sd Cox is to sell sd property to sales sd sum; if there is not enuf to satisfy sd sum the sd Jurdan do oblidge myself to make sd sum good to sd Cox. Wit Bethany Cox, Jno Lewis, Fereby (o) Cox. /s/ Nathan Jourdan. Proven 17 Oct 1799 by Bethany Cox; Henry Key JP. Rec 17 Oct 1799.

p.498-500   Rhinhard Hileman to John Henry Croft. Deed, 4 April 1799, $12, fifty acres, it being one third part of 150 acres on Little Stephens Creek granted to Peter Khune in 1765 and claimed by sd Hireman as his wife Martalaner Hileman's dower. Wit James Blocker, John Blocker Junr. /s/ Rinehard (x) Hileman. Judge Arthur Simkins certifies relinquishment of dower by Martalaner Hileman wife of Rhinhard Hileman. Proven 4 April 1799 by James Blocker; John Blocker; John Blocker JP. Rec 18 Oct 1799.

p.501   Nancy Franklin to Joseph Hightower. Judge Arthur Simkins certifies 13 October 1798 that Nancy Franklin wife of Ephraim Franklin freely released unto Joseph Hightower her interest in fifty acres at Cherokee ponds whereon sd Joseph Hightower now resides which was granted to Ephraim Franklin on 19 November 1772. Wit Arthur Simkins. /s/ Nancy (x) Franklin.   Rec 18 Oct 1799.

p.502-504   William Bobbett to Pleasant Thurmond. Release, 16 May 1799, £90 sterling, 107 acres on Stephens Creek and Savannah river being part of land originally granted to Benjamin Bell bounded by Saml Stalnaker, Holeys land, Richard Tutt Sr, Hiram McDanalds; sold by William McDanald to Jacob Hibbler; by Jacob Hibbler to Wm Bobbett. Wit Alexander Hall, Richd Quarles. /s/ William Bobbett. Proven 16 May 1799 by Richard Quarles; Jas Harrison JP. Rec 21 Oct 1799.

p.504-505   William Wright to Gideon Palmer. Bill of Sale, [no date] $200, one Negro boy Frank. Wit Steven Norris. S Butler. /s/ William Wright. Proven 1 November 1799 by Sampson Butler; Rd Tutt JP. Rec 1 Nov 1799.

p.505-507   James Lowe to John Olliphant. Bill of Sale, 15 December 1795, £17 sterling, Negro boy Charles. Wit Geo H Perrin. /s/ James Lowe. Proven 2 Nov 1799 by G H Perrin; Rd Tutt JP. Rec 2 Nov 1799.

p.507-509   Robert Russell to James Frazier. Deed, 13 July 1799, $37, twelve acres on Rockey Creek of Stephens Creek of Savannah

River, it being part of fifty acres granted to Robert Russell by Gov Wm Bull 21 Dec 1769. Wit Abs Williams, Jno Smith, Andrew Fields. /s/ Robt (x) Russell. Proven 3 August 1799 by John Smith; James Harrison JP. Rec 4 Nov 1799.

p.510-513   James Atcheson to James Frazier. Deed, 27 June 1799, $130,   69 acres on Rockey Creek of Stephens Creek of Savannah river bounded on lines of Charles Williams, James Frazier, Robert Russell, it being part of 600 acres granted to John Earnest Poyas by Gov Wm Bull 18 Jan 1770. Wit Abs Williams, Hezekiah Williams, John Smith. /s/ James Atcheson. Justice William Tennent certifies relinquishment of dower by Elizabeth Atcheson wife of James Atcheson, 25 July 1799; /s/ Betsy (x) Atcheson. Proven 3 August 1799 by Absalom Williams; James Harrison JP. Rec 4 Nov 1799.

p.513-515   George B Moore and wife Sally daughter of Lake Ryan deceased to John & Benjamin Ryan. Satisfaction of an Estate, 2 November 1799, received of John Ryan, Benjamin Ryan Senr & Arthur Simkins Esq executors of will of Lake Ryan decd our full share of real and personal estate of sd Lake Ryan decd. Wit Richard Walpole, John Harden. /s/ George B Moore, /s/ Sally Moore. Proven 5 Nov 1799 by Richard Walpole; Van Swearingen JP. Rec 5 Nov 1799.

p.515-518   Minor Winn of town of Warnsborough, SC, to Thomas Youngblood the elder. Deed, 29 August 1799, $300, 300 acres on Mountain creek of Stephens Creek originally granted to John Hope 28 July 1775; by him conveyed to Jos Kirkland 1777, and by Kirkland to Minor Winn in 1789. Wit Moody Burt, Edward M Blaikley. /s/ M Winn. Proven 12 Oct 1799 by Moody Burt; Russell Wilson JP. Rec 5 Nov 1799.

p.518-539   John Pryor's Certificates. Parish of Wendron, Cornwall. John Prior of this Parish and Elizabeth Cheqwidden of this Parish were married in the church by banns 28 December 1775 by me, Jacob Bullock, vicar. This marriage was solemnized in the presence of John Cheqwidden Anthony Pryor. The mark of P of John Pryor the mark of (S) of Elizabeth Pryor copies from marriage register October 18, 1797. /s/ Richd Gerveys. Wendron Baptisms 1778. John son of Jno Pryor & Elizabeth his wife was baptized May 12, 1778. The above is a copy taken from the Wendron Register October 18, 1797 by me, Richd. In Chancery: Elizabeth Pryor widow John Pryor the son and Mary Pryor the daughter of John Pryor late of Wendron Parish in County of Corn-

wall and Kingdom of England severally make oath, sd Elizabeth Pryor
for herself saith that she the wife of John Pryor she was married in the
Parish Church of Wendron about 22 years ago, that her husband the sd
John Pryor quitted his native home being in the Parish of Wendron
about 18 years ago for America, that she lived with him as such till hs
departure from home, that she had by the sd John Pryor at time of his
departure three children, one son called John Pryor who has lived with
this deponant ever since he was born and now lives with her, and two
daughters one called Ann and another Mary, that while her sd husband
John Pryor was in America she received several letters from him desir-
ing her to come to America and bring the children with her for that he
had considerable property in America that he was able to maintain her
and family in a decent manner. Said John Pryor for himself saith that
he is son of sd John Pryor who died lately in America and that he has
lived with Elizabeth Pryor his mother ever since John Pryor his father
left his native home, that while deponants father lived in America this
deponant & his mother received several letters from him in which his
father desired deponant to come to America. Said Mary Pryor saith she
is daughter of John Pryor late of Wendron parish who died in America,
that she lived with Elizabeth Pryor her mother till capable of getting her
livelihood. Sworn at Helston in Cornwall County 3 September 1798
before Christr Wallis, one of the masters extray in Chancery. /s/ Elizabeth (x) Pryor, /s/ John (R) Pryor, /s/ Mary (P) Pryor.   In Chancery.
Hannibal Thomas, Peter Perry, & Charles Thomas of Parish of Wendron, Cornwall, England, make oath. Hannibal Thomas is Church-
warden of Parish of Windron, knew well John Pryor from his infancy,
that he married Elizabeth Cheqwidden daughter of Thomas Cheqwidden
of sd parish, at time of his departure for America he had three children
who are now all alive, son John Pryor, daughters Ann and Mary; that
he has lately heard that John Pryor is dead in America and has left
considerable property. Peter Perry age about 62 has lived all his life in
Parish of Windron, was well acquainted with John Pryor from infancy;
John Pryor married Elizabeth Cheqwidden dau of Thomas Cheqwidden
of Wendron [words as above]. Charles Thomas was well acquainted
with John Pryor from a child; John Pryor married Elizabeth Cheqwidden dau of Thomas Cheqwidden; was present at the Christening and
was godfather to John Pryor son of sd John Pryor. In Chancery. Henry
Jinkin and John Cheqwidden both of Wendron Parish, Cornwall, England, make oath. Henry Jinkin saith he is Clerk of sd Parish, was well
acquainted with John Pryor, that he was married by Rev Jacob Bullock
late vicar of parish to Elizabeth Cheqwidden dau of Thomas Cheqwidden, and he certifies the copy of church register; also knew Anthony

Pryor the other subscribing witness who is dead. John Cheqwidden saith he was well acquainted with John Pryor [as above], was present at the marriage; knew Anthony Pryor the other witness who is since dead. Notice by Christopher Wallis, notary public, of borough of Helston, before whom appeared Hannibal Thomas, Peter Perry, Chas Thomas, Henry Jinkin, John Cheqwidden all of Parish of Wendron, who several-ly made oath that matters contained in affadavits respecting late John Pryor were sworn before me. Also appeared Elizabeth Pryor widow of John Pryor, and executed a power of attorney to Nicholas Hitching of Helston, postmaster, and John Pryor her son impowering them jointly & severally to transact the affairs of her decd husband. Elizabeth, son John, daughter Mary Pryor severally made oath to matters expressed in the affadavits. Certificate of good character of these persons, 8 Sept 1798. /s/ Chrisr Wallis, notary Publick. John Rowe of Trelil, Wendron Parish, Cornwall, JP, certifies he is well acquainted with these persons who are of good fame and reputation; 8 Sept 1798. /s/ J Rowe. Certi-ficate that bearer John Pryor is son of John Pryor of Wendron, Corn-wall, who left his home about 17 years since and went to America where he settled near Savannah in Georgia in which place he died about six months ago and left his son, the bearer, one of his executors, 18 Oct 1797. /s/ J Rowe. Elizabeth Pryor's power of attorney to son Jno Pryor, 8 Sept 1798. Wit Christ Wallis, Joseph Roberts. mark of Elizabeth Pryor. Articles of agreement between Elizabeth Pryor and Nicholas Hichens; Elizabeth Pryor being unable to pay the expences of her passage to America, hath requested Nicholas Hichens to go to America to endeavour to recover such part of property which she may be entitled to; John Pryor son of sd John Pryor decd by Elizabeth Pryor is to accompany sd Nicholas Hichens; Nicholas Hichens has offered to pay the expences of their passage and for difficulty and trouble which he may be put unto about the recoveryof the property, Elizabeth Pryor hath assigned unto sd Nicholas Huchins one moiety of all such part of share of such property as sd John Pryor might have died possessed of which she may be entitled to as the widow of sd John Pryor decd. Wit Chrisr Wallis, Joseph Roberts. Elizabeth (8) Pryor. Rec 9 Nov 1799.

p.539-540   John Jones and wife Clarey to Jacob Guyton. Deed, 25 October 1799, $5, half acre on Peppers branch of Horse Creek, line of James Jones. Wit Philip Lamar, James Jones. /s/ John Jones, /s/ Clary (x) Jones. Proven 8 Nov 1799 by James Jones; Rd Tutt JP. Rec 8 Nov 1799.

p.540-543   Benjamin Melton and wife Sarah to Eleazar Tharp, schoolmaster. Deed, 26 April 1799, $80, 50 acres on Dry Creek bounded by Robert Whitehead, and Benjamin Melton. Wit Samuel Lewis, James (x) Morgan, Matthew Melton. /s/ Benjamin (x) Malton, /s/ Sarah (x) Melton. Proven 27 April 1799 by James (x) Morgan; J Spann JP. Rec 11 Nov 1799.

p.543-545   Ezekiel Hudnall of Linkhon County, Georgia, to his Grand Children of Edgefield, SC.   Deed Gift, 27 July 1799, for love & goodwill, to Leroy Tibbs Hudnall, man Isaac and girl Sarah with her increase at my decease. Also boy Charles to Daniel Gower Hudnall at my decease. Boy Harry to Stanly Sisen Hudnall at my decease. Also Negro and Negro woman called Jane and Ellick with her future increase to Ezekiel Kemp Hudnall. Also Negro woman Fortune and girl Eady with their future increase at my decease to Elizabeth Shalton Hudnall. Also Negro girl Nise with all her increase to Nancey Foshee Hudnall. Also Negro girl Vilott and Negro girl Rose and their increase at my decease to Martha Middleton Hudnall forever. Wit Jesse Copeland, Samuel (x) Price, Elizabeth Price. /s/ Ezekiel Hudnall. Proven 19 Sept 1799 by Jesse Copeland; Henry Key JP.   Rec 31 Dec 1799.

p.546-548   Henry Champin, planter, to William Burgess. Deed, 29 December 1797, £40 sterling, 94 acres on Lucys branch of Dry Creek, adj James Gilland. Wit Moses (x) Hoetox, Isaac Coe, Joshua Burgess. /s/ Henry (+) Champin, /s/ Elizabeth (+) Champin. Proven 4 Nov 1799 by Joshua Burgess; John Spann JP.   Rec 12 Nov 1799.

p.548-550   Samuel Mays to Jesse Hill. Deed, 5 July 1799, £93 sterling, 250 acres on Stephens Creek bounding on lands of Camel Rogers, Charles Williams, Thomas Goode, same being sold by Wm Tennent sheriff on 7 Aug 1797 for satisfaction of execution against estate of Andrew Williamson decd in favor of Christopher Fitzsimons. Wit Elijah Lyon, Robt Chapman. /s/ S Mays. Proven 13 Nov 1799 by Elijah Lyon; Richard Tutt JP.   Rec 13 Nov 1799.

p.550-552   Thomas Ogle to Samuel Price. Deed, [blank] 1799, $140, 86 acres surveyed for Leroy Tibbs Hudnall and relapsed by sd Ogle bearing date 1 Dec 1796 on Rockey Creek of Stephens Creek bounded by Obediah Henderson, Abraham Williams, & others. Wit Richard (x) Barrett, Philip Holt. /s/ Thomas (T.O.) Ogle.   Proven 15 Oct 1799 by Philip Holt; Rd Tutt JP.   Rec 15 Nov 1799.

p.552-555   John Stephen Mantz to Doby Acred. Deed, 24 September 1799, $150, 100 acres on Hard Labour creek adj lands of sd J S Mantz, Peter Ramby, & Ready. Wit O Ellyson, Geo Merck. Plat shows land of John Stephen Mentz, Readys tract, J Perry's land, Peter Rampsy's line; surveyed 18 June 1799, Abner Perrin D.S. Proven 15 Nov 1799 by O Ellisson; James Harrison JP. Rec 15 Nov 1799.

p.555-558   Thomas Cotton, planter, to Samuel Dennis. Deed, 4 July 1797, £50 sterling, 50 acres north side of the mill pond on Log creek of Turkey Creek of Stephens creek of Sasvannah river. Wit Julius Nichols, William Dennis. /s/ Thomas Cotton. Proven 13 May 1799 by William Dennis; Elkanah Sawyer JP. Rec 15 Nov 1799.

p.558-560   Leonard Nobles of Georgia to John Matthews. Deed, 8 November 1798, $100, 209 acres near the road from Major Hugh Middleton, partly adj widow Mitchell and partly on George Delaughter, on Stephens Creek of Savannah river, granted to Leonard Nobles 1 Jan 1797 by Gov Wm Moultree. Wit Archd Stuart, Dennis Nobles, John Weatherford. /s/ Ld Nobles. Proven 30 March 1799 by John Weatherford; James Cobbs JP. Rec 18 Nov 1799.

p.561-562   Nathan Jordan to his Children Margery Jordan, Abigal Jordan, Leah Jordan, Sarah Jordan, Levy Jordan. Deed Gift, 1 August 1799, goodwill, all I am possessed of and its increase hereafter |not here enumerated| all which property is to remain in my and my wife's hands suring our natural lifetimes and at our deaths to be equally divided. Wit David Burks, Jean (x) Burks. /s/ Nathan Jordan. Proven 20 Nov 1799 by David Burks; Chas Old JP. Rec 20 Nov 1799.

p.562-565   Tomme Keeling Smith & Leonard Waller of Abbeville County, SC, planters, to Benjamin Glover, merchant. Deed, 7 September 1799, £25.16.8, 201 acres, plat 11 Sept 1798 certified by William Caldwell D.S. Wit John M Kellar, Wm Williams. /s/ T K Smith, /s/ Leonard Waller. Plat shows Tender grass lands, lands of Wm Moore, Henry Gady, line of original survey, Thos K Smith's land. Proven 20 Nov 1799 by Jno M Kellar; Rd Tutt JP. Rec 20 Nov 1799.

p.565-567   John Cook, free black man of Village of Campbellton, to William Farbus Taylor, merchant. Bond or Indentures, 17 May 1799, Cook voluntarily binds himself to sd William F Taylor as a servant for five years; Taylor binds himself to find sd Cook & wife her mother and daughter in good & sufficient victuals, cloathing during sd Term. Wit David Barrnett, Charles Covington. /s/ John (x) Cook, /s/ William F

Taylor. Proven 12[13?] Nov 1799; Chas Covington; Wm Garrett JP. Rec 21 Nov 1799.

p.567-578   John Richey & wife Ann of Abbeville to James Campbell of Edgefield. Deed of lease[and release], Abbeville County, 13 November 1792, £60 sterling money, 80 acres joining lands of John Savedge, Richard Brooks, Elisha Brooks, John Murphy[Murphey], originally granted to Ann Brownlee 16 June 1768 on the Kings bounty. Wit John Scogin, Nathan Henderson, Robert Mayson, Hugh Boyd, Ezekiel B Boggs. /s/ John Richey, Ann (x) Richey.   Proven 14 February 1794 by Hugh Boyd; Charles Davenport JP.   Richard Tutt Clerk of Edgefield County Court empowers any two or three Justices of the peace of Abbeville County to take examination of Ann Richey wife of John Richey respecting her right of dower to land conveyed by her husband John Richey to James Campbell, 6 Nov 1795. Certification by Hugh Wardlaw JP, Abbeville County, that Ann Richey freely relinquished her right of dower, 22 November 1795.

p.579-582   Sheriff William Butler to Thomas Weatherington. Sheriffs Titles, 3 September 1799, at suit of Philemon Green against Henry Childs, sheriff directed to sell at Cambridge to highest bidder a tract of land hereinafter described.   William Butler, for [not stated], 200 acres on Horse pen creek bounding on Minor Weatherington, John Todd which sd Henry Childs had at time of the sale. Wit Eugene Brenan, Stanmore Butler. /s/ William Butler Shff 96 Dist. Proven 25 November 1799 by Eugene Brenan; John Blocker JP. Rec 25 Nov 1799.

p.582-584   Arthur H Davis to Jesse Ragin. Deed, 8 April 1797, $100, 110 acres Big Creek of Little Saluda river, granted to sd Arthur H Davis 5 August 1793 by Gov Wm Moultrie. Wit Thomas Berry, Wm (x) Jay, A (x) Jay. Received of Jesse Ragin £10 Sterling the money within mentioned. Wit Thos Berry. /s/ Arthur Davis. Proven 23 Nov 1799 by William Joy; Russell Wilson JP. Rec 25 Nov 1799.

p.584-587   Daniel Bullock, farmer, to Benjamin Watson. Deed, 5 December 1797, £100 sterling, 250 acres, Cane Brake Br of Little Saluda; surveyed by John Douglass, granted to John Burk 1 May 1773 by Gov Wm Bull. Wit John Pope, Joseph Nunn. /s/ Daniel Bullock. Proven 26 Nov1799 by Joseph Nunn; Wm Daniel JP. Rec 29 Nov 1799.

p.587-589   Shemuel Nicholson to Benjamin Watson. Deed, 26 November 1799, $100, 270 acres on Cane brake branch of Little Saluda river joining land where Benjamin Watson now lives, adj Thomas Pulley, Douglas's land, granted by Gov Wm Moultrie 17 Jan 1793. Wit John H Croft, Jas Blocker. /s/ Shemuel Nicholson. Proven 29 Nov 1799 by James Blocker; John Blocker JP. Rec 29 Nov 1799.

p.589-591   Kindred Anderson to Willis Anderson. Deed, 11 March 1799, £50, 100 acres both sides Charleston Road on waters of Saluda, bounded by lands of Jacob Odum, sd land granted to John Anderson. Wit Ezekiel Perry, Levi McDaniel, Davis Williams. /s/ Kindred (x) Anderson. Proven 29 Nov 1799 by Ezekiel Perry; William Daniel JP. Rec 30 Nov 1799.

p.591-594   Peter Jones & wife Polley to John Wilson. Deed, 3 February 1798, £70 sterling, 200 acres, branch of Mountain Creek of Turkey Creek, part of 364 acres granted to James Harrison 3 April 1786; sd 200 acres laid off sw part of original tract. Wit Jos Aiton, Sarah (x) Aiton. /s/ Peter (x) Jones, /s/ Polley (x) Jones. Proven 29 Nov 1799 by Joseph Aiten; Jas Harrison JP. Rec 6 Dec 1799.

p.594-596   Peter Jones to John Wilson. Bond for titles to above, 7 October 1795, Peter Jones bound to John Wilson in sum £100 sterling. condition if above bound Peter Jones shall make unto above John Wilson good and sufficient titles to 200 acres on sw side sd tract, that sd Peter Jones now lives on, above obligation to be void. Wit Joseph Dawson, /s/ Peter (x) Jones. Proven 5 Oct 1797 by Joseph Dawson; James Harrison JP. Rec 6 Dec 1799.

p.596-600   John Glover and wife Polley Glover of Abbeville County to Joseph Collier. Deed, 22 January 1799, £60 sterling, 200 acres on Stephens Creek being part of land originally granted to John Williams bounding on lands of Moses Robertson, Mrs Lowrys land, Jno Martin and sd Joseph Colliers land. Wit John Tolbert, John Bullock. /s/ Jno Glover, /s/ Polley Glover. Plat shows road to Cambridge, Widow Rowan's land, John Martins land, Colliers land; certified by Robert Lang D.S. at request of John Glover. Judge Adam Crain Jones of Abbeville County certifies relinquishment of dowry by Polley Glover, 6 Nov 1799; /s/ Polley Glover. Proven Edgefield, 9 Nov 1799 by John Talbert; Henry Key JP. Rec 6 Dec 1799.

p.600-601   Samuel and William Marsh and others to Samuel Marsh Senr. Receipt, 26 February 1792. Received of Samuel Marsh Senr in his lifetime our parts of his estate, he now being deceased. /s/ Anna

(X) Cotron, /s/ Shiles Marsh, /s/ Elizabeth Marsh, /s/ William Marsh, /s/ Saml Marsh, /s/ Salley Marsh. Proven 9 Dec 1799 by Elizabeth Marsh; Richd Tutt JP. /s/ Elizabeth Marsh. Rec 9 Dec 1799.

p.601-603   Sheriff William Tennent to John Boyd. Bill/Sale, 4 February 1799, at suit James Coursey against William Key & others, sheriff is ordered to sell a Negroe boy named Jack in open sale at Cambridge; struck off to highest bidder John Boyd for $325. Wit Charles Simpkins. /s/ William Tennent Shff 96 District. Proven 8 March 1799 by Charles Simpkins; Hugh Middleton JP. Rec 20 Dec 1799.

p.603-607   William Key to Henry Key Esqr. Deed, 21 December 1799, $1140, 700 acres, being three surveys, one of 200 acres where I now live lying both sides Turkey Creek, originally granted to John Goff by Gov James Glen 7 Oct 1755; another survey of 300 acres granted to Henry Key by Gov Chas Montague 21 May 1772; another survey of 200 acres being part of 400 acres on branch of Turkey Creek granted to Henry Key by Gov Chas Montague 21 May 1772 bounding on William Minter. Wit Wm Wash, Jesse Scruggs, Robt Hatcher. /s/ William Key. Proven 23 December 1799 by Robert Hatcher; John Blocker JP. Rec 23 Dec 1799.

p.608-610   William Key to Henry Key Esqr. Bill/Sale, 21 December 1799, $1330, Negroes: fellow named Jim age 31, wench Alse age 30 and her child named Leah 18 months old, wench named Suck 25 yrs old, boy named Amos 15 yrs old, fellow named Joe 50 yrs old. Wit William Wash, Jesse Scruggs, Robt Hatcher. Proven 23 December 1799 by Robert Hatcher; John Blocker JP. Rec 23 Dec 1799.

p.610-612   William Greenwood Junr of Charleston to John P Bond of Lexington SC. Deed, 18 November 1799, $300, 350 acres in Edgefield County bounding 20 July 1772 when granted to John Caldwell late of Amelia Township, decd, on land of Goodridge Hughes; sold 1792 by Sheriff Samuel Saxon of 96 Dist to sd Wm Greenwood at suit of John Gordan against admr of sd John Caldwell. Wit Danl Smith, Geo Taylor, John Smyth. /s/ Wm Greenwood Junr. Proven Charleston District, 19 Nov 1799, by Daniel Smith; Jacob Drayton JQ. Rec 23 Dec 1799.

p.613-616   Ned Brooks and wife Sevey to Fred Williams. Deed, 2 February 1799, $700, 540 acres on Clouds Creek and Lick Creek running into Little Saluda bounding on lands of Fred Williams, John Baits,

Ned Brooks, Thomas Harrison, Benjamin Fortner, Wm Anderson. Wit Robt Atkins, John Powell, William Puket[Rikel?] /s/ Ned (x) Brooks, Sevey (x) Brooks. Judge Arthur Simkins certifies relinquishment of dower by Sevelity Brooks wife of Ned Brooks. /s/ Sevelity (x) Brooks. Proven 15 November 1799 by John Powell; Elkanah Sawyer JP. Rec 23 Dec 1799.

p.616-619   Isaac Hayne of St. Bartholomews Parish executor of will of Isaac Hayne Decd, to Daniel Bird of Edgefield County. Deed, 12 August 1799, $500,   500 acres on Turkey Creek of Savannah River near Levy Harris granted to Wm Savage & James Simpson 9 Nov 1774, conveyed by them by Wm Anderson 29 March 1776 and by sd Anderson to sd Isaac Hayne decd. Wit Wm Ed Hayne, Wm Roberts. /s/ Isaac Hayne executor to estate of Isaac Hayne decd. Proven, Columbia, SC, 19 March 1799, by William Edward Hayne; Peter Treneau JP. Rec 23 Dec 1799.

p.619-621   Richard Tutt Senr to Charles Barrentine. Deed, 28 December 1799, $100, 188 acres granted to sd Richard Tutt 1 May 1797 by Charles Pinckney Esqr, examined by Peter Bremar pro Secretary. Wit Matthew Mims, Van Swearingen. /s/ Rd Tutt. Proven 28 Dec 1799 by Mat Mims; Van Swearingen JP. Rec 28 Dec 1799.

p.622-624   Richard Tutt Senr to Charles Barrentine. Deed, 28 December 1799, $200, 250 acres on Turkey Creek of Savannah River adj Jno Roberts, James Gunnels, same sold to sd Richard Tutt by Jeremiah Hatcher Sheriff on 1 Oct 1796 as property of John Williams to satisfy an execution in favor of Richard Johnson Junr. Wit Mat Mims, Van Swearingen JP. /s/ Richard Tutt. Proven 28 Dec 1799 by Mat Mims; Van Swearingen JP. Rec 28 Dec 1799.

p.624-627   Peter Morgan to John Burress. Deed, 18 April 1799, $120,   120 acres on Turkey Creek of Savannah R it being part of 600 acres originally granted unto Benjamin Warring 26 Sept 1772. Wit Henry Key, Henry (x) Cox, Triplit (x) Cason. /s/ Peter (x) Morgan. Plat shows Koon Creek, lands of Henry Key, Peter Morgan, Henry Cox, John Barrass.   Proven 4 Oct 1799 by Henry Key; H Middleton JP. Rec 28 Dec 1799.

p.627-630   Peter Morgan to Henry Key Esqr. Deed, 18 April 1799, $232,   232 acres on Turkey Creek of Savannah river, part of 600 acres originally granted to Benjamin Wearing 26 Sept 1772. Wit John Burress, Henry (x) Cox, Triplett (x) Caison. /s/ Peter (x) Morgan. Plat shows Turkey Cr, lands of Peter Morgan, John Burgess(sic). Proven 4 Oct 1799 by John Burress; H Middleton JP. Rec 28 Dec 1799.

p.631-633   Edward Rutledge Esqr of Charleston by his atty John Hunter to Shimuel Nicholson. Bond, 24 August 1799, $2296 to be paid unto Shimuel Nicholson; condition that if Edward Rutledge make title to 1148 acres original grant to Henry Middleton on Little rockey Creek of Stephens Creek bounded at time of survey by land of George Feltmoe Silvenus Stephens Isaac Miller Volentine Kewn(?); titles to be made when second instalment of purchase moeny is paid. Wit Wright Nicholson, John Puckett. /s/ Edward Rutlege by his attorney John Hunter, on stampt paper. Proven 26 Dec 1799 by Wright Nicholson; Wm Daniel JP.   Rec 1 Jan 1800.

End of Edgefield County Conveyance Book 17

p.1-2   John Garrett, Richmond County, Georgia, to William Cox, Edgefield. Deed, 26 June 1799, $150, 150 acres originally granted to John Garrett, on Stephens Creek, lines of Samuel Wills, Dooly. Wit Joseph Thomas, Samuel (S) Hill. /s/ John Garrett. Proven [?] October 1799 by Joseph Thomas; Henry Key JP. Rec 28 December 1799.

p.3-6   Ezekiel Hudnal Junr& wife Martha to Ezekiel Hudnal Senr of Linkhorn County, GA. Deed, 15 August 1799, $1; 462 acres on Benefields Creek where sd Ezekiel Hudnal Junr at present lives adj lands held by Judge Anderson, Jesse Copeland, Enoch Brazeal, James Hagood, Thos Freeman, plat lately made by Edward Collier D.S. Wit Jesse Copeland, Saml (x) Price, Eza (x) Price. /s/ Ezekiel Hudnal, /s/ Martha Hudnal. Plats certified 15 August 1799 by Ezekiel Hudnall Junr show 362 acres and 100 acres. Receipt of Ezekiel Hudnal Senr $700 full consideration. Wit Jesse Copeland, Samuel (x) Price, Elizabeth (x) Price./s/ Ezekiel Hudnal Junr, /s/ Martha Hudnall. Proven 21 Oct 1799 by Jesse Copeland; Alexander Smith, JP. Rec 31 Dec 1799.

p.7-8   Ezekiel Wimberley of Washington County, Georgia, to John Wimberley of Edgefield. Bill/Sale, 17 October 1798, £100.4.8 sterling, Negro man Charles age 30. Wit Frederick Wimberley, Lewis Wimberley. /s/ Ezekiel Wimberley. Proven 6 July 1799 by Lewis Wimberley; John Spann, JP. Rec 31 Dec 1799.

p.8-11   William Norris to Nathan Norris. Deed, 23 December 1799, $300, 750 acres being part of 1000 acres granted to Plowden Weston of Charleston 8 July 1774, conveyed to Wm Norris 5 Nov 1797, bounding on John Walker, William Deshazo, Ned Brooks. Wit John P Bond, S Butler. /s/ William Norris. Judge Arthur Simkins certifies relinquishment of dower by Elizabeth Norris wife of William Norris, 23 Dec 1799; /s/ Elizabeth Norris. Proven 1 January 1800 by Sampson Butler; Rd Tutt CC. Rec 14 March 1800.

p.11-19   Jean[Jane] Wilson to Alexander Hall, planter. L&R, 13 August 1791, £20 sterling, two plantations granted 25 May 1774 unto Jean Wilson by Lt Gov Wm Bull; one of 74 acres on Rocky Creek of Savannah River; the other of 26 acres on branch of Cuffeetown Creek of Savannah River. Wit John Cummin, John (x) Armstrong, James Cockrum. /s/ Jean Wilson[Jain (x) Wilson]. Proven 28 January 1793 by James Cockrum; James Harrison JP. Rec 6 Jan 1800.

p.19-22   John Walls to Benjamin Harrison. Deed, 27 September 1799, $360, 150 acres on Seder Creek, lines of William Murphey, John Spencer; part of 380 acres granted unto James West 6 Feb 1786. Wit Stephen Tillman, Gasper Gallman. /s/ John Walls, /s/ Susannah (x) Walls. Judge Arthur Simkins certifies relinquishment of dower by Susannah Walls wife of John Walls, 16 Oct 1799 ; /s/ Susannah (x) Walls. Proven 6 January 1800 by Stephen Tillman; Wm Garrett JP. Rec 6 Jan 1800.

p.22-25   Amy Cornett, widow, to son Earbin Cornett. Deed of Gift, 16 November 1799, all goods & chattels in her dwelling house on Stephens Creek, delivered before the signing of these presents. Wit Thos Broughton, Hardy (x) Cornett. /s/ Amy (x) Cornett. Proven 4 Jan 1800 by Hardy Cornett; Henry Key JP. Rec 6 Jan 1800.

p.25-31   William Swift of Newberry to Richard Bush Senr of sd county. L&R, 12/13 February 1792, £20 SC money, 312 acres on Beach Creek of South Edisto river bordering on lands of Benjamin Journegen, Edward Couch originally surveyed for John Cronan, other sides vacant, lying below the ancient boundary line south of Saluda river, survey dated 5 Feb 1787, witness Gov Wm Moultrie at Charleston. Wit Richard Bush Junr, John Sills Junr, Christiana Mayson. /s/ William Swift. Proven 3 May 1792 by Richard Bush Junr; Henry King JP. Rec 6 Jan 1800.

p.32-34   Thomas Warren to Israrel Martin. Deed, 4 December 1799, $5 SC money, 100 acres on Clouds Creek [granted by] Gov Wm Moultrie at Charleston 5 Sept 1785. Wit Nathan Norris, Jeremiah (x) Buzbee, Thomas Walker. /s/ Thomas (x) Warren, /s/ Elizabeth (x) Warren. Proven 13 December 1799 by Nathan Norris; Elkanah Sawyer JP. Rec 14 Jan 1800.

p.34-37   John Kirkland and wife Sarah to Zion Davis. Deed, 9 November 1797, £15 lawful money, 50 acres on Dry Creek of Little Saluda being part of 200 acres originally granted Arthur Watson by Gov Wm Moultree. Wit William Brasell, James Brasell, Snoden (x) Kirkland. /s/ John (x) Kirkland, /s/ Sarah (x) Kirkland. Proven 23 Jan 1798 by William Braswell; William Daniel JP. Rec 14 Jan 1800.

p.38-40   Isaac Cox to Zion Davis. Deed, 2 June 1797, £10 sterling, 80 acres adj John Rogers. Wit William Brasell, James Braswell, Henry (x) Champain. /s/ Isaac Cox, /s/ Nancy (x) Cox. Proven

23 Feb 1798 by William Brassell; Wm Daniel JP. Rec 14 Jan 1800.

p.40-43   Thomas Hill to John Hill Senr. Deed, 8 November 1799, $1, [acreage not stated] on Big Turkey Creek of Stephens Creek of Savannah River, the lower corner of tract originally granted Nicholas Glawsear including the grist mill now occupied by sd John Hill Sr. Wit John Blocker Junr, James Blocker. /s/ Thomas Hill. Proven 20 Jan 1800 by James Blocker; John Blocker JP. Rec 20 Jan 1800.

p.43-46   John Dunlap Esqr of Abbeville County, attorney, to Thomas Dozier of Edgefield. Deed, Abbeville County, 25 September 1798, 9000 weight of good inspected tobacco equal to £100, three plantations, titles made by Thomas Farrar late sheriff of Ninety Six Dist; 107 acres on Pen Creek bounded on Bartlett Bledsoe, Wright Nicholson; another tract on Pen Creek of 155 acres bounded by Jeremiah Mobley, Wright Nicholson; another tract of 100 acres on Pen Creek on land of Robert Stark Junr. Wit John Wright, Abraham Dozier. /s/ John Dunlap. Proven -- of March 1800 by Ab Dozier; Richard Tutt CC. Rec 21 Jan 1800.

p.46-51   Thomas Butler, planter, to Reuben Carpenter his son in law and daughter Mary his wife. Deed of Gift, 31 December 1799, goodwill & affection, 51 acres Stephens Creek of Savannah river being part of 300 acres granted unto William Moore by Gov Ch Montague at Charleston 14 August 1772 and by sd Moore conveyed unto Thomas Butler; on Grapeyard Branch, land laid off unto Owen Butler from the original grant, other sides land of original grant. Wit John Hardwick, Arven (x) Butler. /s/ Thomas Butler. Receipt, 31 Dec 1799, before Henry Key JP, for 51 acres, fully satisfyed with as my proportion of the whole of his estate in case he should die intestate; /s/ Reuben Carpenter. Plat dated 3 April 1799; William Coursey D.S. Proven 30 December 1799 by John Hardwick; Henry Key JP. Rec 26 Jan 1800.

p.51-55   Thomas Butler, planter, to son Arven Butler. Deed of Gift, 31 December 1799, love & affection, 52 acres on Grapeyard Branch of Stephens Creek of Savannah River, part of 300 acres granted unto Wm Moore by Gov Ch Montague at Charleston 14 Aug 1772 and by sd Moore unto sd Thomas Butler, bounded by old grant lines. Wit John Hardwick, Reuben Carpenter. /s/ Thomas Butler. Plat 3 April 1799 by Wm Coursey D.S. Receipt 31 Dec 1799 for 52 acres ackd before Henry Key JP, fully satisfyed with my proportion of the whole in case he should die intestate; /s/ Arven (P) Butler. Proven 31 Dec

1799 by John Hardwick; Henry Key JP.   Rec 26 Jan 1800.

p.55-59   William Kilcrease and wife Franky, planter & spinstress, to Daniel Brunson. Deed, 13 November 1799, $300 SC money, 400 acres on branches of Beaverdam of Turkey Creek of Savannah river, crossing Spring branch, adj John Logan, William Coursey, land originally owned by Jacob Bell, Abraham Martins land, being part of 500 acres that James Lyons purchased from William Coursey which was part of two tracts granted unto Wm Coursey. Wit John Lyon, Joseph (x) Brunson. /s/ Wm Kilcrease, /s/ Frances (x) Kilcrease. Proven 29 November 1799 by John Lyons; Henry Key JP.   Rec 28 Jan 1800.

p.59-62   Roger Smith Esqr of Charleston to Peter Morgan. Deed, 1 November 1797, $570, 600 acres on Turkey Creek of Savannah originally granted to Benjamin Waring 26 Sept 1772. Wit Daniel Baugh, Howard R Smith. /s/ Roger Smith. Proven 17 April 1799 by Daniel Baugh; Richard Tutt JP. Plat surveyed for William Anderson 13 March 1772 by A Mayson shows Turkey Creek and two branches, lands of Nimrod Kilchrist, Thos Richards, David Elliham, & McRee. Recorded 5 Feb 1800.

p.62-66   George Ker, merchant of Augusta, Richmond County, Georgia, to William Terry of Edgefield County. Release, 14 April 1798, $85.77, 125 acres on branches of Turkey Creek of Savannah river being part of 160 acres granted unto Lewis Collins whereof 35 acres fell in an old survey, the afsd 125 acres granted and released. Bounded on land granted to Charles Williams, James Coursey, Col Purvess decd. Plat by Wm Coursey D.S. Wit John McFatrick, Pressly Swillivan. /s/ George Ker. Proven 6 February 1800 by John McFatrick; John Blocker JP.   Rec 5 Feb 1800.

p.66-70   Edward Johnson(Johnston) to Edward Prince. Mortgage. Whereas Edward Johnson by his two notes of hand dated 6 and 7 November 1793 stands bound to Edward Prince in sum £50 with legal interest, for better securing of sd notes, 300 acres adj David Andress, Benjamin Sims, Herod Thomson. Wit Wm Tennent, Hugh Middleton. /s/ Edward Johnson. Proven 16 February 1800 by Hugh Middleton Junr; Hugh Middleton JP.   Rec 21 Feb 1800.

p.71-73   Dionysius Oliver to Edward Burt. Deed, 14 November 1799, $250, 271 acres being part of 500 acres originally granted Jacob Fudge on Stephens Creek adj John Stephens, John Robertson, John

Bridges, plat made by James Blocker 28 October 1799. Wit Philip Burt, John Wightt. /s/ Dionysius Oliver. Proven 22 Feb 1800 by John Wightt; Richd Tutt CC. Rec 22 Feb 1800.

p.73-74   George B Moore to William Moore. Bill Sale, 24 July 1798 received from William Moore $300 in full for Negro boy Adam aged 23 years. Wit William Spragins, James (x) Little. /s/ George B Moore. Proven 15 Feb 1800 by James (x) Little; Nathaniel Abney JP. Rec 21 Feb 1800.

p.74-79   Sheriff William Butler to Tolover Bostick. Sheriff Titles, 1 July 1799, at suit of Samuel Savage admr of John Higgins decd against Thomas Heron admr of Tacitus Guillard decd, sheriff seized land to be publicly sold to highest bidder at Cambridge; struck off to Tolover Bostick for £400 sterling, 400 acres originally granted to Andw Carthey, conveyed by his heir at law to John Savage Esqr decd; by him to Tacitus Gillard decd. Wit John Dunlap, Eugene Brenan. /s/ William Butler Sh 96 Dt. Plat shows adj owners William Shaw, William White, Tolover Bostick; certified 29 July 1799 by W Anderson D.S. Proven 1 Feb 1799 by Eugene Brenan; Wm Robertson JP. Rec 25 Feb 1800.

p.79-81   James Morrison to John Stedham. Deed, 15 May 1799, $200, 250 acres on Little Mountain Creek of Sleepy Creek of Savannah River bounded by John Courseys land. Wit Jonathan Clegg, Shadrack (x) Boon. /s/ James Morrison. Proven 22 Feb 1800 by Jonathan Clegg; John Blocker JP. Rec 24 Feb 1800.

p.82-84   William Welsh to Stephen Brown. Deed, 28 January 1800, $130, 91¾ acres Dry Creek being part of 183¾ originally granted unto James Haregrove 5 June 1786 bounding on William Moseley, Widow Hernden, Samuel Dulittle, Benj Joinner. Wit Daniel Baugh, Lucy Baugh. /s/ William (x) Welsh. Proven 28 Feb 1800 by Daniel Baugh; Rd Tutt CC. Rec 28 Feb 1800.

p.84-90   Arthur Watson exr will of Michael Watson decd to Simon Beck. L&R, 28/29 January 1796, £25.10 lawful money, 500 acres originally granted to John Kenny, conveyed by sd Kenny to William Kirkland, and by sd Kirkland to Michael Watson, situate in Colleton County bounding on Moses Powell, M Crawford of Charleston decd, and vacant. Wit Rolan Williams, William McDaniel, Abr Powell. /s/ Arthur (x) Watson. Proven 25 Feb 1800 by William McDaniel; John Spann JP. Rec 3 March 1800.

p.90-94   Simon Beck to William Holstun.   Deed, 25 February 1800, £70, sixty acres being part of land granted to John Kenny 24 August 1770 adj John Spanns line, Floyds corner; another tract of 50 acres granted to sd Beck 2 Sept 1793. Wit Levi McDaniel, William McDaniel, John McDaniel. /s/ Simon (x) Beck. Proven 25 Feb 1800 by Levi McDaniel; John Spann JP. Rec 3 March 1800.

p.94-96   William Holstun to Aaron Asbell. Deed, 26 February 1800, £150, 220 acres, being a tract granted to John Frederick 6 Nov 1786; also 162 acres, it being a tract granted sd John Frederick 6 Nov 1786. Wit Gilbert Falkner, Jeremiah (x) Kish, Josiah (x) Todd. /s/ William Holstun. Proven 26 Feb 1800 by Gilbert Faulkner; John Spann, JP. Rec 3 March 1800.

p.97-99   Evan Stokes to Batte Stokes. Deed, 1 March 1800, $200,   all my right and claims which I now have or hereafter shall have in the estate of my grandfather Richard Stokes deceased which now consists of a Negro woman Esther and her two children named Jeff and Isham; also household and kitchen furniture and plantation utensils. Wit Batte Evans, Edward M Blaikley, Ludwill Stokes. /s/ Evans Stokes.   Proven 3 March 1800 by Batte Evans; Richard Tutt JP. Rec 3 March 1800.

p.99-101   James Barrentine Senr to Enoch Phelps. Deed, 9 September 1799, $150, 175 acres on Turkey Creek of Savannah river adj sd Barrentines home tract, Singleton, John Ryan, Swearingen, surveyed 10 Oct 1792 and granted 4 March 1793. Wit R Roberts, Moses (x) Grier(?). /s/ James (x) Barrentine. Proven 6 March 1800 by Reuben Roberts; Richard Tutt CC. Rec 6 March 1800.

p.101-104   Arthur Watson to Arthur Arrington. Deed, 1 August 1798, $150, 365 acres being part of a tract originally granted to Arthur Watson 17 May 1790 on Dry Creek of Mine Creek joining lands of Samuel Isaac, John Fortner, Christian Currey, Hezekiah Watson, Benjamin Arrington, James Eidson. Wit Arthur Rice Watson, Sanford Collum. /s/ Arthur (A) Watson. Proven 14 September 1798 by Sanford Collum; Elkanah Sawyer JP. Rec 6 March 1800.

p.104-106   Thomas Dalton of Richmond County, Georgia, to William F Taylor of Campbellton. Bill of Sale, 28 September 1799, $325, Negro boy Cuff age about thirteen. Wit Saml Savage, William

Covington. /s/ Thomas (D) Dalton. Proven 6 March 1800 by Samuel Savage; Wm Garrett JP. Rec 10 March 1800.

p.106-107 Elias Morgan to William F Taylor of Campbellton. Bill/Sale, 23 April 1799, $475, Negro man Peter. Wit S Savage Junr, John Wills. /s/ Elias Morgan. Proven 6 March 1800 by Samuel Savage Junr; Wm Garrett JP. Rec 10 March 1800.

p.107-110 Samuel Dennis Junr to Barnabas Grice. Deed, 3 March 1800, $150, fifty acres on Mill Pond, Spring branch, Log Creek of Turkey Creek of Stephens Creek of Savannah river. Wit Stephen Norris, Enoch Phelps. /s/ Saml (x) Dennis. Proven 13 March 1800 by Stephen Norris; Richard Tutt CC. Rec 13 March 1800.

p.110-112 Barnabas Grice to William John Taylor. Deed, 14 March 1800, $85, 10 acres being part of land transfered from Thomas Cotton to Samuel Dennis, by sd Dennis to Barnabas Grise, on waters of Log Creek of Turkey Creek of Stephens Creek of Savannah river. Wit Stephen Norris, T Norris. /s/ Barnabas (x) Grise. Proven 14 March 1800 by Stephen Norris; Rd Tutt CC. Rec 14 March 1800.

p.113-116 Samuel Lewis and wife Nancy, planter & spinster, to Charles Adams, planter. Deed, 5 August 1799, 230 acres on Red bank of Little Saluda bounded by Doctor, Mary Adams, Benjamin Rees, Thomas Carson. Wit John Adams, Joseph (x) McKinney. /s/ Samuel Lewis. Judge Arthur Simkins certifies that Nancy Lewis wife of Samuel Lewis relinquished dower, 5 August 1799; /s/ Nancy (x) Lewis. Proven 12 March 1800 by John (x) Adams; William Robertson JP. Rec 19 March 1800.

p.116-117 David Glenn to Robert Moseley. Bill of Sale, 23 April 1798, Negro woman Fanny about 17 years old. Wit Edward Vann Junr, William White. /s/ David Glenn. Proven 4 Jan 1800 by Edward Vann Junr; John Blocker JP. Rec 21 March 1800.

p.117-118 James Averrett to Robert Moseley. Bill of Sale, 26 November 1799, $180, Negro man Guinea. Wit Charles Waldrom, William G Murphey. /s/ James Averett. Proven 4 January 1800 by Charles Waldrom; John Blocker JP. Rec 21 March 1800.

p.119-121 Dempsey Fields of Buncum County, North Carolina and Thomas Kemp of Edgefield to James Anderson of Columbia County,

Georgia. Indenture, 27 June 1797, £40 sterling, 100 acres on Savannah River granted by Lt Gov Wm Bull to Isaac Lucker 26 July 1774, sold by Isaac Lucker to John Pursell, sold by Pursell to John Smith, and by sd Smith unto Robert Whitton, and sold by Robert Whitton unto Luke Fields; sd Thomas Kemp and Dempsey Fields being the heirs of sd Luke Fields. Wit John Anderson, Elizabeth Foster, John Foster JP, John (x) Rook. /s/ Thomas (x) Kemp, /s/ Dempsey (x) Fields, /s/ Temperance (x) Kemp. Proven 22 March 1800 by John Anderson; H Middleton JP. Rec 26 March 1800.

p.121-124   James Jones and wife Susannah to Jacob Guyton. Deed, 10 November 1799, $15, fifteen acres on Horse Creek adj sd James Jones. Wit Cristifur (x) Coonce, Neal (x) Cone. /s/ James Jones, /s/ Susannah (x) Jones. Proven 20 March 1800 by Neal Cone; John Clark JP. Rec 28 March 1800.

p.124-125   Phebe Covington to James Baker. Dowry, 10 August 1799, Judge Joseph Hightower certifies that Phebe Covington wife of William Covington, being privately examined, declared she freely released unto James Baker her claim of dower in 100 acres which her husband William Covington sold to James Baker, called the Poverty Hill Tract. /s/ Phebe Covington. Rec 28 March 1800.

p.125-127   Mary Jordan to Doctor Joseph Fuller. Bond, March 1793, Mary Gordan bound in sum £500 SC money to be paid to Doctor Fuller, condition Mary Gordan make good titles & conveyance to land granted to sd Mary Gordan including the Haw Pond on the road from Alexander Hanna's to Mr Glover's, after Doctor Fuller has performed the conditions of his bond to Mary Gordan; otherwise to remain in full force. Wit Alexr Downer. /s/ Mary (x) Gordan. Proven 26 March 1800 by Alexander Downer; John Clark JP. Rec 28 Mar 1800.

p.127-130   Richard Freeman and wife Mary to James Newbey. Deed, 12 May 1796, £50 sterling, 100 acres on Wescoats Creek of Savannah River beginning at William Tolberts line, on Solomon Walkers line, on Jesse Copeland. Wit Ezekiel Hudnall, James Freeman, Thos (x) Taylor. /s/ Richard (x) Freeman, /s/ Mary Freeman. Proven 30 December 1799 by Ezekiel Hudnall; Henry Key JP. Rec 24 March 1800.

p.130-132   William Newsome to Alexander Murray Crossle and Mary Henry Crossle. Deed of Gift, 15 February 1800, 5 shillings and love & affection for the son and daughter of my deceased friend Henry Crossle of Augusta, merchant, two Negroes, boy Tom about seven, and girl Clarissa about five or six, children of wench Pat, and the increase of the girl. Wit Lewis Tillman, Barkley Martin. /s/ William Newsom. Proven 24 March 1800 by Barkley Martin; John Blocker JP. Rec 24 March 1800.

p.132-134   Francis Lightfoot, house carpenter, to Tomme Keeling Smith, planter. Deed, 22 March 1800, $62.50, twenty five acres, part of tract whereon I now live adj sd T Keeling Smith and Henry Whites line, land of Henry Gittey. Wit Creswell Moore, John Hamilton. /s/ Francis Lightfoot. Proven 22 March 1800 by Creswell Moore; William Robertson JP.   Rec 24 March 1800.

p.135-139   George White and David Lilly, executors of estate of William White of Abbeville County to Henry White of Edgefield. Deed, 6 February 1800, $1907.50 specie, three tracts containing 381.5 acres; one originally granted to John Murray Esqr of Charleston; conveyed by sd Murray to John Anderson 1766 and bequeathed to Colbert and William Anderson by will of John Anderson dated 16 Nov 1771; also tract originally granted to James Anderson; by him bequeathed to sd John Anderson and by him bequeathed to sd Colbert and William Anderson and by Colbert and William Anderson conveyed to William Moore; the other tract originally granted to William Anderson; by him conveyed to William Moore and the whole three tracts by sd William Moore to William White deceased, and by sd William White deceased left by his will to be sold.   Wit James Gowdey, Walter Childs. /s/ David Lilley, /s/ George White Exors of Estate Wm White. Plat shows Frederick Hards land, Oswell Eves land, road to Island Ford, Spring branch, Cabin branch, Tolover Bosticks land, land granted to Andrew Caitha, and is certified 23 August 1799 by W Anderson, D.S., George White and William White sworn chain carriers. Proven 13 March 1800 by James Gowdey; William Robertson JP.   Rec 24 March 1800.

p.139-141   William Oneal of Johnston County, North Carolina, to William Holstun. Bill of Sale, 17 March 1800, $365, Negro man Bob about age 17. Wit Aaron Asbell, Milley (x) Spann. /s/ William Oneal. Proven 17 March 1800 by Aaron (x) Asbell; John Spann JP. Rec 24 March 1800.

p.142-150   Joseph Jay and wife Mary to William Aaron. L&R, 7 November 1777/7 September 1777, £220 SC money, 192.5 acres being part of a tract of 250 acres laid out for sd Joseph Jay on Saluda river adj land of Joseph King, Patrick McDugle, William Nimon, John Berniters, and vacant land, granted at Charlestown unto afsd Joseph Jay 21 April 1774 by Lt Gov Wm Bull. Wit Joseph King Junr, J King Sr, Hugh Johnson. /s/ Joseph Jay, /s/ Mary (M) Jay. Proven 8 October 1785 by Joseph (x) King; Solomon Pope, JP. Rec 24 Mar 1800.

p.151-153   Reubin Pyles of Laurens County to John Hatcher of Edgefield. Deed, 27 January 1800, £6.15 sterling, 490 acres surveyed for Thomas Beckham 2 May 1786; granted 1 January 1797 to Ayres Goreley, conveyed by sd Gorley unto sd Reubin Pyles. Wit Benjamin Hatcher, Frances Bettis. /s/ Reubin Pyles. Receipt, 27 January 1800 $80 silver as full consideration; Reubin Pyles. Proven 25 March 17-- by Benjamin Hatcher; Van Swearingen JP. Rec 24 Mar 1800.

p.154-158   Richard Glover, farmer, to David Hamilton. Deed, 19 November 1799, $46, 151 acres on Rockey Creek of Savannah river bounded by lands of William Glover, --- King, --- Miller, Thomas Smith, and vacant. Wit Samuel Hall, Wm Sims. /s/ Richard Glover. Justice William Nibbs certifies relinquishment of dower by Susannah Glover wife of Richard Glover, 19 November 1799; /s/ Susannah (x) Glover. Proven 19 November 1799 by William Sims; Wm Nibbs, JP. Rec 24 March 1800.

p.158-160   Samuel Carter to Josiah Langley. Deed, 21 October 1799, $100, 100 acres being part of 1000 acres granted to sd Samuel Carter 3 June 1793 lying on Cuffeetown Creek of Stephens Creek and Savannah river. Wit James Harrison JP, Saml Hall. /s/ Samuel Carter. Proven 25 October 1799 by Samuel Hall; Jas Harrison JP. Rec 24 March 1800.

p.161-163   James Cochram and wife Cathreen to Samuel Hall. Deed, June 1799, £70, 150 acres being part of land granted to James Wilson 2 March 1763 on Cuffeetown and Turkey Creek of Stephens Creek and Savannah river adj land of James Harrison, David Hamilton and the original survey. Wit Gincey (x) Gray, Alexander Patton. /s/ James Cochram, /s/ Cathreen (+) Cockram. Proven 29 June 1799 by Alexander Patton; James Harrison JP. Rec 24 March 1800.

p.164-165   Thomas Warren to Moses Holstun. Deed, 18 January 1800, £4, eight acres being part of land granted John Whi[illegible] 25 May 1790 on Crooked Creek joining land formerly belonging to Wil-

liam Holstun, a tract granted to Moses Hulstun [illegible]. Wit Henry
Fallow, Killiam (x) Cats. /s/ Thomas (x) Warren. Proven 22 March
1800 by William Cates one of the subscribing witnesses; John Spann
JP. Recorded 24 March 1800.

p.166-169   Anthoney Cooper and wife Mary to Thomas Ramsay.
Indenture, 19 September 1793, £40 SC money, 417 acres granted to sd
Anthoney Cooper 7 February 1791 on Reedy Creek of Cuffeetown
Creek adj David Cunningham, Isaac Ramsay, John Murphey, Colonel
Gervey, Eli Thornton, Federick Weaver. Wit James McMillan, Isaac
Ramsey. /s/ Anthoney Cooper, /s/ Mary (x) Cooper.   Proven 12 Janu-
ary 1794 by Isaac Ramsay; James Harrison, JP. Rec 24 March 1800.

p.169-171   Herod Thomson to Charles Chirer[Shirer]. Deed, 16
October 1799, £20, sixty five acres being part of 250 acres granted to
Peter Rush 2 Apr 1772 on Clouds Creek joining Isaac Funderburg's
land and Cannon's land. Wit Isaac Funderburg, Josiah (x) Nobles. /s/
Herod (x) Thompson. Proven 4 March 1800 by Josiah (x) Nobles;
John Spann JP. Rec 24 March 1800.

p.171-174   Jacob Smith and wife Sarah to Jonathan Neal. Deed, 18
February 1800, $50, fifty acres being part of 1000 acres granted to
Jacob Smith 18 March 1793 adj land of John Robbard, Cane Brake
Branch, sd Smith and sd Neal. Wit John Roberts, Jesse (x) Davis,
Henry (x) Corley. /s/ Jacob Smith. Proven 21 February 1800 by Jesse
Davis who made oath he saw Jacob Smith and wife Sarah sign and
acknowledge within deed; Wm Daniel JP. Rec 24 March 1800.

p.174-177   Christopher Shaw to William Morgan. Deed, February
1800, $600,   four hundred acres on fork of Foxes Creek being part of
tract granted to Jas Vessels 13 Nov 1784. Wit Joshua Hammond, Sarah
Hammond. /s/ C Shaw. Justice William Tennent certifies relinquishment of dower by Mary Shaw wife of Christopher Shaw, 15 February
1800; /s/ Mary (x) Shaw. Proven 15 Feb 1800 by Joshua Hammond;
Wm Tennent JQ. Rec 24 March 1800.

p.177-179   John M Dooley of Lincoln County, Georgia, to Philip
Ikner. Deed, 13 December 1799, £50, one hundred acres being a tract
granted Wheaten Pines 13 July 1769. Wit Simeon Perry, Sarah Pitts.
/s/ John M Dooley. Proven 30 December 1799 by Simeon Perry; John
Spann JP. Rec 24 March 1800.

p.179-181   Thomas Caison to Henry Cox. Deed, 22 March 1800,
£50, 100 acres on Coon Creek being part of land granted unto David
Calliham, & part of grant unto Thomas Caison Senr. Wit Jiles Letcher,
Thomas Broughton, Mary Broughton. /s/ Thomas Caison. Plat shows
adjoining land of Triplett Caison and land of Wm Nix. Proven 26
March 1800 by Giles Letcher; James Harrison JP. Rec 24 Mar 1800.

p.182-184   Samuel Carter to Josiah Langley. Deed, 21 October
1799, $200, 200 acres being part of 1000 acres granted to sd Samuel
Carter 3 June 1793 lying on Cuffeetown Creek of Stephens Creek and
Savannah river, adj land of Elizabeth Miller. Wit Samuel Hall, James
Harrison. /s/ Samuel (x) Carter. Proven 25 October 1799 by Samuel
Hall; James Harrison JP.   Rec 24 March 1800.

p.184-186   David Harkins to John McCreless. Deed, 25 September
1799, $300, three hundred two acres below the antient boundery on
Mountain Creek of Turkey Creek. Wit John Hamilton, John Todd.
/s/ David Harkins. Proven 19 November 1799 by John Todd; John
Blocker JP. Rec 24 March 1800.

p.186-188   John Wimberley to John Kent. Deed, 16 November
1796, £50, 350 acres being part of land granted to John Swearingen
17 August 1786, adj Joseph Jones, Shaws Creek. Wit William Hubbard, John Spann, James Hubbard. /s/ John Wimberley. Proven 24
March 1800 by John Spann; Van Swearingen JP.   Rec 24 March 1800.

p.188-190   Willoby Tillery and wife Margaret to John Tillery,
planter. Deed, 1 March 1800, $201, eighty acres on Cedar Creek
of Horns Creek of Savannah river bounded on lands of John Chenie,
David Tillman, John Tillery, William Tillery. Wit William Tillory,
Robert (x) White.   /s/ Williaby (x) Tillory, /s/ Margaret (H) Tillory.
Proven 24 March 1800 by Robert (x) White; John Blocker JP. Rec 24
March 1800.

p.190-192   Benjamin Arrington to Joseph Warren. Deed, 11 August
1798, £10, one hundred acres being part of land originally granted to
Benjamin Arrington, binding on Nead McCartey, Dry Creek, Ninety
Six road. Wit Edward McCartey, Joshua Warren. /s/ Benjamin
Arrington. Proven 28 June 1799 by Edward McCartey; Wm Daniel JP.
Rec 24 March 1800.

p.193-195   John Walker to Simon Beck. Deed, 7 March 1800, £50,

246 acres being part of land granted to Elventon Squires bounding on lands of sd John Walker, Cammells; another tract of 150 acres being part of land granted to sd Elventon Squires 5 Aug 1793 on Beach Creek seperated from original grant by a line agreed on by John Walker and Thomas Adams, land of William Donoho, land which Thomas Adams is now selling to John Walker being on William Donohos line. Wit Matthew Bettis, Frances Walker. /s/ John Walker. Proven 22 March 1800 by Matthew Bettis; John Spann JP. Rec 24 March 1800.

p.195-197   Rolan Williams Senr to Aaron Asbell. Deed, 17 March 1800, £30, forty eight acres being part of land granted to Thomas Adams 6 July 1795. Wit William Holstein, Daniel Pynes. /s/ Rolan Willliams. Proven 24 March 1800 by William Holstein; John Spann JP. Rec 24 March 1800.

p.197-200   John Strother to George King. Deed, 2 April 1796, $30, 100 acres on Big Saluda River, being part of 1000 acres granted to sd John Strother 7 Oct 1793 by Gov Wm Moultrie, adj Margaret Lanes corner, Peter Hawkins line, Chinquepin branch, Fichlands Creek. Wit Thomas Bond, Henry King. /s/ John Strother. Proven 14 May 1796 by Henry King; William Daniel JP. Rec 24 March 1800.

p.200-203   Jeremiah Strother, planter, to Elkanah Sawyer. Deed, 13 March 1798, £10 SC money, 300 acres on Lick Creek of Little Saluda river, bounded on Michael Neywd and vacant land, originally granted to Jeremiah Strother Senr decd 6 April 1756 by Gov James Glen. Wit Jesse Rountree, Clement Cargill. /s/ Jeremiah Strother. Judge Joseph Hightower certifies relinquishment of dower by Elizabeth Strother wife of Jeremiah Strother, 13 March 1798; /s/ Elizabeth Strother. Proven 13 March 1798 by Captain Cargill; Russell Wilson JP. Rec 24 March 1800.

p.203-206   William Mobley and wife Elizabeth to Christopher Whitmon. Deed, 21 November 1799, £20 sterling, 50 acres, being part of 200 acres granted William Waddel 14 August 1772 and conveyed to Jacob Falkner; sd Jacob Faulkner by will left 100 acres to sd Thomas Banks, Ann his wife, and Nathan Garmon, situate on a branch of Clouds Creek known as Claboards Branch. Wit Thomas Harris, Polley (x) Mobbley. /s/ William Mobbley, /s/ Elizabeth (x) Mobbley. Proven 15 March 1800 by Thomas Harrison; Elkanah Sawyer JP. Rec 24 March 1800.

p.206-209   John Carter Green and wife Nancy to William Morgan, planter. Deed, 21 November 1799, $300 SC money, 500 acres , being part of tract granted to sd John Carter and the other to Charles Banks on 21 November 1799 on Horse Creek of Savannah river, adjoining lands of Franklin, John Carter, William Farrance. Wit Joshua Hammond, Enos Howard, Adams Pardue. /s/ John C Green, Nancy (x) Green, Phebe (x) Green. Proven 19 December 1799 by Adams Pardue; Charles Old JP. Rec 24 March 1800.

p.209-211   Jesse Williams to Christopher Wedderman, both of Orangeburgh District. Deed, Orangeburgh District, 26 March 1798, £30, 200 acres on Whetstone branch of Rockey Creek of Saluda bounding on lands of Thomas Warren, Frederick Williams, Jesse Williams, Richard Williams, William Williams. Wit Elkanah Powel, William Williams, John Powell. /s/ Jesse Williams. Proven 5 June 1799 by John Powel; Elkanah Sawyer JP.   Rec 24 March 1800.

p.212-215   Thomas Taylor and wife Creasey to James Newbey of Abbeville. Deed 12 May 1796, £50 sterling, 100 acres on Westcoats Creek of Savannah river adj Thomas Carter, James Brown. Said land was granted to Thomas Taylor 3 October 1791. Wit Ezekiel Hudnall, James Freeman, Pasha (x) Taylor. /s/ Thomas (x) Taylor, Creasey (x) Taylor. Proven 30 December 1799 by Ezekiel Hudnal; Henry Key JP. Rec 24 March 1800.

p.215-217   Roger McCinney, planter, to Tomme Keeling Smith. Deed, 22 March 1800, $75,   25 acres being part of the tract whereon I now live and bounded by sd T K Smiths land, my land, land lately belonging to Wyley Glover. Wit Criswell Moore, John Hamilton.   /s/ Roger McCinney. Proven 22 March 1800 by Criswell Moore; William Robertson JP.   Rec 24 March 1800.

p.217-218   Alexander Oden to Martin Goza. Deed, 1 December 1796, $100, 47 acres, the residue of 371 acres originally granted to me 1 Feb 1790, bounded by Stephens Creek, John Garrett, Scotts branch; the other part of the tract sold to Charles Blackwell and Daniel Barksdale. Wit Charles Blackwell, Mathew (x) Turpin. /s/ Alexr Oden. Proven 18 May 1799 by Matthew (x) Turpin; Hugh Middleton JP. Rec 24 March 1800.

p.218-220   Richard Hampton to Catlett Corley. Deed, 20 December 1790, 10 shillings sterling, 200 acres on Beaverdam creek adj William

West and Banks [blank] and being part of land originally granted to Charles Atkins and conveyed to me by commissioners of confiscated estates. Wit William Renable, William Ham, Joseph West. /s/ R Hampton. Proven 20 February 1797 by William Ham; Elkanah Sawyer JP. Rec 25 March 1800.

p.220-223 Edward Rutledge of Charleston District to James Bullock. Deed, 11 December 1799, £162.10 sterling, 230½ acres on Six Mile creek, being part of tract originally granted to Moses Thompson Esqr 6 March 1750. Wit S Mays, W Drayton. /s/ Ed Rutledge. At request of George Burns, Pr S Mays D.S. made plat of the 230½ acres, same being part of 700 acres granted to Moses Thompson 16 March 1750, laid off 19th March 1798, adj lands of George Burnes, Dan Bullock, James Bullock, Leualen Good, and Ninety Six Creek. Deed proven 25 March 1800 by Samuel Mays; Wm Robertson JP. Rec 25 Mar 1800.

p.223-225 Edward Prince Senr to James Thomas. Deed, 4 January 1800, $200, 150 acres joining land of Capt Daniel Barksdale, James Thomas, & vacant when tract was run out, 1785. Wit Daniel Barksdale, Edward Prince Junr. /s/ Edward Prince Senr. Proven 4 January 1800 by Daniel Barkesdale Esqr; H Middleton JP. Rec 25 Mar 1800.

p.225-228 Philip Lamar to John Hart, planter. Deed, 1 November 1799, $55(sic), 135 acres on Horse Creek, Buzzard branch, Peppers branch, James Jones line. Wit Jacob Carter, George Wallace. /s/ Philip Lamar. Proven 3 December 1799 by Jacob Carter; John Clark JP. Receipt for forty five Dollars it being full consideration money within mentioned; /s/ Philip Lamar. Rec 25 March 1800.

p.228-230 Jacob West to Joseph West. Deed, 2 February 1790, £60 currency, 80 acres Little Saluda at mouth of Clouds Creek adj Catt Corleys land, Thomas Wests line, being part of land originally granted Wm West decd. Wit Richard Hardie, Catlett Corley. /s/ Jacob West. Proven 25 March 1800 by Catlett Corley; Nathaniel Abney JP. Rec 25 March 1800.

p.230-233 Lewis Harris of Augusta, Richmond County, Georgia, and Sarah his wife to Meshack Wrightt of Edgefield. Deed, 10 January 1800, $700, SC money, 150 acres on Savannah river adj Daniel Shaws estate, Walter Taylors land formerly David Zubleys, and land of estate of David Zubley. Wit Abraham Jones, Jos Ware. /s/ Lewis Harris, /s/ Sarah Harris. Justice John Clark certifies relinquishment of dower by

Sarah wife of Lewis Harris [no date]. Proven by Joseph Ware; John Clarke JP [no date]. Recorded 25 March 1800.

p.233-235   Joseph Miller, planter, to John Fox, merchant, of Augusta, Georgia. Deed, 29 August 1799, £200 SC money, 275 acres on Chaveses creek adj Booths land on Dry Creek and George Miller, John Ryan, Garbets land, & Zacheriah James. Wit Benj Hightower, Ads Sanders. /s/ Joseph Miller. Proven 14 October 1799 by Benjamin Hightower; William Anderson JEC. Rec 25 March 1800.

p.235-237   William Moore to John Blaylock Senr. Deed, 17 May 1798, £160 sterling, 250 acres on Bigg Creek originally granted to John Savage 7 June 1769. Wit J Blalock Junr, Zach S Brooks. /s/ W Moore. Proven 3 August 1798 by John Blalock Junr; Nathl Abney JP. Rec 25 March 1800.

p.237-239   Joseph Cunningham to his sister Margaret Frazier, widow & others. Deed Gift, 2 November 1799, love and affection, 241 acres she now lives on, originally granted unto Reuben Frazier by Gov Wm Moultrie 1 May 1786 and 4 November 1793, on Savannah river, for Margaret's life, then to her three sons Daniel Frazier, John Frazier, and William Frazier to be equally divided amongst them. Wit James Baker, Richard Hardy, Daniel Hardy. /s/ Joseph Cunningham. Proven 31 December 1799 by James Baker; Chas Old JP. Rec 25 March 1800.

p.239-242   George Miller to Josey Parker. Deed, 22 March 1800, $128,   178 acres both sides of Muster Fields branch of Savana river originally granted to sd George Miller 1110 acres; adj William Toblers land, George Miller, Parsons. Wit Elihu Williams, Daniel Nail. /s/ George Miller. Recd of Mr Josey Parker $100 in part and his note for $78 when paid will be in full. Wit Elihu Williams, Daniel Neal. /s/ George Miller. Proven 22 March 1800 by Elihu Williams; John Clarke JP. Rec 25 March 1800.

p.242-244   Charles Williams to Littleton Fuller. Deed, 21 February 1800, $309, 103 acres on Rockey branch of Stephens Creek of Savannah river. Wit John Lyon, John Evans. /s/ Charles Williams. Plat shows Stephens Creek, lands of Jesse House, Charles Williams, Abraham Williams land. Proven 21 February 1800 by John Lyon; James Harrison JP. Rec 25 March 1800.

p.244-247   Bowling Deas to Absalom Radford. Deed, 14 February

1800, $100, 150 acres on the road from ridge to Augusta on dreans of Edisto and Mine Creeks, adj Anderson Windsors line where road to Leas Bridge crosses sd line, 40 yards north of sd Radfords house, to Poseys line, to Absalom Landrums line to Bibby Bushs line, to Gamillians line, including the plantation where sd Absalom Radford now lives being part of land formerly granted to Rolan Williams; conveyed from him to sd Deas. Wit Willis Federick, Patan (x) Bland. /s/ Bowling (x) Deas. Proven 11 March 1800 by Willis Frederick; William Daniel JP. Rec 25 March 1800.

p.247-249   Edward Rutledge of Charleston District to George Burns. Deed, 11 December 1799, £162.10 Sterling, 469½ acres on Six Mile Creek, it being part of land originally granted to Moses Thompson Esqr 6 March 1750. Wit S Mays, W Drayton. /s/ Edward Rutledge. This land not warranted against Mrs Martin Dower[Power?] /s/ Edward Rutledge. Proven 25 March 1800 by Colonel Samuel Mays; Wm Robertson JP.   Rec 25 March 1800.

p.249-251   Samuel Stalnaker and wife Druscilla to William Holloway, planter. Deed, 31 December 1796, £50, 216 acres on a branch of Rockey creek of Savannah river on road from Long Cain to Campbellton bounded by lines of William Evans, James Cockram; being originally granted to sd Saml Stalnaker. Wit William Evans, John Lyon. /s/ Samuel Stalnaker, /s/ Druscilla (x) Stalnaker.   Proven 24 March 1800 by William Evans; Wm Robertson JP. Rec 25 Mar 1800.

p.251-254   William Key to John Boyd. Deed, 10 November 1799, William Key justly indebted in two bonds making in whole $6,000 with condition of payment of $3,000 in two payments; for better securing of sd bonds, sd William Key hath granted unto John Boyd three tracts of land: 200 acres on Turkey Creek whereon William Key now resides; 300 acres granted to Henry Key; 200 acres granted to sd Henry Key, also four Negroes, James, Moses, Else, & Sook unto John Boyd; condition that if William Key pay unto John Boyd afsd sums of money with the interest thereon, then this present writing shall be void.   Wit Eli Garnett, Jas Garnett, John Grimany. /s/William Key. Proven 11 Novr 1799 by James Garnett; H Middleton JP.   Rec 25 March 1800.

p.255-257   Martin Goza to Elijah Abston. Deed, 26 February 1800, $150, 371 acres, part of tract originally granted to Alexander Oden 1 Feb 1790 bounding on Stephens Creek, land claimed by Jeff Sharpton, Scotts branch; other part of sd tract sold to Charles Blackwell and

Daniel Barkesdale. Wit Jacob Clackler, Richard (x) Skipper. /s/ Martin Goza. Justice William Tennent certifies relinquishment of dower by Amy Goza wife of Martin Goza, 15 March 1800; /s/ Amy (+) Goza. Proven 15 March 1800 by Jacob Clackler; H Middleton JP. Rec 25 March 1800.

p.257-258   William Exum to Bibby Bush. Deed of Sale, 13 July 1799, $150, Negro girl named Rodey and her increase. /s/ William Exum. Acknowledged 13 July 1799 by William Exum; John Spann JP. Rec 25 March 1800.

p.259-260   Bibbey Bush to Isaac Bush. Deed, 18 January 1800, £50,   342 acres granted to sd Bibbey Bush 13 April 1792 on head of Mine Creek of Saluda River bounded by lines of Elisha Barrentine, Rolan Williams and vacant land at time land was run. Wit Francis Walker, Prescott Bush. /s/ Bibbey Bush. Proven 25 Jany 1800 by Prescott Bush; John Spann JP.   Rec 25 March 1800.

p.260-262   Isaac Bush to Bibbey Bush. Deed, 18 January 1800, £50,   500 acres surveyed for sd Bibby Bush 15 August 1797 on head branches of South Edisto River bounded by lines of Gomillion, Tilley, Elventon Squire, Bibby Bush, Frederick Holmes, William Bush. Wit Francis Walker, Prescott Bush. /s/ Isaac Bush. Proven 25 Jany 1800 by Prescott Bush; John Span JP.   Rec 25 March 1800.

p.262-264   William Bush to Bibbey Bush. Deed, 25 January 1800, £50, 155 acres surveyed for Wm Bush 15 August 1797 on branches of Saluda river bounded by lines of Walton, and vacant. Wit Rolan Williams, Isaac Bush, Henry Holemon. /s/ William (x) Bush. Proven 25 Jany 1800 by Rolan Williams; J Spann JP.   Rec 25 March 1800.

p.264-266   David Glover to John M Dooley of Linkcoln County, Georgia. Deed, 23 April 1799, $300,   344 acres originally granted to Paley Gibson. Wit Rd Tutt, John Lyon. /s/ David Glover. Proven 27 March 1800 by John Lyon; Richard Tutt Clerk/Court.   I assign the within to Marstin[Marston] Clay for value received March 26th 1800. Witness Thomas P Martin. /s/ J M Dooley. Proven 27 March 1800 by Thomas P Martin; Richard Tutt CC.   Rec 27 March 1800.

p.266-267   John Garrett of Richmond County, Georgia, to Samuel Hill. Deed, 26 June 1799, $15,   nine acres originally granted to John Garrett, on Stephens Creek butting on Sanderfers old line. Wit Joseph

Thomas, William (x) Cox. /s/ John Garrett. Proven 15 Octr 1799 by Joseph Thomas; Henry Key JP. Rec 26 March 1800.

p.268-269   Josiah Crews to Samuel Hill. Deed of Sale, 8 January 1799, $420, Negro woman Judah, Negro girl Hannah. Wit Hughes Moss, Cornelius Jeter. /s/ Josiah Crews. Proven 19 March 1799 by Hughes Moss; Henry Key JP. Rec 26 March 1800.

p.269-271   William Reed of Linkhorn County, Georgia, to William Mellot. Deed, 8 January 1800, $300, 100 acres on main road from Augusta to old wells bridge granted to Fielding Ryandols 3 April 1786; also 147 acres on waggon road from piney woods house to Augusta which was granted to John Ryan 1 Jan 1787. Wit A Herndon, William Ingram. /s/ Wm (W) Reed. Proven 26 March 1800 by William Ingram; James Cobbs JP. Rec 26 March 1800.

p.271-273   John Garrett of Richmond County, Georgia, to Samuel Hill. Deed, 25 June 1799, $150, 150 acres originally granted to John Garrett butting on Stephens Creek and on Susannah Glantons land. Wit Joseph Thomas, William (x) Cox. /s/ John Garrett. Proven 15 October 1799 by Joseph Thomas; Henry Key JP. Rec 26 March 1800.

p.273-274   Obriant Smith of Charleston to Thomas Carter. Deed, 13 January 1800, $250, 500 acres bounding on land of Moses Callaham, Thomas Carter, and unknown. Wit Stanmore Butler, Rebeccah Anderson. /s/ Obrien Smith by his attorney W Anderson. Proven 26 March 1800 by Stanmore Butler; John Blocker JP. Rec 26 March 1800.

p.275-276   Solomon Lucass to William Mellit. Deed, 13 March 1800, $480 SC money, 111¼ acres being part of 300 acres originally granted to Richard Kirkland 20 July 1772 on Chaveses Creek, inclosing one acre purchased from Phill May Junr for a mill seat. Wit James (x) Gardner, William Ingram. /s/ Solomon (x) Lucass. Proven by 26 March 1800 William Ingram; James Cobb JP. Rec 26 Mar 1800.

p.277-278   John Wilkerson of Pitt County, North Carolina, to James Moseley. Bill of Sale, 17 March 1800, $350, Negro girl Moll age 13 or 14. Wit William Ingram, Daniel Wooten. /s/ John Wilkerson. Proven 26 March 1800 by William Ingram; Van Swearingen JP. Rec 26 March 1800.

p.278-280   John Abney to Paul Abney. Deed, 11 February 1800, $100, 425 acres being part of 900 acres originally granted to said John Abney on Tosetys Creek of Saluda River, adj land of James Carson now belonging to Major Thomas Butler. Wit William W Abney, James Barnes. /s/ John Abney. Proven 11 February 1800 by William Abney; Nathaniel Abney JP. Rec 26 March 1800.

p.280-282   John Abney to James Barnes. Deed, 11 February 1800, $35, fifty acres originally granted to John Dean on the Bounty and conveyed by George Dean brother and heir at law to sd John Dean to sd John Abney on branch of Tosetys Creek of Saluda River bounded by lands of Paul Abney, James Summers, John Abney, Kennedy, and vacant. Wit Paul Abney, William (S) Abney. /s/ John Abney. Proven 11 Feb 1800 by Paul Abney; Nathaniel Abney JP. Rec 26 Mar 1800.

p.282-284   John Jolley, planter, to Kammel[Camel] Clegg. Deed, 14 October 1799, $150, 150 acres being part of 500 acres granted unto Thomas Carson, sd part divided from remainder, John Quattlebaums land, Sleepey Creek, Little Stephens Creek. Wit William (x) Marlow, Charles Brooks. /s/ John (x) Jolley. Proven 15 Jan 1800 by William Marlow; John Blocker JP. Rec 26 March 1800.

p.285-287   Alexander Alexander of Spartanburg County, SC, to David Thompson. Deed, 24 January 1800, $260, 200 acres on Little Gunnels creek of Stephens Creek of Savannah river bounded by lands of Dempsey Bussey at time of survey 5 Jan 1773 for Peter Guynn and granted to him 13 April 1773 by Gov Wm Bull. Wit Larkin (I) Logan, Tho Moore. /s/ Alexander Alexander. Spartenburgh District, Justice Thomas Moore certifies relinquishment of dower by Ester Alexander wife of Alexander Alexander, 24 January 1800; /s/ Esther Alexander. Proven 26 March 1800 by Larkin (x) Logan; H Middleton JP. Rec 26 March 1800.

p.287-289   Presley Bland and wife Martha to Andrew Gmelin. Deed, 24 January 1800, $300, 416 acres on branches of Shaws Creek of South Edisto river which was granted to sd Presley Bland by Gov Chas Pinckney 1797. Wit Ezekiel McClendon, Jacob Fannin. /s/ P Bland. Proven 26 March 1800 by Ezekiel McClendon; Van Swearingen JP. Rec 26 March 1800.

p.289-292   Joshua Hammond to Christopher Shaw. Deed, February 1800, $1000, several tracts of land adjoining the Cherokee ponds; one contains 200 acres and was granted unto Henry Sizemore 26 Sept 1772; another is part of 100 acres which was granted to Jethro Rountree on 26 July 1774 containing 80.5 acres, 19.5 being sold out of sd hundred to Sarah Tarrance; the other is 352 acres which was granted to Francis Settle on 5 February 1787, 15 acres of which being now held by James McQueen and in an older grant than sd Settles is hereby excepted. Wit William Morgan, James McDaniell. /s/ Joshua Hammond. Judge William Tennent certifies relinquishment of dower by Sarah Hammond the wife of within named Joshua Hammond, 15 Feb 1800; /s/ Sarah Hammond. Proven 15 February 1800 by William Morgan; Wm Tennent JQ. Rec 26 March 1800.

p.292-294   Jesse Pitts to David Orsbourn. Deed, 28 September 1796, $100, 175 acres on Little Saluda river, being part of tract of 650 acres granted to me Jesse Pitts 1 June 1792; sd 175 acres bounded by lands of Charles Fushee, Joel Brown, Francis Posey, Repts Orsbourn. Wit Joel Brown, William Orsbourn. /s/ Jesse Pitts. Proven 4 March 1800 by Joel Brown; William Daniel JP. Rec 26 March 1800.

p.295-296   John Norwood to Tolover Bostick. Bill of Sale, 23 February 1796, $70 SC money, Negro boy named Hell about age seventeen. Wit J McCrackan. /s/ John Norwood. Proven 3 October 1799 by James McCrackan; Wm Nibbs JQ. Rec 26 March 1800.

p.296-301   Henry Geddes of Charleston, storekeeper, to John Loftin [Lofton]. L&R, 27/28 January 1790, £4.10 SC money, fifty acres, granted 7 August 1786 on Bird Creek joining Mc Andersons land, surveyed for Cornelius Loftin and granted to Henry Geddes. Wit John Kenady, Robert Geddes. /s/ Henry Geddes. Proven 8 February 1793 by John Kenady; James Harrison JP. Rec 27 March 1800.

p.302-307   John Brooks Junr of Orangeburgh District to Samuel Brooks of Edgefield. L&R, 16 November 1792, £35 SC money, 98.5 acres being part of tract of 100 acres on Lick Creek of Clouds Creek which was granted to Silas Carter and from him conveyed to James Hayes 1782 and from him to sd John Brooks 1792; also unto Samuel Brooks for £10 sterling, another tract containing 23 acres being part of two tracts one containing 128 acres which was granted to John Thomas Fairchild and conveyed from him to William Brooks and the other a part of tract granted to William Brooks and transfered from him to sd John Brooks 1799, sd 23 acres bounds on William Fairchilds land. Wit Thomas Walker, James Muirehead, Edward Johnston. /s/ John

Brooks Junr. Proved Orangeburgh District 9 March 1793 by Thomas Walker; J Thomas Fairchild JP. Rec 28 March 1800.

p.307-309   Thomas Rodgers, farmer, to William Rodgers. Deed, 28 February 1800, $100, land on Beaverdam Branch originally granted to Thomas Rodgers for 397 acres in 1793, bounded on Henry Burkhalters land, other sides vacant. Wit Alexr Downer, N Hukens.   /s/ Thomas Rodgers. Proven 26 March 1800 by Alexander Downer; John Clark JP. Rec 28 March 1800.

p.309-314   William Smith, house carpenter, to Edmund Holleman, planter. Bill of Sale, 29 January 1800, Marriage hath been solemnized between afsd Wm Smith and Nancy Norwood widow of John Norwood deceased, and sd William Smith being desirous that goods which were conveyed by sd John Norwood to sd Nancy Norwood then wife of John Norwood should still be vested in trust for the benefit of Nancy Smith formerly Norwood, and whereas Wm Smith is willing to make over in trust for use of Nancy Smith other goods as was agreed on between sd William Smith and Nancy Smith previous to the marriage, Now William Smith for five shillings SC money paid before delivery of these presents, receipt acknowledged, hath granted unto sd Edmund Holloman Negroes: Negro Lydda and her three children, girl Lockey, boy Jack, girl Harriott; wench Molley, wench Jenney, wench Hannah, wench Phillis, boy Willis, together with bed and furniture, plantation utensils, horses, cattle, hogs, waggon, unto sd Edmund Holleman, to permit sd Nancy Smith to use above granted goods during lifetime; in case Nancy Smith should not survive William Smith her husband, Edmund Holleman is to stand possessed of goods afsd to use of persons Nancy Smith shall by will appoint. In case Nancy Smith should survive afsd William Smith her husband, then Edmund Holleman agrees the will of sd Wm Smith reconveys goods afsd to Nancy Smith. Wit Daniel Huff, Geo (x) Spozar. /s/ William Smith. Receipt of William Smith for five shillings from Edmund Holleman. Proved 5 April 1800 by Daniel Huff; Richard Tutt CC. Rec 5 April 1800.

p.314-315   David Glenn to John Olliphant. Bill of Sale, 23 April 1798, $350, Negro woman Rachel. Wit Wm Hagens, Folton Mims. /s/ David Glen, /s/ Robert Glenn. Proven 5 April 1800 by William Hagens; Rd Tutt CC. Rec 5 April 1800.

p.315-318   William Tennent to Ephraim Ferrel. Sheriffs Titles, 6 August 1798, at suit of Ephraim Ferrel against John Fudge, Sheriff sold land publicly to highest bidder for ready money at Cambridge; struck off to Ephraim Ferrell for $120, 300 acres on Little horse Creek being part of land originally granted to Jacob Fudge decd and willed by sd Fudge to John Fudge. Wit Stanmore Butler, J Hatcher. /s/ William Tennent Shff 96 District. Proven 8 April 1800 by Jeremiah Hatcher; Rd Tutt, CC. Rec 8 April 1800.

p.318-320   Richard Bush Junr to Isaac Bush. Bill Sale, 14 April 1798, $500, Negro girl Vilet about age eighteen, horse, mare and personal propperty belonging to sd Richard Bush Junr; condition Richard Bush pay by two years the full sum of $500 with lawful interest to sd Isaac Bush. Wit Bibby Bush, John (x) Bush. Proven 10 April 1800 by Bibby Bush; John Span JP. Rec 6th April 1800.

p.320-321   John Tillory to Isaac Brunson. Deed or Mortgage, 10 April 1800, $103.12½, Negro girl Cate age thirteen, 140 acres land whereon I now live on Horns Creek, mare, cattle, hogs, furniture; condition if John Tillory pays Isaac Brunson $103.12½ with lawful interest upon first January next ensuing then Bill of Sale to be void. Wit William Wash. /s/ John Tillory. Proven 12 April 1800 by William Nash[Wash?]; Richard Tutt CC. Rec 12 April 1800.

p.322-324   Robert Retherford to William Moore. Bill of Sale, 6 March 1800, £30 SC money by two notes of hand dated 6 March 1800, Negro boy Ned age six,; if Robt Retherford pay unto Wm Moore £30 SC money by 25 December 1801 this Deed of Sale shall be void. Wit Gilson Yarbrough, S Butler. /s/ Robert Retherford. Proven 20 March 1800 by Gilson Yarbrough; Nathaniel Abney JP. Rec 21 Apl 1800.

p.324-325   William Turner to Barnett Barnes. Deed, 15 April 1799, for value received, Negro boy Sam. /s/ Wm (x) Turner. Condition of above sail is such that if Wm Turner do pay unto Barnett Barnes before 15 December next $60 silver, above sail to be void. Wit Theophilus Favor, William Barnes. /s/ Wm (x) Turner. Proven 31 Jany 1800 by Theophilus Favours; Nathl Abney JP. Rec 21 April 1800.

p.325-328   Margaret Gomillan, planter, to grandson Joseph Jones. Deed Gift, 4 November 1799, love & affection and 25¢, 100 acres granted to Margaret Carpenter 12 December 1798 on Augusta road near head branches of Edisto; condition sd Margaret Gomelon occupy sd premises as long as she live. Wit Thos Swearingen, Enoch Phelps. /s/ Margaret (x) Gomelon. Proven 25 March 1800 by Thos Swearingen;

Van Swearingen JP.   Rec 24 April 1800.

p.328-334   William Washington, planter of Laurence County, SC, to Isaac Mazyck Weston of Charleston.   Mortgage, 1 April 1800, Washington's bond $1000 Federal money, condition, payment of $500 with lawfull interest to be paid at different periods; Washington sells for one year 1000 acres between Savannah river on Bigg and Dry Creek branches of Little Saluda bounding at original survey on John Savage, John Chanys widow, Marshall & James Chaneys land, and William Chaney and other owners not known; above land was granted to Paul Mazyck by Gov Wm Bull 15 Oct 1771.   When payment is made, bond shall be of none effect. Wit John White, John Cummings. /s/ William Washington. Proven 1 April 1800 by John White; John Mitchell JP. Rec 24 April 1800.

p.335-341   John Ryan to Thomas Swearingen. L&R, 8/9 December 1794, £50 sterling, 593 acres, Paces Branch of Shaws Creek, bounded by Thomas Swearingen, Abraham Odom and Van Swearingen, except 21 acres. Wit Van Swearingen Junr, Richard Burton. /s/ John Ryan. Proven 24 April 1800 by Van Swearingen; James Cobbs JP. Rec 24 April 1800.

p.341-344   John Garrett and Catherine Garrett of Augusta, Georgia, to Charles Powell of Edgefield. Deed, Georgia, 24 January 1800, $225, 100 acres in Edgefield known as the Chalk Hill tract, and #22 in the plat laid down of the Chickasaw Indians land which was forfeited to SC and sold by the Commissioners of that State unto John Garrett. Wit Joseph Hightower, David Butler JP. /s/ John Garrett, Catherine Garrett. Richmond County, GA, Justice David B Butler certifies relinquishment of dower by Catherine Garrett wife of John Garrett, 24 January 1800; /s/ Catherine Garrett. Proven, Edgefield, 19 April 1800 by Joseph Hightower; Charles Old JP.   Rec 30 April 1800.

p.344-345   William Morgan to Christopher Shaw. Bill of Sale, 19 December 1799, $350, Negro boy age 16 named Briton. Wit Wm Gray, Matthew Stoker. Proven 21 April 1800 by Matthew Stoker; Charles Old JP.   Rec 30 April 1800.

p.345-348   Sinclair David Gervais Esqr, barrister of Charleston, to Hughes Moss, planter. Release, 6 December 1799, $300, 300 acres on Beaverdam about two miles south from Turkey creek called Springfield, bounded on the late Robert Mevill, John Logan, Thomas Good,

which Titles are to take effect on the death of Mrs Ann Franks formerly
Mrs Ann Allen, widow and relict of John Allen, being part of a survey
in Edgefield near Turkey Creek. Wit John Lyon, Henry L Gervais. /s/
Sinclair D Gervais. Proven 26 April 1800 by John Lyon; Henry Key
JP. Rec 3 May 1800.

p.348-350   Deed on these pages is X'd out "because it is wrong."

p.350-353   Daniel Mazyck to George Youngblood, planter. Deed, 3
December 1799, Daniel Mazek, eldest captain in the late second regi-
ment of foot of SC on continental establishment commanded by Lieut
Colonel Francis Marion, £125 sterling, 150 acres which was surveyed
for Robert Lang 26 January 1773 and granted 4 May 1775, conveyed to
sd Daniel Mazyek 1776 on Mine Creek a branch of Little Saluda river
bounding at time of survey on Joseph Dawes; also 150 acres surveyed
for Daniel Ravinel Junr 25 May 1774 and granted to sd Daniel Ravinel
Junr 4 May 1775 and conveyed by him 1775 on Mine Creek of Little
Saluda River bounding on Daniel Ravinels land, Robert Langs land;
also 200 acres which was surveyed for Daniel Ravinel Junr 26 May
1774 and granted him 4 May 1775 and conveyed by him to sd Daniel
Mazyck 1775 on Mine Creek of Little Saluda river bounding on John
Cottons land, Daniel Ravinels land. Wit Tho Winstanley, Danl James
Ravenel. /s/ D Mazycke. Justice Peter Frenau certifies that Mrs Sarah
Mazycke wife of Daniel Mazycke relinquished right of dower, 13
February 1800. Proven 13 February 1800 by Daniel James Ravenel;
Peter Frenau JP. Rec 3 May 1800.

p.354-356   John McTeer and wife Ann of Beaufort District, SC,
planter, to Samuel Carter of Edgefield, planter. Deed, 4 February
1800, £80 SC money, 150 acres on Hawtree Creek since called
Cuffeetown Creek of Stephens Creek and Savannah River surveyed 24
March 1757 for John Stout granted to John Stout by Gov Wm Littleton
13 Oct 1759. Wit Lemuel Vasser, Jno Gooding. /s/ John McTeer, /s/
Ann McTeer. Beaufort District, Justice John Lightwood certifies the
relinquishment of dower by Ann McTeer wife of John McTeer, 6
February 1800; /s/ Ann McTeer. Proven, Beaufort District, by Lemuel
Vasser, 5 February 1800; Jno Lightwood JP.   Rec 5 May 1800.

p.357-358   Moses Westberry of Georgia to Samuel Carter. Deed,
20 December 1799, £25, 100 acres originally granted Robert Brown 13
Sept 1774 on a branch of Cuffeetown Creek of Stephens Creek of
Savannah river bounded by Nicholas Mikler, Henry Strum and vacant

land when surveyed. Wit Edward Harrison, John (x) Couch. /s/ Moses Wesbery. Proven 20 December 1799 by Edward Harrison; James Harrison JP. Rec 4th May 1800.

p.359-361   Thomas Walpole to Thomas Berry. Deed, 1 May 1800, $500, 125 acres on Horns Creek on line of John Gray, old road from Augusta to Island Ford of Saluda, old Field of Fair Hills, plat thereof made by E Bowling Stark for Saml Marsh, part of tract sold by Theodore Stark to Saml Marsh. Wit Saml Marsh, Willis McClendon. /s/ Thos Walpole. Justice Arthur Simkins certifies relinquishment of dower right by Frances Walpole wife of Thomas Walpole, 7 May 1800; /s/ Frances Walpole. Proven 7 May 1800 by Samuel Marsh; Arthur Simkins JQ. Rec 7 May 1800.

p.361-363   Francis Lightfoot, house carpenter, to William Moore son of Richard, planter. Deed, 22 March 1800, $17.50, seven acres on a small branch of Henleys Creek being part of land on which I now live bounded by land surveyed for Robert Beaty, Henry Getty, William Wrightt, and adj tract I now live on. Wit John McCool, John Martin. /s/ Frans Lightfoot. Proven 6 March 1800 by John Martin; William Robertson JP. Rec 10 May 1800.

p.363-365   Daniel Bird to Joseph Rairden[Rairdaine] and Timothy Rairden[Rairdaine]. Deed, 8 May 1800, $500, 500 acres on waters of Turkey Creek of Savannah River near Levy Harris granted to Wm Savage and James Simpson 9 Nov 1774 conveyed by them to William Anderson 1776 and by sd Anderson to Isaac Hayne. Wit John Morris, William Rairdaine Proven 8 May 1800 by John Morris; John Blocker JP. Rec 12 May 1800.

p.365-367   Barnabas Grice to David McBride. Deed, 3 May 1800, $200, forty acres, being part of 50 acres conveyed from Thomas Cotton to Samuel Dennis; from sd Dennis to Barnabas Grice, sd 40 acres on Spring branch to its mouth, crossing creek, running on brow of hill. Wit Mat Mims, Moses (O) Grice. /s/ Barnabas (x) Grice. Proven 13 May 1800 by Matthew Mims; Rd Tutt CC. Rec 13 May 1800.

p.368-370   West Harris to Peter Utz. Deed, 8 April 1800, $80, sixty acres part of tract originally granted to James Williams by Gov Wm Bull 12 Oct 1770 on Little Stephens Creek of Savannah river, crossing Long Cain Road. Wit Stephen Norris, Jeremiah Strother. /s/ West Harris. Proven 26 May 1800 by Stephen Norris; Richard Tutt JP.

Rec 26 May 1800.

p.370-372   William Guirey of Ogle Thorp County, Georgia, to James Garrett of Campbellton, Edgefield County. Deed, 13 September 1799, $250, Lot #2 in Campbellton. Wit Abel Keyes, John Longmire. /s/ William Guirey. Proven 7 May 1800 by John Longmire; William Garrett JP. Rec 26 May 1800.

p.372-376   Robert Brooks to Edmund Holleman. Deed, 20 May 1800, $300, 127 acres on branches of Turkey Creek of Savannah River bounded by land granted to Thomas and Chs Williams & Lewis Collins, being part of 160 acres granted to Lewis Collins by Gov Chas Pinckney 4 July 179(?), by Collins 127 acres was conveyed to Aaron Thomalan 1794 and by Aaron Thomalan to Matthew Cockerham 1794 and by Matthew Cockerham unto sd Robt Brooks 1795. Wit Daniel Wilson, Milley Tutt. /s/ Robert (x) Brooks. Justice William Nibbs certifies relinquishment of dower by Annise Brooks wife of Robert Brooks, 22 May 1800; /s/ Annise (x) Brooks. Proven 21 May 1800 by Daniel Wilson; Wm Nibbs JQ. Rec 26 May 1800.

p.376-377   Item on these pages was X'd out.

p.377-379   Alexander Downer, architect, to Abraham Ardis. Deed, 4 July 1797, $180,   185 acres bounding on Joseph Fuller, Leigh Anstiegen, Thomas Rogers, Alexander Downer and Leonard Myer, being part of grant to sd Alexander Downer 5 June 1786. Wit Cradk Burnell, John Clark JP. /s/ Alexr Downer. Justice John Clark certifies relinquishment of dower by Margaret Downer wife of Alexr Downer, 4 July 1797; /s/ Margaret (m) Downer. Proven 28 May 1800 by Craddock Burnell; Rd Tutt CC. Rec 28 May 1800.

p.380-382   Joseph Fuller, physician, to Craddock Burnell. Deed, 27 May 1800, 147 acres in New Winsor Township being part of land granted to sd Joseph Fuller 7 March 1791, at time of survey bounded by Alexander Downer, Thos Rogers, Myers Old, Joshua Lockwood, Lud Williams, David Zubbley, Leonard Myers. Wit Jacob Zink Junr, Abraham Ardis. /s/ Joseph Fuller. Proven 28 May 1800 by Abraham Ardis; Rd Tutt CC. Rec 28 May 1800.

p.382-384   Cornelius Dysert, physician of Richmond County, Georgia, to Cradock Burnell. Deed, 21 September 1799, £50 sterling, fifty acres in New Winsor being part of land granted to Alexander

Downer and conveyed to Lamuel Young admr of Wm Evans and from sd Lamuel Young to Cornelius Dysert, at time of survey adj Henry Jones, Daniel Shaw, Lud Williams. Wit James Haregrove, James C Dysart. /s/ C Dysart. Proven 11 March 1800 by James Haregrove; Charles Old JP. Rec 28 May 1800.

p.384-387   Lemuel Young of Augusta, Georgia, to Cornelius Dysart of same place. Deed, 28 July 1799, whereas William Evans on 23 Mar 1786 entered covenant with Cornelius Dysart in which he was bound within twelve months to make title unto Cornelius Dysart for a tract of 58 acres adj lines of Daniel Shaw, Lud Williams, Henry Jones, unless an older grant for sd land disannuls Alexander Downeys grant for same, in which case sd Evans bound himself to pay unto sd Cornelius Dysart seventeen guineas with lawful interest from date of agreement; whereas Dysart is satisfyed there is not elder title to sd land, and title of Alexander Downer and those claiming under him will be complete, and whereas sd Lemuel Young married daughter and heiress of sd William Evans, is admr of his estate, and desires to do justice to Cornelius Dysart, Now this indenture witnesseth that Lemuel Young for consideration afsd and $1, grants unto Cornelius Dysart 50 or 58 acres in Edgefield County, being part of land granted unto Alexander Downer 5 June 1786, conveyed to Lemuel Young. Wit George Watkins JP, Cradock Burnell, Seaborn Jones. /s/ Lemuel (L) Young. Proven 28 May 1800 by Cradock Burnell; Rd Tutt CC. Rec 28 May 1800.

p.388-390   Dempsey Hughes of Washington County, Georgia, to William Killcrease. Deed, 21 November 1797, £30 sterling, 50 acres on a branch of Loyds creek of Stephens Creek of Savannah river being part of land originally granted to Thomas Key adj John Kilcrease. Wit Moses (x) Meze, C H Coursey. /s/ Dempsey (x) Hughs. Proven 5 May 1798 by Charles Coursey; Henry Key JP. Rec 2 June 1800.

p.390-402   Samuel Williams to William Todd. L&R by way of Mortgage, bond 6/7 April 1798, $274, condition for payment of $137, and further sum of five shillings sterling paid before sealing of these presents, 334 acres on Turkey and Rockey creeks of Savannah river. If Samuel Willliams pay unto Wm Todd $137 according to above condition, anything herein contained shall be null and void. Wit Daniel Bird, John Todd. /s/ Samuel Williams. Proven 13 May 1800 by Daniel Bird; Jno Blocker JP. "I assign over to John Williams all my right of the within indenture this 21st day of May one thousand eight hundred. Test Jesse Blocker, Michael Blocker. /s/ William Todd. Proven 21

May 1800 by Jesse Blocker; John Blocker JP.   Rec 30 May 1800.

p.403-405   William Cochran to Frederick Slappey. Deed, 6 January 1800, £80, 100 acres originally granted to Jacob Glaninbury November 1756 in Granville now Edgefield county on Cuffeetown Creek of Stephens Creek of Savannah river. Wit James McMillian, William Wagner. /s/ William (x) Cochran. Justice William Nibbs certifies relinquishment of dower by Nancy Cochran wife of William Cochran, 6 January 1800; /s/ Mary (x) Cochran. Proven 24 May 1800 by William Wagner; James Harrison JP.   Rec 6 June 1800.

p.406-408   William Bexley and wife Barbara Bexley to Martin Utz. Deed, 26 March 1800, $85, 84 acres part of four undivided tracts granted John Jacob Messer Smith, Kune & Shewmaker, the whole containing 584 acres. Wm and Barbary Bexley sell 84 acres or one seventh of above lands, it being three legatees part of sd land as shall be divided by law between them and the other heirs of sd Messer Smith. Wit Henry (x) Timmerman, Peter (x) Utz, John Henry Croft. /s/ William Bexley, /s/ Barbary (x) Bexley. Justice Arthur Simkins certifies relinquishment of dower by Barbary Bexley wife of William Bexley, 7 June 1800; /s/ Barbary (x) Bexley. Proven 7 June 1800 by Peter (x) Utz; Arthur Simkins JQ.   Rec 7 June 1800.

p.409-411   William Bexley and Barbary Bexley to Peter Utz. Deed, 26 March 1800, $160, 200 acres on Sleepy Creek adj land of Peter Dorn, granted to John Jacob Messer Smith 6 April 1773. Wit Henry (x) Timmerman, John Henry Croft, Martin (x) Utz. /s/ William Bexley, Barbary (x) Bexley. Justice Arthur Simkins certifies relinquishment of dower by Barbary Bexley, 7 June 1800; /s/ Barbary (x) Bexley. Proven 7 June 1800 by Martin Utz; Arthur Simkins JQ.   Rec 7 June 1800.

p.411-414   William Prichard to John Cogbourn. Deed, 12 November 1799, $400, 150 acres on Turkey Creek adj James Coursey, being part of 250 acres originally granted to John Rutledge Esqr 16 December 1784. Wit A Edmonds, A Cogbourn. /s/ William Prichard. Proven 11 June 1800 by Aaron Cogbourn; Richard Tutt Clerk of Court. Recorded 4 June 1800.

p.414-416   John Carter & Thomas Lamar to Jesse Rountree. Deed, 2 January 1800, $300, 134 acres. Wit Melines C Leavenworth, John Glover. /s/ John Carter, /s/ Thos Lamar. Plat shows Big Horse Creek, and adjoining land of Thos Lamar. Plat certified as being the 134 acres

whereon John Rountree now lives, and part of a tract of 1090 acres cer-
tified by Bonnett Craft the 26 May 1783 late Chickasaw Indian Land,
December 21, 1799; /s/ Tho Cargill D.S.   Proven 31 May 1800 by
John Glover; William Garrett JP.   Rec 12 June 1800.

p.416-419   John Carter to Jesse Rountree. Deed, 2 January 1800,
$350, 635 acres bounded on Horse Creek, except such parts as may
lye within the lines of land granted unto Samuel Glover. Wit Melines
Leavenworth, John Glover. /s/ John Carter. Proven 31 May 1800 by
John Glover; William Garrett JP.   Rec 12 June 1800.

p.419-421   John Carter and Thomas Lamar to Jesse Rountree.
Deed, 2 January 1800, $350, 227 acres agreeable to platt hereunto
annexed. Wit Melines C Leavenworth, John Glover. /s/ John Carter,
/s/ Thos Lamar. Plat shows adjoining lands of Philip Lamar, Ayers
Goreley, Thos Rogers, and Tobler's ford; plat certified by Thos Cargill
DS, 277[sic] acres being part of 500 acres originally granted to John
Howell, lying on Horse Creek; 20 Decr 1799. Proven 31 May 1800 by
John Glover; William Garrett JP.   Rec 12 June 1800.

p.421-424   Philip Lamar to Jesse Rountree. Deed, 2 January 1800,
$200, 106 acres bounded agreeable to a plat hereunto annexed. Wit
John Carter, John Glover. /s/ Philip Lamar.   Plat shows adjoining
owners John Howell, Philip Lamar; certified 18 Decr 1799 by Thomas
Cargill DS; land lay on Big Horse Creek, part of 400 acres originally
granted to Philip Lamar 7 Nov 1785. Proven 31 May 1800 by John
Glover; William Garrett JP.   Rec 12 June 1800.

p.424-426   Eliza Mary Leger and Eliza L Hutcheson of Charleston
to Jiles[Giles] Chapman. Deed, 19 February 1800, £40 sterling, 250
acres on Clouds Creek adj land of John Carlin, other sides vacant at
original grant to Adam Hond Doringer 8 March 1755, sold 1766 by
Roger Pinckney to John Ward & Peter Leger. Wit Edward Croft,
Adam Effurt. /s/ Eliza M Leger, /s/ Eliza L Hutcheson. Proven 15
March 1800 by Adam Efurt; Elkanah Sawyer JP.   Rec 28 June 1800.

p.427-428   James Fletcher, planter, to Margett Frazer. Deed Gift, 5
May 1800, love & affection towards Margarett Frazier & her four children Daniel, John, William & Patsey Frazier, mare, colt, bed, furniture; to Daniel, John, William & Patsy one Negro woman Tiner, cattle,
horse, hoggs, sheep, [other items], absolutely without any manner of
condition. Wit Jas Baker, John R Bartee. /s/ James Fletcher. Proven

6 May 1800 by James Baker; Charles Old JP.   Rec 4 July 1800.

p.428-430   Mary Wade to Richard Johnson.   Relinquishment of
dower, 15 January 1800, land granted to Jonn Wade my late husband
23 June 1774 which tract my son sold unto Richard Johnson for $40 to
me paid.   Wit Andrew (x) White, Ephraim Ferrel. /s/ Mary (x) Wade.
Proven 15 January 1800 by Andrew White; James Cobbs JP.   Rec 7
July 1800.

p.430-433   Obediah Kilcrease, planter, to young son Abraham
[Abram] Kilcrease.   Deed Gift, 3 April 1799, 130 acres I live upon on
Beaverdam of Turkey Creek of Savannah river being part of two tracts,
one of 100 acres granted unto me whereof I sold a part thereof unto
John Witt, a part of a tract that I purchased from John Wild which was
part of 1000 acres granted to Edward Van that Witt purchased from
Wm Coursey the whole bounded by land granted unto William Minter
[Winter?] and part of the original grant and part of the tract granted
unto [illegible].   Condition sd Obediah Kilcrease is to enjoy the above
premises during his lifetime.   Wit: Thomas Broughton, Riddich Bozemore. /s/ Obediah (x) Kilcrease.   Plat shows the two tracts and adjoining land of Thurmond, Witt, & Wm Minter.   Proven 11 May 1799 by
Thomas Broughton; Henry Key JP.   Rec 7 July 1800.

p.433-435   Joshua Hammond to Sarah Tarrance.   Deed, 15 February
1800, $30, nineteen acres two rods thirty perches near Cherokee Ponds
on the Augusta road.   Wit William Morgan, C Shaw. /s/ Joshua Hammond.   Justice William Tennent certifies relinquishment of dower by
Sarah Hammond wife of Joshua Hammond, 15 February 1800; /s/
Sarah Hammond.   Proven 14 June 1800 by Christopher Shaw; Chs Old
JP.   Rec 7 July 1800.

p.436-438   Francis Lightfoot to John Hamilton.   Deed, 22 March
1800, bond of Lightfoot, obligated to Hamilton $700; condition pay-
ment of $350 with lawful interest; secured by 149 acres where Francis
Lightfoot now lives; if payment is made, these presents to be null and
void.   Wit J Martin, Daniel Goodman. /s/ Francis Lightfoot.   Proven
14 July 1800 by John Martin; Wm Robinson JP.   Rec 15 July 1800.

p.438-440   Francis Lightfoot, house carpenter, to His Children.
Deed Gift, 22 March 1800, love & affection for children named Henry
B Lightfoot, Pattey Lightfoot, Elizabeth Lightfoot, Polley Lightfoot,
Sukey Lightfoot, Nancy Lightfoot, to Henry B Lightfoot mare & colt;

dau Patty 12 neat cattle & 12 sheep; dau Elizabeth 2 beds & furniture; dau Polley 2 beds & furniture, daus Sukey & Nancy to be equally divided all remainder of household furniture; also to Henry my plantation tools and carpenters tools. Wit John Martin, John Hamilton. /s/ Francis Lightfoot. Proven 14 July 1800 by John Hamilton; William Robinson JP. Rec 15 July 1800.

p.441-444   Benjamin Crookshanks formerly of South Carolina but now of the Indian Nation to John Furey of Augusta, Richmond County, Georgia, tanner. Deed, 9 December 1799, $200 lawful money, 400 acres granted to John Crookshanks bequeathed by John Crookshanks to his three sons John, David & Benjamin Crookshanks jointly as coheirs by will 10 March 1765; divided: John 150 acres; David 150 acres; remaining 100 acres to Benjamin butting on Davids line. Wit Drury Pace JP, Samuel Melson, Mary (x) Pace. /s/ Benjamin (O) Crookshanks. Proven 18 June 1800 by Samuel Melson; Chas Old JP. Rec 18 July 1800.

p.444-447   John Corley to James Riley. Deed, 20 March 1800, $300, 150 acres on Big Creek of Little Saluda binding on lands sold to Mullicon Norwood by Abner Corley, one Root, Chysor, Christy. Wit Richard Tear, Elijah Riley. /s/ John Corley. Proven 31 May 1800 by Richard Tear; Nath Abney JP. Rec 28 July 1800. Justice Wm Butler certifies that Mary Corley wife of John Corley relinquished dower, 23 June; /s/ Mary (x) Corley. Rec 28 July 1800.

p.447-449   John Corley to Mullican Norred. Deed, 24 December 1799, £50 paid by Abner Corley, Big Creek of Little Saluda, land originally granted unto John Higdon or held under the name of Higdons land in boundaries from Higdons old line to Big Creek to Poplar log Place. Wit Geo Story Park, Jas Riley, Richard Tear. /s/ John Corley. Justice William Butler certifies relinquishment of dower by Mary Corley wife of John Corley, 23 June 1800; /s/ Mary (x) Corley. Proven 2 June 1800 by James Riley; Nathl Abney JP. Rec 28 July 1800.

p.449   William Moore to James Caison. Indorsement 20 January 1800, William Moore relinquishes title to within instrument a deed being completely satisfyed. Wit Francis Higgins. /s/ William Moore. Rec 24 July 1800.

p.449-452   James Carson and wife Sarah to Nathaniel Spragens. [Spraggins]. Deed, [date omitted] 1800, £30, 55 acres being part of

288 acres granted to sd James Carson on Tossiters Creek bounded by land of Thomas Butler, Cullen Lark, John Abney, and land owned by James and Sarah Carson. Wit Joel Abney, John Kay[?] /s/ James Carson. Justice William Butler certifies relinquishment of dower by Sarah Carson wife of James Carson, 13 June 1800; /s/ Sarah Carson. Proven 14 April 1800 by Joel Abney; Nathaniel Abney JP. Rec 24 July 1800.

p.452-454   William Moore to James Carson. Deed, 12 April 1800, £20, 55 acres being part of 288 acres originally granted to James Carson on Tositers Creek bounded by lands of Thomas Butler, James & Salley Carson, Cullen Lark. Wit Gilson Yarbrough, Nathaniel Spragins. /s/ Willm Moore. Proven 14 April 1800 by Nathaniel Spragins; Nathl Abney JP. Rec 24 July 1800.

p.454-457   Ezekiel Pennington, planter, to Morris[Maurice] Calliham, planter. Deed, 12 March 1800, £50, 33 acres part of 105 acres being part of 305 acres granted to Sanford Keziah on Turkey and Stephens Creek. Wit Thomas Broughton, Thomas Caison, Mary Broughton. /s/ Ezekiel Pennington. Plat represents 33 acres being part of 105 acres bought of Minor Kilcrease the son and heir of John Kilcrease who bought sd 105 acres of Sanford Keziah who has a grant for 305 acres granted 23 June 1774. Plat shows adj owners Robert Mitchell, Kilcrease, Wm Reed, Wm Thomas. Proven 12 July 1800 by Thomas Caison. Rec 18 July 1800.

p.457-459   William Morris to Stephenson Campbell. Deed, 17 February 1800, $30, two acres on west side of Ninety Six road, it being part of a larger tract originally granted to Joseph Lewis. Wit Edward Burt, Philip Burt, Moody Burt. /s/ William (x) Morris. Proven 18 Feb 1800 by Moody Burt; Van Swearingen JP. Rec 30 July 1800.

p.459-461   Jeremiah Mobbley[Mobley] Senr, planter, to Edward Mobbley [Mobley]. Deed, 15 February 1799, £5, 75 acres being one half of the land granted to Jeremiah Mobley Senr by Wright Nicholson lying on both sides of the branch bounded on land formerly Robert Starks, & Theophilus Goodwin's land. Wit Lewis Mobley, Martha (x) Frederick. /s/ Jeremiah Mobley. Proven 8 July 1800 by Lewis Mobley; William Daniel JP. Rec 30 July 1800.

p.461-463   Jeremiah Mobbley Senr, planter, to Jeremiah Mobbley Junr. Deed, 15 February 1799, £5, 75 acres being one half of the land granted Jeremiah Mobbley Senr by Wright Nicholson, on the north side of the branch binding on Josiah Howels and John Bledsoes land. Wit Lewis Mobley, Martha (x) Fedrick. /s/ Jeremiah Mobley. Proven 8 July 1800 by Lewis Mobley; William Daniel JP. Rec 30 July 1800.

p.463-466   George Grizel to John Williams Hendrick. Deed, 1800, $700,   135¼ acres being part of 150 acres granted to Job Red and by sd Red conveyed to William Harvey Senr bounded by Savannah river, other sides vacant when surveyed. Another tract of 110 acres granted to William Harvey Senr, sold by executors of sd Wm Harvey at public auction, purchased by Zepheniah Harvey, from sd Zepheniah conveyed to George Grizzle and on the upper side joining the above mentioned 135¼ acres, on the lower side joining Fields land. Wit Anderson (x) Turpin, Eliza Middleton. /s/ George Grizzle. Justice William Tennent certifies relinquishment of dower by Sally Grizzle wife of within George Grizzle, 28 July 1800; /s/ Sally (x) Grizzle. Proven 9 July 1800 by Anderson (x) Turpin; Hugh Middleton JP. Rec 1 Aug 1800.

p.467-469   Josiah Frisbe to Thomas Butler. Bond, 25 March 1785, Josiah Frisbe bound unto Thomas Butler in sum £500 sterling; condition title to be made to 320 acres being part of 640 acres sd Frisbee is now settled on surveyed by Harewood Jones, adj Federses Spring branch, Swift Creek; rights to be made 12 months from date, then obligation to be void. Wit Wm Renolds, Peggy Reynolds. /s/ Josiah Frisbee. Proven 25 March 1799 by William Reynolds and Peggy Reynolds; Henry Key JP.   Rec 26 July 1800.

p.469-471   Hilliry Philips of Hancock County, Georgia, Planter, to Robert Ware. Deed, 7 December 1799, five shillings, 50 acres being part of 220 acres originally granted Hilliry Philips bounded at time of original survey on land of Amos Roberts and John Davis, other sides vacant. Wit Zepheniah Harvey, Nehemiah Harvey, John Moore. /s/ Hilliry Phillips. Proven 22 Feb 1800 by John Moore; William Tennent JP.   Rec 1 August 1800.

p.471-474   James McDaniel, planter, to Robert Ware. Deed, 11 April 1796, $650, 319 acres in two tracts on road from Augusta to Fort Charlotte on Savannah river and Stephens Creek, one tract bounded at time of original survey by land of John Davis, John Sullivant, Hilliry Philips and was granted to Amon Roberts 3 April 1786 by Gov Wm Moultre; the other tract bounded at time of original survey by lands of Amon Roberts, Hilliry Phillips and was granted to

John Davis 5 Sept 1785 by Gov Wm Moultrie; sd tracts were sold by
sd Amon Roberts and John Davis respectively to William Brooks and
by Wm Brooks to James McDaniel. Wit Wm Tennent, Hugh Middleton
Junr. /s/ James McDaniel. Proven 11 Feb 1799 by Hugh Middleton
Junr; H Middleton JP. Rec 1 Aug 1800.

p.474-476   George B Moore of Georgia to Benjamin Journegan.
Deed, 2 July 1798, $100, fifty acres originally granted to Lacon Ryan
decd 8 July 1774 on Shaws Creek of Edisto river. Wit Isaac Kirkland,
Benj Ryan Junr, William Swearingen. /s/ George B Moore. Proven 6
October 1798 by Benjamin Ryan Junr; Vann Swearingen JP. Rec 4
Aug 1800.

p.476-478   William Harden to John Harden. Bill Sale, 6 May 1800.
William Whitton & Thomas Wash of Virginia for $325 sell to William
Harden of Edgefield County, a Negro woman Clary/Clara. Wit Thos
Holleway, John Harden. Assignment of title to John Harden 4 August
1800; wit Eugene Brenan, Thos Holleway; /s/ Wm Harden. Proven 4
Aug 1800 by Thos Holleway; Rd Tutt CC. Rec 4 Aug 1800.

p.478-480   Reuben Pyles of Laurens County to John Dicks. Deed,
16 January 1800, one hundred and half Dollars, 100½ acres being part
of land surveyed by Samuel Burgess containing by original grant 1317
acres which tract was after relapsd by Ayres Goreley and by him
conveyed unto Reuben Pyles. Wit Ambrose Foster, Mary (x) Williams.
/s/ Reuben Pyles. Proven 23 January 1800 by Ambrose Foster; John
Clark JP. Rec 5 August 1800.

p.481-484   Mrs. Jemimah Hix wife of Joseph Hix to Henry Pay.
Dower, 22 July 1799, deed for 52 acres witnessed by Michael Brooner
and Robt Melton being near the muster field branch opposite Beech
Island and originally granted to Robert Lang DS and from him con-
veyed to Joseph Wood and from Wood to sd Joseph Hix, bounded by
Robert Lang, Parsons, Woods part of same tract, James Gray; Henry
Pay hath paid unto Mrs Jemimah Hix $100, who conveyed her right of
dower in sd land. Wit Michael Broone, Robert Melton. /s/ Jamima (x)
Hix, /s/ Joseph Hix. Receipt for $100 signed by Joseph Hix. Proven 7
June 1800 by Michael Brooner; John Clark JP. Rec 5 Aug 1800.

p.484-487   Joseph Hix, planter, and Jamimah his wife to Henry Pay,
planter. Deed, 22 July 1799, $100, fifty two acres near the muster
field branch opposite Beech Island, original tract of 344½ acres granted

to Robert Lang DS, from him conveyed to Joseph Wood, from Wood to sd Joseph Hix, bounded by Robt Lang, Joseph Wood, Parsons, Jas Gray. Wit Michael Brooner, Robert Melton. /s/ Joseph Hix, /s/ Jamimah (x) Hix. Proven 7 June 1800 by Michael Brooner; John Clark JP. Rec 5 Aug 1800.

p.488-491   Reuben Pyles of Laurens County to George Miller. Deed 25 January 1800, $377, 377 acres both sides Long Branch of Town Creek, being part of an old survey made by Samuel Burgess and surveyed for him 3 March 1786 which tract was afterwards relapsed by Ayres Goreley and conveyed to sd Reuben Pyles by sd Ayres Goreley. Wit John Burgess, Daniel Nail[Neal]. /s/ Reuben Pyles.   Proven 12 July 1800 by Daniel Nail; John Clark JP.   Rec 5 Aug 1800.

p.491-493   Nathan Johnson of Logan County, Kentuckey, to John Olliphant. Bond, 15 November 1894, £500 sterling, for the true pay-ment of which I bind myself; condition if Nathan Johnson hath con-veyed to John Olliphant by deed 279 acres, if above bound Nathan Johnson shall keep harmless sd John Olliphant and defend same from Nathan Johnson Senr, above obligation to be void, else to remain in full force. Wit George H Perrin. /s/ Nathn Johnson Junr. Proven 11 Aug 1800 by George H Perrin; Rd Tutt CC.   Rec 11 August 1800.

p.493-496   Peggy Merdock to William Perrin Senr. Deed, 8 August 1800, $100, fifteen acres on Hard Labour Creek of Stephens Creek and Savannah river bounded on lands of George Perrins heirs, Henry Zimmerman decd, originally granted to Philip Zimmerman decd and by him willed to Henry Zimmerman decd; from him conveyed to Joseph Murdock the husband of Peggy Murdock. Wit Lelly[Letty?] Perrin, G H Perrin. /s/ Peggy Murdock. Proven 9 Aug 1800 by G H Perrin; Rd Tutt CC.   Rec 9 Aug 1800.

p.496-498   Peggy Murdock to William Perrin Senr. B Sale, 8 August 1800, $200, [livestock and household goods]. Wit Lelly Perrin, G H Perrin. /s/ Peggy Murdock. Proven 9 August 1800 by G H Perrin; Richard Tutt CC. Rec 12 August 1800.

p.498-499   Peggy Murdock to William Perrin Senr. Deed of Sale, 8 August 1800, $250, Negro girl Milly with her future increase. Wit Lelly Perrin, G H Perrin. /s/ Peggy Murdock. Proven 9 August 1800 by G H Perrin; Richard Tutt CC.   Rec 12 Aug 1800.

p.500-502   William Prichard to John Blocker. Deed, 8 June 1797, $10, 250 acres granted to William Prichard 1784 on Log Creek of Turkey Creek below the antient boundry line. Wit James Blocker, John Blocker Junr. /s/ William Prichard. Proven 14 August 1800 by John Blocker Junr; Richard Tutt CC.   Rec 14 Aug 1800.

p.502-503   Lydia Leach, single woman, to John Blocker. Bill of Sale, 20 February 1797, $75, mare, filley, cows & calves, heffer. Wit James Blocker, John Blocker Junr. /s/ Liday (x) Leach.   Proven 14 August 1800 by John Blocker Junr; Rd Tutt CC. Rec 14 Aug 1800.

p.503-505   Lydia Leach, single woman, to John Blocker, planter. Bill of Sale, $100, 100 acres on Turkey Creek granted to Mary Base- hart 23 Jany 1773 and descended by heirship to sd Lydia Leach.   Wit James Blocker, John Blocker. /s/ Lydia (x) Leach.   Proven 14 Aug 1800 by John Blocker Junr; Rd Tutt CC.   Rec 14 Aug 1800.

p.506-508   John Ewing Calhoun of St. Johns Parish, SC, attorney at law, to Richard Hardie of Little Saluda in Ninety Six Dist. Deed, 24 April 1798, £61.5 sterling, 245 acres both sides of Daylings Creek of Little Saluda known by No 4 in Platt of Charles Atkins land sold by Commissioners of Forfeited Estates bounded by Tobias Meyers land. Wit Geo Fluker, Moses Matthis. /s/ John E Colhoun. Proven 15 Mar 1800 by Moses Matthis; Russell Willson JP.   Rec 15 August 1800.

p.508-510   Willis Anderson to Archibald Yarbrough Senr. Deed, 18 November 1799, $200,   100 acres known as Starks old place which land was granted to John Anderson on both sides Charleston Road bounded by lands of Jacob Odom, Ravenells land, William Bell, which land sd Yarbrough now lives on. Wit Doctor Perry, Ezekiel Perry, Ezekiel (x) Wimberley. /s/ Willis Anderson. Proven 18 August 1800 by Doctor Perry; Rd Tutt CC. Rec 18 Aug 1800.

p.510-514   Drury Mims Senr to Livington Mims. Deed, 2 August 1800, $400, 410 acres in two tracts of land adjoining each other, one of 240 acres on Shaws Creek a branch of Edisto river bounded by lands of James Barrentine, David Burk, Rice Swearingen, Abigail Jones, Samuel Walker, surveyed for him sd Drury Mims 30 April 1788 and granted 7 July 1788 by Gov Thos Pinckney; other tract containing 170 acres on Shaws creek bounded by Rebecca Starks and Abigail Jones's and vacant land at time of survey, surveyed for him sd Drury Mims 2 Feb 1790 and granted 7 Jan 1793 by Gov Wm Moultrie. Wit Mat

Mims, Rd Tutt. /s/ Drury Mims. Proven 17 Sept 1800 by Mat
Mims; Rd Tutt CC. Rec 17 Aug 1800.

p.514-516   John Ewing Colhoun of Pendleton County, attorney at
law, to Moses Matthews[Matthis], planter, of Edgefield. Deed, 27
November 1798, £128.14 sterling, 429 acres on Little Saluda river,
#5 in the platt of John Ewing Colhouns land made by William
Anderson Esqr on a resurvey, bounded by lands of George Fluker, sd
Matthis, Richard Hardie, Jacob Pope. Wit W Anderson, Jno Cotney.
/s/ Jno E Colhoun. Proven 22 February 1800 by W Anderson; William
Robertson JP. Rec 15 Aug 1800.

p.517-520   Thomas Bazemore to Edward Cartledge. Deed, 24
March 1800, $900, two plantations containing 150 acres each; one
being part of 300 acres granted to David Calliham decd on Stephens
Creek bounded by lands of sd Bazemore, David Calliham Jr, Elisha
Robertson; 150 acres on Stephenses Creek bounded on Elisha Robert-
son, David Calliham, Ebenezer Sterns, & unknown. Wit Thos Willing-
ham, Richard Searls, Nancy Cartledge. /s/ Thos Bazemore. Proven 14
Aug 1800 by Thomas Willingham; Henry Key JP. Rec 20 Aug 1800.

p.520-523   John Chields[Chiles] Senr of Abbeville District to John
Marshall Moore. Deed, 24 February 1800, £60 SC money, 100 acres
granted by Gov Wm Bull 2 May 1770 unto James Beaty on a branch of
Hanleys Creek of Ninety Six Creek adj lands of Wm Robinson Esqr,
William Shaw, Henry Getty, Benjamin Glover, Wm Moore, John Hamilton. Wit George White, Catlett Conner. /s/ John Childs Senr. Justice
William Nibbs certifies relinquishment of dower by Maryan Chiles wife
of John Chiles Senr, 5 February 1800; /s/ Mary Ann (x) Chiles. Proven
25 Feb 1800 by Catlett Conner; Wm Nibbs.   Rec 26 Augt 1800.

p.524-528   James Campbell (Red head) to John Marshall Moore.
Deed, 28 February 1800, $448.75, eighty nine and three fourths acres
on a branch of Cuffeetown Creek being part of 100 acres originally
surveyed for Joseph Drews bounding on land originally surveyed for
John McClure and Roger McKinney, John Savage. Wit Robt Marsh,
Roger McKinney. /s/ James Campbell.   Plat certified 24 Oct 1799 by
W Anderson D.S. Justice William Nibbs certifies relinquishment of
dower by Hopy Campbell wife of James Campbell, 1 April 1800; /s/
Hopy (8) Campbell. Proven 1 April 1800 by Robert Marsh; Wm Nibbs
JQ.   Rec 26 August 1800.

p.528-532   Benjamin Glover to John Marshall Moore. Deed, 10
April 1800, $500, two hundred and one acres, sett of titles made by
Thomas Keeling Smith and Leonard Waller to sd Benjamin Glover
bearing date 7 September 1799. Wit John McKellar, Richd Moore. /s/
Benj Glover. Justice William Nibbs certifies relinquishment of dower
rights by Polley Glover wife of Benjamin Glover, 10 April 1800; /s/
Polley Glover.   Proven at Cambridge, 10 April 1800, by John Mc-
Kellar; Wm Nibbs, JQ. Rec 28 Aug 1800.

p.532-535   Bowling Deas to Jonathan Weaver[Wever]. Deed, 20
August 1800, $25, fifty acres on Rocky Creek of Savannah river adj
lands held by sd Wever, being part of 246 acres granted Joseph Lewis
by Gov Chas Pinckney 2 March 1789, conveyed from him to William
Smith and from Smith to sd Dees. Wit Absalom (x) Radford, Willis
Fedrick, Joseph Lewis. /s/ Bowling (x) Dees. Proven 20 August 1800
by Absalom Radford; William Daniel JP.   Rec 1 Sept 1800.

p.535-537   Derick Holsenbake to George Delaughter. Deed, 22
January 1800, $600, 400 acres on Mill Creek of Big horse Creek, a
tract granted to Isaac Kirkland and when surveyed bounded on Peter M
Coverless's [McCoverless?] land. Wit Martin Hitt, George Anderson.
/s/ Derick Holsonbake. Proven 17 April 1800 by George Anderson;
Chas Old JP.   Rec 1 Sept 1800.

p.538-541   John Kenneday to William Rowan. Mortgage, 23 August
1800, Kennedy indebted unto Rowan in several sums amounting to
$963, for more sure payment on or before 1 January 1804, Kennedy
grants Rowan 642 acres on Waiscoat Creek of Savannah river being
part of land granted to sd William Rowan and whereon sd John Kennedy now lives.   Provided John Kennedy truly pay to Wm Rowan
$963 then present writing shall be void.   Wit Wm Evans, Thos Evans.
/s/ John Kennedy. Proven 29 August 1800 by William Evans; James
Harrison JP.   Rec 2 Sept 1800.

p.541-543   John Kennedy to William Rowan. Bill Sale, 17 January
1800, $40, [livestock and household goods], provided John Kennedy
shall pay unto William Rowan $40 with interest on or before 17 Jany
next then present bill of sale shall be void. /s/ John Kennedy. Proven
29 August 1800 by William Evans; Jas Harrison JP.   Rec 2 Sep 1800.

p.543-544   Samuel Gardner to John Gardner. Bill Sale, 20 December 1799, five Negroes: Tiller, Porter, Milley, Juday, Dafney. [Price

of Negroes was not mentioned.] Wit Wm Pursell, Wm Quarles, Wm Wright. /s/ Samuel (x) Gardner. Proven 15 February 1800 by Wm Pursell; Matt Martin JP. Rec 12 Sept 1800.

p.545   State of South Carolina, Edgefield District. Justice Wm Nibbs certifies relinquishment of dower rights by Sarah Bozemore wife of Thos Bozemore, 25 March 1800; /s/ Sarah (I) Bozemore. This Dower refers to the tract of land recorded in this same Book at pages 517 to 520, sold by Thos Bozemore to Cartledge.

End of Edgefield County Conveyance Book 18

CANNON, Lucy 8 9   -- 96
CANTEY, James 63
CAPEHART, Henry 8
CAPS, Barnabas 67 Elizabeth 58
Matthew 32 58
CAREW, John 15 Susannah 15
CARGILL, Captain 98 Clement 5
24 40 98 Patsey 24 Thomas 115
CARLIN, John 73 115
CARNS, Peter 7
CARPENTER, Margaret 108
Mary 88 Reuben 88
CARSON, Charles 44 69 James
29 36 37 44 49 57 66 71 105 117
118 Robert 37 Salley 71 118
Sarah 117 118 Thomas 92 105
William 48   -- 45
CARTER, Aaron 20 Dudley 4
Jacob 100 John 4 38 65 66 69 99
114 115 Samuel 2 5 95 97 110
Silas 38 106 Thomas 49 99 104
CARTHEY, Andrew 90
CARTLEDGE, Edward 123
Nancy 123 Samuel 40   -- 125
CASE, William 68
CASEY, Levi 26
CASHAW COUNTY, SC 19
CASON, James 49 Joseph 29
Robert 36 Thomas 2 Triplit 84
William 29
CASSITY, Peter 62
CATES, William 96
CEDAR BRANCH 41
CEDAR CREEK 13 52 97
CHADOWICK, Lazarus 9
CHADWICK, David 32
CHALK HILL TRACT 109
CHALWIN, Joseph 26
CHAMPAIN, Henry 87
CHAMPIN, Elizabeth 79 Henry
79
CHANDLER, Joel 26

CHANEY, James 109 Marshall
109 William 109
CHANY, John 109
CHAPMAN, Giles/Jiles 115
Robert 79 William 38
CHARLESTON 1 5 19 25 31 38
39 41 50-52 63-66 73 83 85-90
94 95 100 102 104 106 109 115
CHARLESTON ROAD 25 34 59
68 82 122
CHASTAIN, -- 29
CHATHAM COUNTY, GA 24
66
CHATWIN, Joseph 32
CHAVES CREEK 9 23 33 40 62
68 72 101 104
CHEATHAM, Gutridge 4 John 4
Peter 4
CHENIE, John 97
CHEQWIDDEN, Elizabeth 76 77
John 76 77 78 Thomas 77
CHEROKEE PONDS 75 105 116
CHICKASAW INDIAN LAND
115 Indians 58 109
CHIELDS, John 123
CHILDRESS, Ann 52 Phebe 52
CHILDS, Henry 81 John 123
Walter 94
CHILES, John 123 Mary Ann/
Maryan 123
CHINEY, John 4
CHINQUEPIN BRANCH 98
CHIRER, Charles 96
CHRISTIAN, Gideon 71 Jesse 71
CHRISTMAS, Richard 74
CHRISTON, Gideon 4
CHRISTY, -- 117
CHYSOR, -- 117
CLABOARDS BRANCH 98
CLACKLER, Jacob 103 John 4
CLAHELD, Jacob 67
CLAIGG, Cammell 30

COTRON, Anna 83
COTTON, Didamia 46 Jemimah 46 John 46 110 Rebeccah/ Rebeckah 46 Salley 46 Thomas 80 92 111
COUCH, Edward 20 69 87 John 111
COULTER, David 29 30
COURSEY, Allen 3 Charles 113 James 83 89 114 John 90 Robert 73 W 7 William 3 4 9 20 30 31 33 39 42 48 56 73 88 89 116 --8
COURT HOUSE ROAD 13
COURTNEY, Alishabah/Elishabah 21 James 21
COVERLESS, Peter 124
COVINGTON, Charles 46 80 81 John 33 Phebe 93 William 50 58 92 93
COWAN, Elenor 45 George 58
COWBREY, John 5
COWDREY, John 71
COX, Bethany 75 C 16 Christopher 74 Fereby 75 Henry 84 85 97 Isaac 87 Nancy 87 William 24 86 104
COY, John 21
CRABTREE, James 64 John 42 50 51 William 50 54 64
CRADDOCK, Cornelius 47
CRAFT, Bonnett 115
CRAFTON, Samuel 26 28 29 32 33 39 46 61 62
CRANE, William 20
CRAWFORD, Daniel 23 52 56 M 90
CREWS, Josiah 104
CROFT, Edward 115 John 75 82 114
CRONAN, John 87
CROOKED BRANCH 44
CROOKED CREEK 95 RUN 34

CROOKSHANKS, Benjamin 117 David 117 John 117
CROSSLE, Alexander 93 Henry 94 Mary 93
CROUTHER, Isaac 33
CROW, William 38
CROWE, Samuel 3
CROWTHER, Isaac 3
CRUCOD RUN 13
CUFFEETOWN/CUFFEYTOWN CREEK 2 5 20 26 46- 48 54 57 59 60 64 86 95-97 110 114 123
CULBREATH, Joseph 3 27
CULLENS, Federick/Frederick 29
CULPEPER, Joseph 13 14
CUMBERLAND RIVER 64
CUMMIN, John 86
CUMMINGS, James 14 John 109
CUNNINGHAM, David 15 96 John 20 44 Joseph 39 101
CURLS, Thomas 3
CURREY, Christian 69 74 91
DABBS, Jesse 55
DAGNEY, Samuel 7 -- 74
DALTON, Thomas 91 92
DANIEL, Daniel 14 Elias 30 James 14 John 61 William 9 14 18 22 25 27 28 41 45 52 56 60 61 65 68 70 73 81 82 85 87 88 96 97 98 102 106 118 119 124
DANNEL, William 41
DARBEY, Benjamin 38
DARGAN, William 15
DARRELL, Edward 64
DAVENPORT, Charles 81
DAVIDSON COUNTY, TN 64
DAVIS, Arthur 81 Jesse 96 John 1 21 119 120 Thomas 34 W 54 William 51 Zion 52 87
DAWES, Joseph 110
DAWSON, Joseph 82

ENGLAND 77
ESKRIDGE, A 17 Austen 43 67
ESSARY, Abner 40
ESTAR, Samuel 54
ETHEREDGE, Abel 27 Benjamin 12 13 Lewis 26 27 Lott 13 Samuel 12 13 Sarah 13 William 27
EVANS, Batte 60 91 Humphrey 8 John 101 Thomas 47 124 William 1 31 47 102 113 124   -- 41
EVE, Oswell 66 94
EVELEIGH, Col 72
EVELY, -- 13
EXUM, Lucy 12 69 William 103
FAIR HILLS 111
FAIRCHILD, J 107 John 12 38 William 106
FAIRFIELD COUNTY 14
FALKNER, Gilbert 91 Jacob 98
FALL CREEK 10
FALLOW, Henry 96
FANNIN, Jacob 43 105
FARQUHAR, James 57 Thomas 54 William 57
FARRANCE, William 99
FARRAR, Thomas 28 88
FAULKNER, Gilbert 91 Jacob 98
FAUQUIER COUNTY, VA 12
FAVOR/FAVOURS, Theophilus 108
FEDERICK, John 9 Lewis 9 Mary 9 Willis 41 102
FEDERSES SPRING BRANCH 119
FEDRICK, Martha 119 Willis 124
FELBACH, Peter 22
FELTMOE, George 85
FERNED, -- 73
FERREL/FERRIL, Ephraim 12 34 107 108 116
FICHLANDS CREEK 98

FIELD, -- 46 119
FIELDS, Andrew 76 Dempsey 92 93 Luke 93
FINDLEY, Charles 9 James 58 John 72 Moses 24
FITZSIMMONS, Christopher 54 79
FIVE NOTCHED ROAD 45
FLAT SPRING BRANCH 14
FLEMING, James 51
FLEMMON/FLEMMONS, James 51 William 51
FLETCHER, James 115 Thomas 62
FLEY, Samuel 20
FLOREN, William 52
FLOYD, Grandboy 68   -- 91
FLUKER, George 122 123
FOREMAN, George 56 Isaac 23
FORESTER, David 16
FORGEE, John 33
FORT CHARLES 47
FORT CHARLOTTE 119
FORTENBURGH, Jacob 49
FORTNER, Benjamin 84 John 27 91
FORTUNE, Joseph 47
FOSETYS CREEK 2
FOSTER, Ambrose 120 Elizabeth 93 John 93
FOWL CREEK 10
FOWLER, Edward 41 Mary 41
FOX, James 69 John 9 34 101
FOXES CREEK 96
FRAKLIN, Edmund 59
FRANKLIN, Anne 1 Charles 32 33 70 Edmond 9 Ephraim 1 75 Isham 1 Nancy 75   -- 99
FRANKS, Ann 110
FRASER, James 63   -- 51
FRAZER, Margett 115
FRAZIER, Benjamin 20 Daniel

rick 71 John 71 82 114 115 Joseph 50 Mary 50 Polley 82 124 Richard 95 Samuel 115 Susannah 95 William 72 95 Wyley 99 --93
GMELIN, Andrew 105
GODFREY, Benjamin 44
GODWIN, Nathan 6
GOFF, John 83
GOMELON, Margaret 108
GOMILLAN, Margaret 108 -- 103
GOOD, Leualen 100 Thomas 109
GOODALE, Thomas 23 66
GOODE, Mackness 7 32 Thomas 54 William 43 orphans 73
GOODIN, -- 4
GOODING, John 110
GOODMAN, Daniel 116
GOODWIN, Charles 58 59 Theophilus 118
GOODWYN, John 14
GORDAN, John 83
GORDAN/JORDAN, Mary 93
GORELEY, Ayres 95 115 120 121
GORMAN/GORMON John 2 21 44 67
GOSSETT, Isaac 41 John 41
GOUEDY, Betcy 15 16 James 15 16 Robert 15
GOUGE, Joseph 6
GOWDEY, James 53 94
GOZA, Amy 103 Martin 26 32 99 102 103
GRANBEE 48
GRANVILL COUNTY, VA 67
GRANVILLE, Charles 70
GRANVILLE COUNTY, SC 12 43 54 56 58 63 114
GRAPEYARD BRANCH 88
GRAY, Gincey 95 James 60 120 121 John 111 Josiah 7 William

109 -- 60
GREAT SALUDA RIVER 69
GREEN, John 99 Nancy 99 Phebe 99 Philemon 81 Thomas 51 William 33
GREEN COUNTY, GA 18 48
GREEN COUNTY, TN 64
GREENWOOD, William 83
GRICE/GRISE, Barnabas 92 111 Moses 111
GRIER, Moses 91
GRIFFETH/GRIFFETHS, David 37 39 Joseph 37 38 39
GRIFFIN, John 62 Joseph 38 William 9 40
GRIFFIS, John 16 17 Nicholas 16
GRIM, John 72 Laurence 72 73
GRIMANY, John 102
GRIZEL, Georgia 119
GRIZZEL, George 46
GRIZZELL, George 45
GRIZZLE, George 119 Sally 119
GRUBER, John 42
GUIGNARD, James 59 62 63
GUILLARD, Tacitus 90
GUIREY, William 112
GUNNELS, James 84   -- 69
GUNNELS CREEK 32 59 60
GUYNN, Peter 105
GUYTON, Jacob 74 78 93
GWINN, John 39
GWYN, Martin 64
HACKNEY, Joseph 71
HAGENS, William 107
HAGOOD, James 39 86
HALFWAY SWAMP 25 27 29 53 55 74
HALL, Alexander 75 86 J 29 John 26 29 Judith 70 Samuel 20 95 97 Thomas 26 William 57
HAM, William 100

MATHER, Memoah 22
MATHEWS, Lewis 35
MATTERSON COUNTY, VA 12
MATTHEWS, John 80 Moses 123
MATTHIS, Moses 122 123
MAULDIN, Caleb 70
MAY, James 40 62 68 John 14
Mary 68 Phill 9 23 39 40 68 104
Sarah 9
MAYES, John 49 Samuel 22
MAYS, Mattox 74 Nancy 4 S 17
28 39 55 Samuel 4 22 23 38 40
53 54 55 79 100 102 Stephen 73
MAYSON, A 89 Christiana 87
James 72 John 50 Robert 81
MAZEK, Daniel 110
MAZYCK, Daniel 43 110 Paul 109
MAZYCKE, Daniel 110 Sarah 110
McBRIDE, David 111
McCARTEY, Edward 10 52 97
James 10 John 14 Nead 97
William 11
McCARTY, William 11
McCARY, Richard 5 42
McCINNEY, Roger 99
McCLENDON, Ezekiel 105
Willis 111
McCLURE, John 123
McCOMBS, Robert 40
McCOOL, John 111
McCOOMBS, Robert 25
McCOVERLESS, Peter 124
McCOY, Elizabeth 9 John 49
McCRACKAN, James 106
McCRELESS, John 15 53 97
McCUTCHEN, Robert 51 53
McDANALD, Hiram 75 William 75
McDANIEL/McDANIELL,

Hiram 37 James 45 46 106 119
120 John 24 91 Layah 24 Levi 82
91 William 90 91 -- 48
McDANOLDS, William 37
McDARNEL, -- 68
McDOLE, Peter 25
McDONALD, Alexander 47
McDOUGALL, Robert 52
McDOWALL, Abel 25 Patrick 25
William 16
McDUGLE, Patrick 95
McFATRICK, John 89
McGINNIS, Thomas 9
MCHAN, Luke 55
McKELLAR, John 124
McKIE, Michael 67
McKINNEY, Benjamin 7 Mary 7
Mordecai 5 Roger 123
McMILAN/McMILLAN, Alexander 35 James 23 40 52 56 65
McMILLIAN, Abner 57 James 57 114
McMILLION, Alexander 34
McMURDY, Robert 66
McQUEEN, James 58 106
McREE, -- 89
McTEER, Ann 110 John 110
MEAGLER, Joseph 54 57
MEDCALFE, Henry 43
MEDLOCK, Stephen 48
MEE, George 28
MEES, Major 23
MEGHEES, David 23
MEHL, Peter 30
MELLIT, William 104
MELLOT, William 104
MELSON, Samuel 117
MELTON, Benjamin 27 78 79
Mathew/Matthew 7 79 Robert
120 121 Samuel 37 Sarah 78 79
MENTZ, John 80
MERCK, Conrad 64 George 64

80 Margaret 64
MERDOCK, Peggy 121
MERRELL, William 62
MESO, Moses 73
MESSER, Samuel 11 William 15
MEVILL, Robert 109
MEYER, Tobias 122
MEYERS, Leonard 66 Michael 23
MEZE/MEZO, Moses 73 113
MICHALS, Barbary 54
MIDDLE CREEK 16
MIDDLETON, Aggy 65 Eliza 57 64 65 119 H 2 9 45 47 85 93 100 102 103 105 Henry 30 85 Hugh (as justice) 28 33 39 46 83 89 99 119 120 (personal) 8 22 57 58 64 65 80 Philadelphia 8 Samuel 57
MIGLER, Conrad 54 Peter 54
MIKLER, Nicholas 110
MILES, Aquila/Aquilla 3 60
MILL CREEK 44 69 124
MILL POND 92
MILLER, Catharine/Catherine 25 67 Elizabeth 25 97 George 47 101 121 Isaac 85 John 25 Joseph 101 Miller 34 50 -- 95
MILLS, William 62
MILNER, Smith 69
MIMMS/MIMS, Briton 8 29 35 47 62 Drury 62 122 123 Folton 107 Livington 62 122 Mat 62 123 Mathew/Matthew 8 16 62 84 111 Tingnell 62
MINE CREEK 11 20 25 91 102 103
MINTER, Anne 3 William 3 83 116
MISCAMPBELL, James 54
MITCHELL, James 53 55 John 74 109 Robert 118 Widow 80 William 47

MOBBLEY/MOBLEY, Edward 118 Elizabeth 98 Jeremiah 88 118 119 Lewis 118 119 Polley 98 Rachel 25 William 22 98
MONDAY, James 47
MONK, John 63 64
MONTAGUE, Charles 7 18 30 31 43 83 88 Governor 18 23
MOORE, Agness 43 Benjamin 67 Creswell 94 Criswell 99 David 13 60 Davis 5 35 George 37 38 76 90 120 Green 40 Isbal 43 James 38 43 John 40 42 119 123 124 Joseph 23 Mary 38 Richard 111 124 Robert 43 Sally 76 Thomas 105 William 13 37 38 40 43 71 80 88 90 94 101 108 111 117 118 123 -- 29
MORES CREEK 11 31
MORGAN, Ann 57 Anne 3 Cary 24 Eli 37 Elias 92 Enos 36 Evan 1 36 37 Evin 57 James 79 Ozias 36 37 Peter 3 39 46 57 84 85 89 William 50 96 99 106 109 116
MORRIS, Grissin 17 John 7 17 111 Joseph 27 Marget 45 Rachel 7 William 118
MORRISON, James 71 90
MORRISS, Viott 36
MORTON, Joseph 57
MOSELEY, James 104 John 21 Joseph 21 Robert 92 William 44 90
MOSELY, Edward 54 Robert 50 Thomas 13 William 44
MOSS, Hughes 104 109
MOULDEN, Archabel 39
MOULDING, Tyre 38
MOULDON, -- 28
MOULTRE, William 52 53 119
MOULTREE, William 2 8 19 20 39 49 80 87

119 Thomas 47 William 2 119
REAH, Lucy 62
RHODES, William 52
RICHARDS, Thomas 89
RICHARDSON, Abraham 65
David 53 William 67 Wine-
fred/Winifred 65   -- 1
RICHEY, Ann 81 John 81
RICHLAND COUNTY 14 62
RICHLAND CREEK 9 13
RICHMAN, Jacob 14
RICHMOND COUNTY, GA 1
23 32 41 46 69 86 89 91 100 103
104 109 112 117
RIDGE ROAD 47
RIGHT, Abigal 72 Thomas 51
William 68
RIKEL, William 84
RILEY, Elijah 117 James 117
Moses 7
RIPLEY, Ambrose 62 73
Ambrous 48
RITCHY, Dan 49
ROBBARD, John 96
ROBERSON, John 2 Thomas 2
ROBERTS, Amon 47 119 120
Amos 119 Anne 34 Daniel 57
Jeremiah 34 John 84 96 Joseph 78
Leroy 50 Reuben 11 91 Roy 72
Thomas 34 William 57 84
ROBERTSON, Elisha 123 George
19 James 47 John 46 89 Joseph
55 56 59 Moses 82 Peter 7 74
Russell 59 Sam 19 Susan 52 Will
69 William 11 25-27 45 46 51-53
68 90 92 94 99 100 102 111 123
ROBINET, Widow 53
ROBINSON, Jacan 13 Joseph16
William 21 41 42 44 53 116 117
123
ROBISON, Joseph 59
ROCKEY CREEK 17 28 29 30

36 41 48 51 54 55 63 64 71 75
76 79 95 99 101 102 113
ROCKY CREEK 54 63 86 124
RODES LAND 50
RODGERS, Daniel 47 Thomas
107 William 107
ROE, John 38
ROGERS, Camel 79 Daniel 54 56
58 Elijah 21 Elisah 21 Elisha 21
James 12 Jean/Jeane 21 John 87
Michael 32 Thomas 112 115
Ulysses/Ulyssus 50 62 Williams
12
ROLTON, Talton 41
ROOK, John 93
ROOT, -- 117
ROPER, Benjamin 4 David 4
Samuel 11 William 11
ROSS, Hugh 1
ROUNDTREE, Jesse 58
ROUNTREE, Jesse 58 98 114
115 Jethro 106 John 115
ROW, Benjamin 27 James 20
ROWAN, James 48 Margaret 48
Mrs 82 William 36 48 124
ROWBUCK, Robert 53
ROWE, Benjamin 44 45 James 7
20 John 1 29 41 78
ROWELL, Edward 23
ROWLAND, David 60 61
RUSH, Daniel 2 5 David 2 5
Peter 96
RUSSELL, Arnold 63 Robert 75
76
RUTLEDGE, Edward 27 85 100
102 John 114 Mary 27   -- 16
RYAN, Benjamin 38 76 John 38
76 91 101 104 109 Lacon 120
Lake 76 Sally 76
RYANDOLS, Fielding 104
RYANS MILL 59
RYLES, -- 59

79 Easter 6 Ellick 79 Else 102
Esther 91 Estther 30 Fanny 92
Flora 55 Fortune 79 Frank 35 65
75 Glasgow 69 Grace 56 Guinea
92 Hana 36 Handy 61 Hannah 11
65 104 107 Harriott 107 Harry 79
Hell 106 Isaac 61 69 79 Isham 91
Jack 30 32 43 83 107 Jacob 34 41
James 102 Jane 67 79 Jeff 44 91
Jenney 48 107 Jenny 41 62 Jim
67 74 83 Jinney 55 Joe 26 49 56
83 Joseph 32 62 Juda 44 Judah 55
104 Juday 124 Jude 8 47 Landy
26 Leah 83 Let 45 Letty 32 Lewis
24 Liddy 43 Lockey 43 107 Lotty
32 Luce 6 Lucy 55 Lues 12
Lydda 107 Milley 11 65 124
Milly 121 Moll 104 Molley 32
107 Molly 2 43 Moses 8 59 69
102 Nancy 65 67 Nanny 69 Ned
108 Nick 8 Nise 79 Pat 8 67 94
Pegg 8 Peregrin 33 Peter 32 62
65 74 92 Philles 20 Phillis 22 36
49 107 Pol 67 Polley 29 Porter
124 Press 29 Primas 73 Princess
28 Rachel 62 67 107 Reuben 33
61 Rodey 103 Rose 6 11 16 79
Salley 29 Sam 12 29 108 Sampson 55 Sarah 79 Sook 102 Steph-
en 19 Stepney 5 Suck 83 Susy 74
Tannstan 62 Tiller 61 124 Tiner
115 Tom 11 94 Tunstan 62 Vilet
108 Vilott 79 Violet 62 West 32
Willis 107 Wilson 45
SLEEPY CREEK 33 61 90 105
114
SLOAN, John 25
SLURRING, William 52
SMART, William 14
SMEDLEY, John 18 Thomas 18
SMITH, Alexander 86 Daniel 83
Howard 89 Jacob 9 10 19 52 59
68 96 James 36 59 John 34 35 61
66 76 93 114 Luke 34 35 36 74
Messer 20 51 114 Moses 51
Nancy 107 Obriant/Obrien 104
Robert 53 55 Roger 39 52 89
Saffie 10 Sarah 96 Thomas 66 95
124 Tomme 94 99 William 16 35
56 107 124
SMITHER, Jacob 52
SMITHERS, -- 69
SMYTH, Andrew 15 Betsy 16
John 83 Mary 16 Matilda 15 16
SNOWDEN, Thomas 30 33
SNYDAR, -- 56
SOUTH EDISTO RIVER 87 103
105
SPAN/SPANN, Francis 11 12
Henry 11 J 11 70 49 79 James 11
13 John 11 12 21 26 52 56 65 66
67 79 86 90 91 94 96 97 98 103
108 Milley 94
SPARTANBURG COUNTY 105
SPENCER, John 9 87 Shepherd
70 -- 9
SPOZAR, George 107
SPRAGENS, Nathaniel 117
SPRAGGINS, Nathaniel 117
SPRAGINS, Nathaniel 118 Wil-
liam 43 90
SPRATT, John 51
SPRING BRANCH 36 68 89 92
111
SPRINGFIELD 109
SQUIRE, Elventon 103
SQUIRES/SQUYARS, Ann 28
Elventon 28 98 William 28
STACHER, Amos 69
STALNAKER, Adam 11 Druscil-
la 102 Drusilla 47 Samuel 37 47
75 102
STARK, E Bowling 111 Rebecca
122 Robert 22 28 88 118

119 120
TENNESSEE [TENECY] 16 64
TERKY CREEK 44
TERREL, Ephraim 74
TERRY, John 4 48 50 Stephen 48
William 50 89
THARP, Catey/Caty 13 Eleazar
78 Eleazor 13 Elizabeth 13
Zacheus 13
THIEL, John 41
THOMALAN, Aaron 112
THOMAS, Bushead 25 Charity
58 Charles 77 78 Elizabeth 32 64
Hannibal 77 78 James 16 25 31
32 100 Joseph 86 104 Mary 27 51
William 118
THOMPSON, David 105 Herod
22 96 Moses 100 Robert 16
Samuel 16
THOMSON, David 41 59 Herod
89 96
THORN/THORNE, Hightower 61
THORNTON, Eli 96
THREEWITTS, John 41
THURMOND, Pleasant 75   -- 73
116
TIDDERS, William 24
TIGAR BRANCH 59 62
TILLERY/TILLORY, John 97
108 Margaret 97 Williaby/ Willo-
by 97 William 97
TILLEY, -- 103
TILLMAN, Daniel 52 54 David
56 97 Elizabeth 56 Lewis 52 94
Stephen 87
TIMBERMAN, Henry 61 Peter
61
TIMMERMAN, Henry 114
TINNEY, William 26
TOBLER, John 69 William 101
-- 69   ford 115
TODD, Jean 20 John 26 81 97

113 Josiah 91 William 20 113
TOLBERT, John 16 82 William
17 93
TOM, John 33
TOMLIN, Jacob 30 James 17
TONEY, William 21
TONSEY, -- 22
TOOTEWINE, Simon 10
TOSETYS CREEK 105
TOSITERS/TOSSITERS/TOSSE-
TIES CREEK 71 118
TOWN CREEK 41 73 121
TOXSEY, -- 22
TRAVIS, Barrott 24 25
TRAYLOR, Thomas 50 72
TRELIL, ENGLAND 78
TRENEAU, Peter 84
TRICE, John 49
TROTMAN, Thomas 29
TROTTER, Jeremiah 4 John 38
66 Joseph 44 Nathan 4
TRUWIT/TRUWITT, Edmond 42
TUCKER, J 16 Joseph 5 60
Landon 17
TUDDOR, William 5
TURKEY CREEK 3 13 17 25 26
29 34 39 40 42 46 48 51 56 73
80 82-85 89 91 92 95 97 102 109
110-114 116 118 122
TURKY CREEK 4
TURNER, George 56 Harris 12
William 108   -- 73
TURPIN, Anderson 119 Mathew/
Matthew 57 99
TUTT, Barbara 34 Benjamin 12
28 39 47 Milley 112 Richard 2 4
6 8-11 16 18 20 26 29 31 32 34-
37 39-41 46-48 50 52 55 56 58
60-62 64-66 68 69 72 74 75 78-
81 83 84 86 88-92 103 107 108
111-114 120-123
TUTTS OLD ROAD 48

WINGATE, Isaac 23
WINN, Minor 76
WINSTANLEY, Thomas 110
WINTER, William 116
WINTON COUNTY 33
WISE, Henry 1
WITT, John 116 Martin 24 Mills 73
WOLECON, Daniel 23
WOLF, James 27
WOOD, Daniel 23 Jeremiah 23 24 Joseph 23 120 121
WOODS, Nicholas 7
WOOTAN, Joab 49
WOODEN, Daniel 104
WRAY, Henry 45
WRIGHT, John 88 M 56 Thomas 51 William 31 68 75 125
WRIGHTT, Meshack 100 William 111
WYNN, Charles 69
YANCEY, Charles 9
YARBOROUGH, Mr 6
YARBROUGH, A 67 Archibald 122 Gilson 38 53 71 108 118
YEATES, Abraham 71 72 Thomas 72
YORK COUNTY 40
YOUNG, Elizabeth 72 Hugh 1 Lamuel/Lemuel 113 Mary 9 72 William 1
YOUNGBLOOD, Amy 68 Elizabeth 68 George 55 110 Isabella 68 Jacob 26 James 30 68 Jeremiah 29 30 Rebecca 68 Susannah 29 30 Thomas 68 76 Winnefred 68
ZIMMERMAN, Henry 61 121 Philip 121
ZINK, Jacob 112
ZINN, J 34 -- 1
ZUBBLEY, David 112

ZUBLA, David 73 -- 73
ZUBLEY, David 100